Making Signs,
Translanguaging
Ethnographies

ENCOUNTERS

Series Editors: Jan Blommaert, *Tilburg University, The Netherlands,* Ben Rampton, *Kings College London, UK,* Anna De Fina, *Georgetown University, USA,* Sirpa Leppänen, *University of Jyväskylä, Finland* and James Collins, *University at Albany/SUNY, USA*

The Encounters series sets out to explore diversity in language from a theoretical and an applied perspective. So the focus is both on the linguistic encounters, inequalities and struggles that characterise post-modern societies and on the development, within sociocultural linguistics, of theoretical instruments to explain them. The series welcomes work dealing with such topics as heterogeneity, mixing, creolization, bricolage, cross-over phenomena, polylingual and polycultural practices. Another high-priority area of study is the investigation of processes through which linguistic resources are negotiated, appropriated and controlled, and the mechanisms leading to the creation and maintenance of sociocultural differences. The series welcomes ethnographically oriented work in which contexts of communication are investigated rather than assumed, as well as research that shows a clear commitment to close analysis of local meaning making processes and the semiotic organisation of texts.

All books in this series are externally peer-reviewed.

Full details of all the books in this series and of all our other publications can be found on http://www.multilingual-matters.com, or by writing to Multilingual Matters, St Nicholas House, 31-34 High Street, Bristol BS1 2AW, UK.

ENCOUNTERS: 12

Making Signs, Translanguaging Ethnographies

Exploring Urban, Rural and Educational Spaces

**Edited by
Ari Sherris and Elisabetta Adami**

MULTILINGUAL MATTERS
Bristol • Blue Ridge Summit

DOI https://doi.org/10.21832/SHERRI1916
Library of Congress Cataloging in Publication Data
A catalog record for this book is available from the Library of Congress.

Library of Congress Cataloging in Publication Control Number: 2018026962

British Library Cataloguing in Publication Data
A catalogue entry for this book is available from the British Library.

ISBN-13: 978-1-78892-191-6 (hbk)
ISBN-13: 978-1-78892-190-9 (pbk)

Multilingual Matters
UK: St Nicholas House, 31-34 High Street, Bristol BS1 2AW, UK.
USA: NBN, Blue Ridge Summit, PA, USA.

Website: www.multilingual-matters.com
Twitter: Multi_Ling_Mat
Facebook: https://www.facebook.com/multilingualmatters
Blog: www.channelviewpublications.wordpress.com

The policy of Multilingual Matters/Channel View Publications is to use papers
that are natural, renewable and recyclable products, made from wood grown in
sustainable forests. In the manufacturing process of our books, and to further
support our policy, preference is given to printers that have FSC and PEFC Chain
of Custody certification. The FSC and/or PEFC logos will appear on those books
where full certification has been granted to the printer concerned.

Typeset by Deanta Global Publishing Services Limited.
Printed and bound in the UK by the CPI Books Group Ltd.
Printed and bound in the US by Thomson-Shore, Inc.

Contents

Contributors

Elisabetta Adami holds a PhD in English Linguistics and is a University Academic Fellow in Multimodal Communication at the School of Languages, Cultures and Societies, University of Leeds, UK. Her research specialises in social semiotic multimodal analysis. Her more recent publications include journal articles, edited special issues and volumes on sign-making practices in place (on the social semiotics of renovation/gentrification, and on disembodied multimodal communication in superdiverse spaces) and in digital environments (on the aesthetics of web design and interactivity, on YouTube video interaction, on the affordances of mobile devices and on sign-making in social media). She is editor of *Visual Communication*.

Arlene Archer has a PhD in Applied Linguistics and is the director of the Writing Centre at the University of Cape Town. She is the convener of the South African Multimodality in Education research group (see https://samultimodality.wordpress.com/). She has recently co-edited four books on multimodality and writing – *Changing Spaces: Writing Centres and Access to Higher Education in South Africa* (2011); *Multimodal Approaches to Research and Pedagogy* (2014); *Multimodality in Writing* (2015); *Multimodality in Higher Education* (2016) – and has been awarded a British Academy Fellowship to investigate the changing nature and forms of writing in a digital age.

Samua Mango Aworo is a teacher and farmer, as well as Safaliba language and political activist. He teaches Safaliba at the English-Arabic Primary School in Mandari, Ghana. He also farms yam, maize, cassava, tomatoes, beans and peppers for his family and the local market. He has been active in School for Life, a complementary education program that brings functional literacy and numeracy to rural Ghanaian children who do not attend school. He speaks Safaliba, Dagaare, Vagla, Jula, Gonja, English and French. He is the second vice-chairperson for the Bole-Bamboi constituency of the Convention Peoples Party (a Socialist Party founded by Nkrumah).

Felix Banda is a Senior Professor in the Linguistics Department, University of the Western Cape. His research interests include sociolinguistics, linguistic landscapes, language practices in society and education, Bantu linguistics, multimodality, critical media and material culture of migration studies. His recent publications include a co-edited monograph *A Unified Standard Orthography of South-Central African Languages* (2015), and articles 'Linguistic landscapes and the sociolinguistics of language vitality in multilingual contexts of Zambia' (*Multilingua* 36 (5), 595–625, with Hambaba Jimaima, 2017) and 'Language policy and orthographic harmonization across linguistic, ethnic and national boundaries in Southern Africa' (*Language Policy* 15, 257–275, 2017).

Jeff Bezemer is Professor in Communication and co-director of the Centre for Multimodal Research at UCL Institute of Education. He started his academic career at Tilburg University, the Netherlands, where he completed a PhD on multilingualism in primary education. Since 2004, he has held academic posts at UCL Institute of Education and Imperial College London and has led funded research projects on multimodal communication in a variety of different settings. His current focus is on inter-professional communication in health care settings. His latest books include *Introducing Multimodality* (with Carey Jewitt and Kay O'Halloran) and *Multimodality, Learning and Communication: A Social Semiotic Frame* (with Gunther Kress), both published by Routledge in 2016.

Anders Björkvall is Professor of Swedish at Örebro University, Sweden. His research interests range from multimodality, social semiotics and discourse analysis to the ethnography of artefacts and texts. Anders has also published in the fields of literacy and learning, often with a focus on children's semiotic uses of technology. His latest publications include a paper on methodology – 'Critical genre analysis of management texts in the public sector: Towards a theoretical and methodological framework' – and a co-edited book: *Advancing Multimodal and Critical Discourse Studies: Interdisciplinary Research Inspired by Theo van Leeuwen's Social Semiotics* (Routledge).

Jan Blommaert is Professor of Language, Culture and Globalization and director of Babylon (Center for the Study of Superdiversity) at Tilburg University, the Netherlands. He also holds appointments at Ghent University (Belgium) and the University of the Western Cape (South Africa). His work in sociolinguistics, discourse analysis and linguistic anthropology has focused consistently on processes of globalization and their effects, notably on forms of social inequality. In recent work, he has addressed the interaction between online and offline zones of social life as an area inviting new forms of theoretical imagination.

Jessica Bradley is Lecturer in Education in the Institute of Childhood and Education at Leeds Trinity University, UK. Her doctoral research is based in the School of Education at the University of Leeds and part of the AHRC-funded Translation and Translanguaging project. Her research focuses on communicative practices in collaborative community arts and street theatre as well as on the intersection of evaluation and research in educational outreach and engagement. Her recent publications include writing about engagement processes in higher education arts and languages and ethnographic research. She is co-editing a book for Multilingual Matters with the working title *Translanguaging as Transformation* (with Emilee Moore and James Simpson).

Ofelia García is Professor of the PhD programs in Urban Education and Latin American, Iberian and Latino Cultures at the Graduate Center of the City University of New York. García has published widely in the areas of sociology of language, language policy, bilingualism and bilingual education. She is the general editor of the International Journal of the Sociology of Language and the co-editor of Language Policy (with H. Kelly-Holmes). Among her best-known books are *Bilingual Education in the 21st Century: A Global Perspective* and *Translanguaging; Language, Bilingualism and Education* (with Li Wei), which received the 2015 British Association of Applied Linguistics Award. Her website is www.ofeliagarcia.org.

Samantha Goodchild is a PhD candidate at SOAS University of London, UK, and Research Assistant at the University of Leeds, UK. Her doctoral research is part of the Leverhulme-funded Crossroads project: Investigating the unexplored side of multilingualism in the Casamance, Senegal. Her research concerns multilingual communicative practices, examining the link between repertoires and mobility using linguistic ethnographic methods. She is currently co-editor of the *SOAS Working Papers in Linguistics, vol 19* with Miriam Weidl. She is co-founder and co-director of *Language Landscape*, a not-for-profit company and website, www.languagelandscape.org, mapping and promoting the world's linguistic diversity through academic engagement and outreach programmes.

Hambaba Jimaima holds a PhD in linguistics from the University of the Western Cape, Cape Town, South Africa. He is a lecturer and Head of Department, Department of Literature and Languages in the School of Humanities and Social Sciences at the University of Zambia. His research interests revolve around semiotics, sociolinguistics, syntax and the extended view of multimodality, predicated on language production and consumption in the public spaces. His recent publications include "Linguistic landscapes and the sociolinguistics of language vitality in multilingual contexts of Zambia," *Multilingua,*De Gruyter Mouton vol 36/5: 595–626, 2017 (with Felix Banda) and Semiotic Ecology of linguistic landscapes in rural Zambia, *Journal of Sociolinguistics*19/5: 643–670, 2015 (with Felix Banda).

Gunther Kress is Professor of Semiotics and Education at the UCL Institute of Education, University of London. His interests are in communication and meaning (-making) in contemporary environments. His broad aims are to continue developing a social semiotic theory of meaning-making and (multimodal) communication; and, in that, to develop a theory in which communication, learning and identity are entirely interconnected. Part of that agenda is developing apt tools for the 'recognition' and 'valuation' of meaning-making. His publications include *Language as Ideology*; *Social Semiotics*; *Reading Images: The Grammar of Graphic Design*; *Multimodality: A Social Semiotic Approach to Contemporary Communication*; and, most recently, *Multimodality, Communication, Learning: A Social Semiotic Frame*.

Diane Larsen-Freeman is Professor Emerita of Education and Linguistics, Research Scientist Emerita and former director of the English Language Institute at the University of Michigan. She is also Professor Emerita at the Graduate SIT Institute in Brattleboro, Vermont and a Visiting Senior Fellow at the University of Pennsylvania. Her recent books are *Complex Systems and Applied Linguistics* (2008, with L. Cameron), winner of the MLA's Kenneth Mildenberger Book Prize, the third edition of *Techniques and Principles* (2011, with M. Anderson) and the third edition of *The Grammar Book, Form, Meaning, and Use for English Language Teachers* (2015, with M. Celce-Murcia).

Lorato Mokwena is an early career academic at the University of the Western Cape, South Africa. She holds a PhD in Linguistics from the University of the Western Cape, South Africa, where she currently is a linguistics lecturer. She is a 2010 Mellon Mays Undergraduate Fellow and served as a graduate assistant for this fellowship. She is also a former fellow at the Centre for Humanities Research. Her current research interests include rural linguistic landscapes, semiotic remediation, and repurposing as well as oral linguascaping.

Emilee Moore is a Serra Húnter Fellow at the Universitat Autònoma de Barcelona. She is mainly interested in language practices in multilingual and multicultural educational contexts from a perspective that integrates linguistic ethnography, interactional sociolinguistics, ethnomethodology and sociocultural learning theories. She helps develop primary and secondary school teachers who are prepared to educate children and youth in contexts of linguistic diversity. She is a member of the GREIP Research Centre at the Universitat Autònoma de Barcelona and co-convenor of the AILA Research Network on Creative Inquiry in Applied Linguistics.

Nirukshi Perera is a sociolinguistic researcher affiliated with Monash University, Australia. She won the Australian Linguistic Society/Applied Linguistics Association of Australia Michael Clyne prize for Best Thesis on Immigrant Bilingualism and Language Contact and the Australian PhD Prize for Innovations in Linguistics (joint winner) in 2018. She is interested in the connections between language, culture, religion and identity for South Asian migrants, particularly for second-generation youth, investigated via ethnography and discourse analysis. She has published papers in the *Journal of Multilingual and Multicultural Development* and *Multilingua: Journal of Cross-Cultural and Interlanguage Communication*.

Paul Schaefer completed his PhD on aspects of Safaliba grammar in 2009 at the University of Texas at Arlington. He is a linguistics and translation consultant with GILLBT, the Ghanaian affiliate of SIL International, and has worked with representatives of several different languages of northern Ghana in orthography development and literacy efforts.

He serves as an advisor to the "Safaleba Karembo Yala" (Safaliba Language Program) based in Mandari, Ghana. Since 2014 he has collaborated with Ari Sherris, Samua Mango Aworo, and others to help develop community-oriented educational materials toward a goal of improved educational outcomes for Safaliba elementary school pupils.

Ari Sherris is Associate Professor of Bilingual Education in the College of Education and Human Performance at Texas A&M University-Kingsville. During 2015–2016, he was Fulbright Scholar at the University of Education, Winneba, Ghana. Prior to that, he was Research Associate at the Center for Applied Linguistics in Washington, DC, and he has held appointments at King Abdullah University of Science and Technology in Saudi Arabia, and at Teachers College Columbia University. His book *Language Endangerment: Disappearing Metaphors and Shifting Conceptualizations* (2015), co-edited with the late Elisabeth Piirainen, is published by John Benjamins. His CV and publications are at https://tamuk. academia.edu/AriSherris.

Miriam Weidl is a PhD student at SOAS, University of London, where she writes her PhD thesis on multilingualism in the Casamance, southern Senegal, within the project 'Crossroads –Investigating the unexplored side of multilingualism' (see https://soascrossroads.org/). Her research focus is on sociolinguistics, linguistic ethnography and languaging with multimedia approaches in highly multilingual and multicultural settings (see e.g. *MAXIME – Languaging without Boundaries* (2016)). She recently co-edited the SOAS Working Papers in Linguistics 19 with Samantha Goodchild and additionally works as linguist, researcher and teacher trainer within 'LILIEMA – Language independent literacies for inclusive education in multilingual areas'.

Acknowledgments

A book is the product of many people. First and foremost, we are deeply grateful to the people and communities across the globe who opened their worlds, their discourses and their ways of making meaning to the researchers who authored the empirical chapters in this book. Thank you!

At the same time, of course, we extend our heartfelt thanks to the researchers themselves! Their planning, data collecting, analyzing, writing and re-writing are at the center of our conversations – however seminal still – about how to bring together social semiotics and complexity theory.

Every book like this has birth pains. It is indelibly etched within our spirited passions that Jan Blommaert, Ofelia García, Gunther Kress and Diane Larsen-Freeman – the contributors of our 'bricolage' – gave generously their time and advice in sensitive, knowledgeable and caring ways, believing that we could navigate this journey – even when we doubted ourselves – moving us to think differently, to continue to take risks. Many, many thanks!

We would also like to thank the entire production team at Multilingual Matters for their expert advice and encouragement on details related to timetables and production. Moreover, we would like to single out Anna Roderick, Florence McClelland and Sarah Williams for their professionalism and great patience meeting our needs.

We are deeply grateful to the Encounters series editors at Multilingual Matters – Jan Blommaert, Ben Rampton, Anna De Fina, Sirpa Leppänen and James Collins – for honoring us through the inclusion of our volume in their distinguished series. Jan's guidance, in particular, was thoughtful, caring and wise at important junctures. Thanks also to the anonymous reviewer who provided insightful and punctual feedback on a first draft of the manuscript.

This monograph would never have come to be in its current form were it not for Elisabetta and Ari's serendipitous meeting and subsequent conversations – between talks and over drinks during their attendance at the Symposium on Translanguaging and Repertoires across Signed and Spoken Languages at the Max Planck Institute for the Study of Religious and Ethnic Diversity in Göttengen, Germany, in June 2016. There, we also met some of the chapter contributors to this volume (Samantha Goodchild, Niru Perera and Miriam Weidl), whose papers and their connections with ours gave Ari the idea of an edited volume. Thus, we wish to thank Annelies Kusters, Ruth Swanwick and Max Spotti, who organized and invited us to take part in the symposium.

Finally, each of us is deeply thankful to the other for making the process that generated this volume a wonderful learning experience, both intellectually and personally.

Foreword

Jeff Bezemer and Gunther Kress

This book marks an important shift in linguists' understanding of meaning-making in the contemporary world. Until fairly recently, their focus was firmly on 'language', i.e. speech and writing. While this is still the case in some branches of linguistics, a *multimodal* perspective has gained significant ground among ethnographically oriented linguists seeking to advance understanding of meaning-making through documenting and analyzing concrete instances of representation and communication. As linguistic ethnographers exploring urban and rural, educational and other institutional spaces, they are acutely aware that there is very little empirical material 'out there' that qualifies as 'pure language'. Aside from some speech-only phone conversations and writing-only literary texts, the goings-on they witness rarely involve speech or writing alone, if at all (the former is already being replaced by video calls). Thus, linguists need multimodality to produce apt accounts of and theorize meaning-making.

As well as drawing attention to texts that do not involve any signs made in speech or writing (which may well account for the majority of human interaction), multimodality invites linguists to explore how speech and writing each combines with other modes. The sites explored in this book provide many richly discussed examples in this regard. Take the semiotic landscape of the marketplace. Instead of exploring vendors' use of writing, 'multimodalists' might consider their entire stall as the semiotic product to be analyzed, highlighting that writing operates alongside three-dimensional spatial arrangements used by vendors, for example, to classify their produce, to highlight their best deals, displaying their adherence to institutional norms and regulations, demanding attention from an audience, etc. Instead of exploring the use of speech alone, the multimodalist might also consider how vendor and customer negotiate prices or pass objects using combinations of gaze, gesture, speech and movement of their bodies. Without attention to all the semiotic resources in play, accounts of sign-making cannot be satisfactory, if the aim is to attempt to understand how meaning-makers constitute and reconstitute meaning out of the plurality of the distinct resources available to them.

With that comes an evaluation of speech or writing as just two of often very many means of making meaning. And with that shift is a realization that modes other than speech or writing may be central in whatever it is that is being transacted. That leads to a far-reaching assessment of the contemporary semiotic landscape – one not at all easy to accomplish.

The shift toward multimodality is prompted by a fading away of previously (relatively) stable social arrangements. They had produced a degree of certainty and predictability about meaning-making, and perhaps made it possible not to attend to all the semiotic means involved. This book contributes to the building of a much-needed account of the new social arrangements – and of the semiotic 'look' of these, in different parts of the world. It allows readers to explore what is general and what is particular about the resources and principles of meaning-making that are identified across quite different spaces – a temple or a school. The empirical examples and their discussions invite – maybe even force – readers to rethink old assumptions about communication. The examples challenge us to examine, review, revise and, in some case, jettison *terms* that, until recently, were entirely taken for granted, and seemed reliable and apt.

Take Saussure's use of the terms 'language' and 'langue'. The former refers to what we would now call a specific *mode* – speech – and the latter to one *socially and culturally specific realization* of that mode, e.g. 'French'. Yet, why define 'French' exclusively in terms of the speech resources developed by the French? (Never mind the different kinds of French across the globe!) One alternative is to describe the *semiotic repertoire* that communities have developed in response to their social needs. That would include its speech resources as much as its resources of gesture, its image resources and so forth, giving recognition to the distinct 'French-ness' of a gesture, say, or the distinct 'Japanese-ness' of an image or the distinct use of image among Instagrammers. Indeed, instead of the 'language' of a 'nation' (as one possible focus), we might refer to the semiotic resources of specific communities, regional and global, dominant and marginal. This new conception would include a set of principles for what mode to use in what circumstances, and the compositional principles understood and employed by members of that community.

There are more, urgent questions still. What, now, actually constitutes a community? What semiotic resources 'belong to' which community?

Is it possible and useful to trace the social and cultural origins of the constituent elements of a semiotic product like a market stall? What might their provenance tell us about the identities of its designer? And how should we describe the semiotic resources and principles involved in meaning-making in spaces marked by diversity and mobility? What, now, is the place of 'code' and 'language', 'mixing' and 'switching'? What new terms – 'semiotic resource', 'sign complex', 'multimodality', 'translanguaging' – might be needed to produce apt accounts of communication under these circumstances? Which of these terms is incompatible with the premises of multimodality, reflecting 'old' school thinking about speech and writing? This book provides overwhelming evidence to counter many of these old, still widespread notions of 'language': 'language is the principal means of communication'; 'language is the principal marker of social and cultural diversity'; 'language is mostly "symbolic" (and therefore needs to be learned), whereas image and gesture are mostly "iconic" and "indexical"', i.e. they simulate or point at the visible world (and are therefore universally understood).

All of these questions highlight the pressing need for a new set of *meta-communicative resources* that recognize both multimodality in its interrelation with the social, technological and semiotic changes of the past three decades or so. These meta-communicative resources for multimodality are themselves multimodal. As well as apt 'names', contributors to the book use the resources of image, for example, to represent, analyze and comment on communication. Without such resources for 'transcription', or rather, *transduction*, to use a more generic term, much semiotic work will remain unnoticed, unspeakable, invisible. What to think, for example, of the work involved in fashioning an artifact out of a water bottle and other materials to hand? How do we document, render visible, classify and name the range of communicative resources and the ways in which they were combined in this instance? This book makes some important inroads in this important and relatively unexplored territory.

The achievement of this book rests precisely in this: in raising fundamental theoretical and methodological questions, it challenges those who engage with it in much-needed debates about multimodal meaning-making as well as the shape of the contemporary social and semiotic world.

1 Unifying Entanglements and Dynamic Relationalities: An Introduction

Ari Sherris and Elisabetta Adami

This volume is a polyphonic coming together and going beyond, both in explorations and theorizations of communication and language (or of how we make meaning and communicate).

Traces of the unifying entanglements that hold this book together are in the title's nonfinite verb forms: 'mak*ing* signs', 'translanguag*ing* ethnographies' and 'explor*ing* urban, rural and educational spaces' – they resonate, chime and address do*ing*, mov*ing* and chang*ing* rather than stasis. The knowledge in each of the seven empirical chapters (Chapters 3 through 9) that comprise the lion's share of words is about explor*ing* sign-mak*ing* and translanguag*ing* from smaller pieces of larger ethnographic datasets. One way to conceptualize the entanglements is to cluster them as follows: three chapters explore making signs (Chapters 3 through 5) in urban (Chapter 3), rural (Chapter 5) and both rural and urban contexts (Chapter 4). Two additional chapters explore translanguaging (Chapters 8 and 9), each in rural Africa, with one in an educational space (Chapter 9) and the other through an outdoor linguistic landscape study (Chapter 8). Finally, two further chapters resonate with explorations of both sign-making and translanguaging in urban educational contexts (Chapters 6 and 7).

An additional way to construct meaning across the chapters is through the moves implied in a (re)centering of discourses from the periphery. Where relevant, Adami's (Chapter 3) and Banda, Jimaima and Mokwena's (Chapter 5) ethnographies might be interpreted as suggesting that researchers in multilingual contexts explore the possible central role that artifacts-as-signs might play in their research, particularly in contexts where linguistic meaning-making due to constraints of linguistic comprehensibility prevail; Archer and Björkvall's research (Chapter 4) suggests the adaptability of a concept of repertoire from translanguaging as a centering move in their study of circulating discourses around upcycled artifacts-as-signs; Bradley and Moore (Chapter 6) suggest semiotic transformation as a centering move possibly leading to a dynamic conceptualization of translanguaging around artifacts-as-signs; Perera (Chapter 7), Goodchild and Weidl (Chapter 8) and Sherris, Schaefer and Mango (Chapter 9) center the communicative resources of translanguaging and work the spaces of translanguaging repertoires in contexts that themselves are not central research sites and more traditional sociolinguistic and sociopolitical takes on their research would stress code-switching across separate and distinct language categories. If sign-making is at bottom relational, entangling and dynamic, it is no less political. As such, each chapter might be viewed as a political re-centering of ethnographic research agendas in urban, rural and educational spaces.

Because ethnography does not occur in a theoretical vacuum, no matter the extent to which an emic understanding grounds the endeavor, short narratives on broad questions with theoretical ramifications were solicited from major theorists on sign-making/social semiotics (Gunther Kress), translanguaging (Ofelia García), exploratory/radical sociolinguistics/social theory (Jan Blommaert) and Complex Dynamics Systems Theory (Diane Larsen-Freeman). The resulting *bricolage* piece (Chapter 2) embodies its title 'Communicating beyond Diversity' in its very process of co-construction; by entexting[1] into writing what we foresee as a mutually influencing practice of theoretical discussion, it shows, we hope, the immensely rich and useful opportunities and outcomes of pursuing a dialogue across these important theories. A complex subject positioning across these theories is to take a heterarchic approach (discussed briefly below and in Chapter 10) to tools and research methods across timescales, spaces, practices, bodies and the material world. As such, a complex dynamic turn as metaphor (Blommaert, 2015, 2016) or as metatheory (Larsen-Freeman, 2017; Bricolage) represents directions to guide a complexity turn in ethnography (Agar, 2004a, 2004b). Social semiotics (Hodge & Kress, 1988; Kress, 2010; van Leeuwen, 2005) discusses complexity and change with respect to meaning-making, suggesting a mutual process of influence between social semiotics and ethnography (Dicks *et al.*, 2011).

For Elisabetta, coming from a social semiotic perspective (Hodge & Kress, 1988; Kress, 2010; van Leeuwen, 2005) onto meaning-making, the book shows the coming to a meeting space of two recent areas of thinking that, each from its end, started questioning well-established traditional assumptions on the way in which language and communication work. On the one end, by looking at the situated practices of language use, the latest sociolinguistic research into superdiversity and applied linguistic research on (trans)languaging (for the most recent works in the area see Arnaut *et al.*, 2016; Canagarajah, 2017, 2018; Creese & Blackledge, 2018; García *et al.*, 2017; Hua *et al.*, 2017; Vogel & García, 2017; Wei, 2017) is not only questioning national language codification as the most useful lens to investigate meaning-making today, but it is also coming unavoidably to engage with the multimodality of communication; quite simply, if we want to observe how people communicate and make meaning in actual practices and contexts, we realize that we need to factor in how we gesture, how we smile and frown, how we use objects, images and our bodies, along with how we speak and write. And, when we do so, the whole process appears in its fluidity and complexity, rather than as the result of selecting and combining pre-given inventories of (nationally codified) rules and signs. On the other end, the latest semiotic research, in the increasingly multifaceted and stratified theoretical and empirical body of work in social semiotic multimodality, is faced with the need to tackle issues of 'culture', when confronted with today's transnational dynamics and flows of people and signs (Adami, 2017; Hawkins, 2018). While social semiotics multimodality has had an innovative influence and effect on the ways in which we look at language, as one (not necessarily the most sophisticated and norm-providing) of the resources that we use to communicate, it still needs to develop and refine its theoretical, methodological and analytical apparatus to account for today's trans- inter- and cross-cultural dynamics of meaning-making. The chapters addressing sign-making in this volume are a first attempt at doing so.

For Ari, yet another way to conceptualize the entanglements (Barad, 2007) is through a Complex Semiotic Heterarchic Theory. As such, the many labors of love published in this volume are but snapshots of continuous movement and changes in their making, translanguaging and exploring. They are, perforce, dynamic, mobile, porous, soft-assembled and co-constructed (Larsen-Freeman, 2017a,b) with materials, voices, discourses, lyrics, scripts, transcriptions, objects and any number of ways we label the relationalities within and between the discours*ing* in all the chapters of this book, including the theoretical ones. The meaning within each chapter emphasizes a continuously emerging meaning-making or 'effects' (Chapter 2), making it unnecessary to decide if change or sign-making are in some modernist hierarchy, some metatheory with sign-making or change beyond or higher than the other. A heterarchy also discounts a homoarchy, which would only be one path or patterning. This thinking, perhaps, is promoted through a concept of the world as an undifferentiated manifold – materially and relationally. Heterarchy is also promoted when we conceptualize relationalities as Martin Buber has done. In *I and Thou*, Buber (1923/1970) traces relationalities through 'encounter' and 'experience', where the former is our closest relation of ecological wholeness in ways not unlike the conceptualizing of posthumanism we live within when we are one with our most embodied sense of self and we let go of the aggrandizement of the human endeavor (following on Pennycook, 2018); whereas 'experience' conceptualizes our more analytical proclivities to relationalities of valuing, parsing, ranking, researching, etc. – albeit drawing on the enlightened spaces of encounter (de-centering the anthropomorphic) with our environment, or commons, and our learning, living and sign-making. One doesn't have to construct Buber's I-thou/I-it as a binary or even as a continuum; it is enough to know with our 'nerves of knowledge' as Doris Lessing (1962: 515) suggests in her novel *The Golden Notebook* that we compartmentalize knowledge and we de-compartmentalize it and in so doing we hold both 'encounter' with (and embodiment of) the undifferentiated manifold of our existence/environment and we hold (tell and re-tell) 'experience' of its differentiation; and that these two move heterarchically. Additionally, as translanguaging moves into a de-privileging of language toward conceptions of social semiotic repertoires of meaning-making and communication, it moves into a heterarchic framing of relationalities, which are ways of seeing, knowing and meaning-making in this volume. As such, translanguaging (Canagarajah, 2011; García, 2009; Vogel & García, 2017) moves into and through Buberian encounter from pre-translanguaging conceptions of language in structural conceptions to poststructural conceptions that de-center language though a more holistic understanding of semiotic modes or resources.

Overview of This Book

In what follows, we introduce the scholarship in our book. Elisabetta Adami and Ari Sherris in Chapter 2 have assembled a 'bricolage' of ideas, by asking 10 questions to Jan Blommaert, Ofelia García, Gunther Kress and Diane Larsen-Freeman. The four theorists provide concise answers on the way they conceptualize communication, language, culture, the role of power, society and individual agency, as well as on how their views can be useful for teaching, on what they believe to be the most crucial issues today and, in the last question, on how their own views resonate with those of the others. By positioning the stances of these four theorists on the same page for the same topics, the Bricolage presents itself as the start of an extremely fruitful dialogue, and offers readers the possibility of identifying common threads, intertwinings, overlappings, entanglements and synergies as well as differences, a few of which are hinted at by Adami and Sherris in the concluding paragraphs.

In Chapter 3, Elisabetta Adami's analysis of sign-making practices is conducted in a butcher shop in Leeds Kirkgate Market in the UK. The market, in an urban setting, is among Europe's oldest operating markets. The chapter identifies accommodation and responsiveness to a burgeoning socio-cultural and linguistically diverse demographic on the part of the butcher toward his customers. From a fine-grained social semiotic analysis, the chapter raises important theoretical and methodological hypotheses for future research (e.g. on the ready availability and deployment of nonverbal resources in culturally and linguistically diverse spaces and on the necessity of integrating social semiotic multimodality and ethnography in the analysis of artifacts-as-signs).

Arlene Archer and Anders Björkvall in Chapter 4 explore the discourses of upcycled artifacts from discarded plastic bottles (i.e. a doorway curtain, a shopping center installation, light fittings, jewelry and animal trophy heads), communication, materiality and practice. Findings trace social semiotic meaning-making in fluid and situated discourses across local and global contexts. A concept of repertoire from a theory of translanguaging is adapted to analyze the complexity of circulating discourses identified that valorize the upcycled artifacts.

Felix Banda, Hambaba Jimaima and Lorato Mokwena (Chapter 5) transgress the dominant narrative in linguistic landscape research to investigate the social semiotic remediation of Chinese signage in two rural Zambian landscapes while developing a theory of semiotic linguistic landscape that incorporates material ethnography as a methodology in a study based on interview and photograph data. Findings indicate repurposing and semiotic remediation as go-to strategies by interlocutors 'reading' signage in multilingual contexts where signage might become a reference point or a territorial marker.

Jessica Bradley and Emilee Moore (Chapter 6) conduct fine-grained analyses of the converging processes of translanguaging, multimodality and resemiotisation among youth engaged in street art in Slovenia and spoken-word poetry in the North of England. Findings indicate that a linguistics lens is insufficient: embodied and musical modes contribute a richer representation of the data. Moreover, semiotic transformation, the authors argue, is necessary as both a conceptual lens and an analytical tool, deepening an understanding of the dynamic nature of translanguaging.

Nirukshi Perera in Chapter 7 explores the intersection of two semiotic modes – gesture and spoken translanguaging – among second-generation migrant Sri Lankan Tamil Hindu youth (aged 13–15 years) interacting with each other and with their first-generation migrant teacher in a Tamil-medium religious school in urban Australia. The chapter argues that just as a translanguaging lens acknowledges language fluidity, future developments in gesture might develop a similar lens, challenging future research in poststructuralist semiotics.

In Chapter 8, Samantha Goodchild and Miriam Weidl investigate the fluid use of languages and perceptions about language in two case studies in rural areas of the Casamance region of southwestern Senegal. The first case study focuses on a conversation among five women harvesting rice; the second conversation takes place among three men and one woman constructing mud bricks. The data is rich in fluid translanguaging and the authors argue it suggests open, dynamic and shifting perceptions of spoken and observed language practices by the Senegalese interlocutors themselves, throwing into question the Global North's bounded notion of languages as a socially situated realistic theory of what people do, or think they do with language.

Ari Sherris, Paul Schaefer and Samua Mango Aworo in Chapter 9 reflect on the paradox of translanguaging for a minoritized, unrecognized indigenous language struggling to simultaneously achieve a bounded, structural identity like recognized Ghanaian indigenous languages with status in government schools *and* an open, dynamic identity to facilitate bilingual literacy in a remote rural area of Ghana. The authors discuss the role of translanguaging in excerpts from Safaliba oral tradition, hip-hop, community and classroom texts. They suggest a complex dynamic positionality based on Kenneth Lee Pike's (1972[1959]) early positionality on language.

Finally, the 'Heterarchic Commentaries' of Chapter 10 are a genre where Ari and Elisabetta imagine the next steps in complexity theory and social semiotics based on research from Chapters 3 through 9 in the spirit of inclusiveness for diverse ways of knowing. In its inclusiveness, the chapter aspires to sustained varied commentaries as open, constructive imaginaries for future research and a more heterarchic positionality. Our layout is somewhat like Joshua Solomon Soncino's 1484 first folio pages of the Talmud with commentary surrounding an object of study. Indeed, medieval traditions of the Talmud at their best brought commentaries to the same page generating material and spatial proximity to suggest that through the interaction of diverse voices and dialogue, the complexity of the human spirit, the complexity of enquiry and the complexity of reflection might be celebrated, blended, elaborated on and pushed back against in chronotopic mashups (Bakhtin, 1981; Blommaert, 2015) of heteroglossic entanglements and relationalities.

Note

(1) Blommaert (2005) defines entextualization as "the process by means of which discourse is successively decontextualized and recontextualized and thus made into a 'new' discourse" (pp. 251–252).

References

Adami, E. (2017) Multimodality and superdiversity: Evidence for a research agenda. *Tilburg Papers in Culture Studies* 177, 1–28.

Agar, M. (2004a) We have met the other and we're all nonlinear: Ethnography as a nonlinear dynamic system. *Complexity* 10 (2), 16–24.

Agar, M. (2004b) An anthropological problem: A complex solution. *Human Organization* 63 (4), 411–418.

Arnaut, K., Blommaert, J., Rampton, B. and Spotti, M. (eds) (2016) *Language and Superdiversity*. New York: Routledge.

Bakhtin, M.M. (1981) *The Dialogic Imagination: Four Essays*. Austin, TX: The University of Texas Press.

Barad, K. (2007) *Meeting the Universe Halfway: Quantum Physics and the Entanglements of Matter and Meaning*. Durham, NC: Duke University Press.

Blommaert, J. (2015) Chronotopes, scales, and complexity in the study of language in society. *Annual Review of Anthropology* 44, 105–116.

Blommaert, J. (2016). From mobility to complexity in sociolinguistic theory and method. In N. Coupland (Ed.), *Sociolinguistics: Theoretical Debates,* (pp. 242–262). Cambridge, UK: Cambridge University Press.

Buber, M. (1923/1970) *I and thou*. New York: Simon and Schuster.

Canagarajah, S. (2011) Codemeshing in academic writing: Identifying teachable strategies of translanguaging. *The Modern Language Journal* 95, 401–417.

Canagarajah, S. (ed.) (2017) *The Routledge Handbook of Migration and Language*. London: Routledge.

Canagarajah, S. (2018) Translingual practice as spatial repertoires: Expanding the paradigm beyond structuralist orientations. *Applied Linguistics* 39 (1), 31–54.

Creese, A. and Blackledge, A. (eds) (2018) *The Routledge Handbook of Language and Superdiversity*. London: Routledge.

Dicks, B., Flewitt, R., Lancaster, L. and Pahl, K. (2011) (eds.). Multimodality and ethnography: Working at the intersection. *Qualitative Research* 11 (3, special issue).

García, O. (2009) *Bilingual Education in the 21st Century: A Global Perspective*. Malden, MA: Wiley Blackwell.

García, O., Flores, N. and Spotti, M. (eds) (2017) *The Oxford Handbook of Language and Society*. Oxford: Oxford University Press.

Hawkins, M.R. (2018) Transmodalities and transnational encounters: Fostering critical cosmopolitan relations. *Applied Linguistics* 39 (1), 55–77.

Hodge, R. and Kress, G. (1988) *Social Semiotics*. Cambridge: Polity Press.

Hua, Z., Otsuji, E. and Pennycook, A. (eds) (2017) Multilingual, multisensory and multi-modal repertoires in corner shops, streets and markets. *Special Issue of Social Semiotics* 27 (4), 383–532.

Kress, G. (2010) *Multimodality. A Social Semiotic Approach to Contemporary Communication.* London: Routledge.

Larsen-Freeman, D. (2017a). The fractal shape of language. A presentation at the 18th World Congress of Applied Linguistics. 27 July.

Larsen-Freeman, D. (2017b) Complexity theory: The lessons continue. In L. Ortega and Z.-H. Han (eds) *Complexity Theory and Language Development: In Celebration of Diane Larsen-Freeman* (pp. 11–50). Amsterdam/Philadelphia, PA: John Benjamins.

Lessing, D. (1962) *The Golden Notebook.* New York: Simon and Schuster.

Pennycook, A. (2018) *Posthumanist Applied Linguistics.* New York: Routledge.

Pike, K.L. (1972 [1959]) Language as particle, wave, and field. In R.M. Brend (ed.) *Kenneth L. Pike: Selected Writings* (pp. 129–143). The Hague: Mouton.

van Leeuwen, T. (2005) *Introducing Social Semiotics.* London: Routledge.

Vogel, S., & García, O. (2017). Translanguaging. In G. Noblit (ed.), *Oxford Research Encyclopedia of Education.* Oxford: Oxford University Press. https://ofeliagarciadotorg.files.wordpress.com/2018/01/vogelgarciatrlng.pdf

Wei, L. (2017) Translanguaging as a practical theory of language. *Applied Linguistics* 39 (2), 9–30.

2 Communicating Beyond Diversity: A Bricolage of Ideas

Jan Blommaert, Ofelia García, Gunther Kress,
Diane Larsen-Freeman
Bricoleurs: Elisabetta Adami and Ari Sherris

We asked Jan Blommaert, Ofelia García, Gunther Kress and Diane Larsen-Freeman to respond to 10 questions in a succinct and cogent style for a general audience. We provided time for each to read each other's texts, revise their own and then address Question 10. When all questions were addressed, each author could go back, re-read the texts they wrote and shift these again. Here are their answers, displayed in alphabetical order of author.

(1) How would you introduce your current thinking or theoretical stance?

Jan Blommaert:

In a few words: encompassing, explorative and radical. I embarked some years ago on the project of critically evaluating and, whenever required, reformulating (or formulating, if you wish) social theory for a society in which social lives now continually cross from online into offline spaces and back. This new online infrastructure, in my view, is a fundamental shift in the basic 'operating system' of society, comparable to the mass circulation of printed book and newspapers, of the telegraph and telephone, of radio, cinema and TV, and of computers. There are entirely new ways in which people engage and interact with knowledge, artifacts, groups and ultimately with themselves – all of which demand new forms of social imagination, I base the explorative theorizing on recent insights into sociolinguistics (very broadly taken here), using (and radically implementing) the assumption that every form of social action is a form of interaction, and that insights into forms of interaction can provide us with a reliable foundation for social theory.

Gunther Kress:

I am interested in meaning in social interaction of any kind. As social arrangements (which had provided – and been mirrored by – the framings of 'traditional' disciplines) are fraying and beginning to disappear, they are giving way to hazily emergent new arrangements and different framings. Tools are needed for description and analysis to meet three requirements. First, a (at this time necessarily provisional) redrawing of the boundaries of a new and newly integrated account of meaning-making, together with criteria that support that integration. This domain can no longer be characterized in terms of existing disciplines: that is, no further recourse to any combination of multi-, inter-, cross-, trans-, etc. Second, the development of tools with the explanatory power to account for emerging social arrangement(s) and posing apt questions in the newly framed domain. Third, an ordering of theoretical terms, both at the general level of a community (that is, applying to all social practices and domains), and at the level of specific modes (applying to the materially distinct semiotic means of that domain). The framing account will include meanings that have not as yet been given full recognition, nor made theoretically evident.

Ofelia García:

I work on issues of language in society, especially in education. I believe that schools are responsible for the perpetuation of constructions of language that exclude language minoritized people. Thus, I work on re-politicizing language, while shaping ways in which schools might educate all equitably.

In many ways, my work belongs in the borderlands, as Gloria Anzaldúa says, of disciplines and thinking. Resting on my early work with Joshua Fishman, I have taken what I have called a critical post-structuralist stance on language in society (García *et al.*, 2017). As such, my stance on language and education goes beyond the functional one of much work in applied linguistics. My work attempts to expand the discussion beyond structural aspects of named standardized language that have been reified to structural issues in society and the tools by which institutionalized hierarchies of power are established. As a Latinx woman, born in Cuba and raised in NYC, my work pays attention to how colonialism and nation-state formation have shaped the construction of language in education. And yet, because my work is situated in schools, and I have deep respect for teachers and students, I attempt to frame the work so as not to leave teachers and students behind.

Diane Larsen-Freeman:

My interests lie in understanding language, its learning and its teaching. When I first encountered Complex Dynamic Systems Theory (CDST), it challenged how I had been taught to think about language. Instead of conceiving of language as an idealized, bounded system, as the theory in which I was trained would have it, I came to see (for my purposes) a more useful emic conception of language as an open system, continually being transformed by its users within a specific spatial-temporal context and by its internal self-organizing dynamics. When conceiving of language thusly, there was no need to posit an innate language organ, a competence-performance distinction or preformationism. These constructs gave way to ecological thinking, featuring contextualized meaning-making, interconnected multilevel systems, environmental affordances, non-linearity, unfinalizability, historicity and, above all, emergentism. CDST is a theory of and for our times because it is fundamentally a nonreductionist theory of change. As such, it is especially useful to those interested in language use/development/learning/teaching/evolution. While some social scientists and humanists might object to CDST because of its origin in the physical sciences, CDST can be thought of as metatheory, which is transdisciplinary and which can inform thinking about symbolic systems as well as natural ones.

(2) What is your notion of meaning/meaning-making?

Jan Blommaert:

Meaning in its traditional (linguistic) sense is one of the many effects of social (inter)action, and quite often a nonlinear one (an outcome that cannot be predicted from initial conditions). I have replaced 'meaning' almost entirely by 'effect', and I attempt to examine specific kinds of effects emerging from specific kinds of (online-offline) actions. Meaning-as-effect is grounded in (some degree of) recognizability, and this recognizability is usually not a feature of the resources we use alone, but more of the practices we deploy them in. Which is why 'yes' can mean 'no' and 'darling' can sound like a threat depending on what happens in the interaction in which these words are being used.

Gunther Kress:

The term 'meaning' points to a mediating relation between 'the world', an individual's semiotic work in making sense of that world and the always provisional 'outcome' of this process of mediation. *Meaning* largely refers to this third aspect, the result of bringing together an individual's semiotic resources, enabling her/him to describe and order significant phenomena of all kinds in the world. Semiotic resources are *socially produced* and are *culturally available* for members of a community, and are used in social actions. Signs are both *social* (given the resources drawn on) and *individual* (given the individuals' agency in choice from the resources, and constant re-making). *Signs*, the constitutive elements of *meaning*, are never 'used' but always newly made, as the product of ceaseless *new making* of meaning. In the semiotic work of sign-making, *signifieds* ('elements of significance') are joined with *signifiers* (material means apt for making *signifieds* evident). *Signs* are the material realization of socially significant phenomena – whether objects or events. They are the result of an agent's momentary material *fixing* and *framing* of immaterial *semiosis*. In networks of relations, signs make up the always up-to-date meaning resource of the sign-maker: both as a record of experience and action in the social world and as resources to be used in new (inter-)action.

Ofelia García:

I believe that language refers to the human capacity to make meaning, and not to standardized named languages taught and legitimized in political states and schools. Meaning-making is for me the most important activity of human beings. I conceive of human beings as people who make meaning for themselves, for their lives, for the lives of others, always from their own positionality.

Meaning-making is what drives learning, not the acquisition of a standardized named language. And yet, schools create the barrier of a named language measured through standardized assessments that evaluate content achievement only through one (or two) standardized named languages. Without the barrier of this language construction, language minoritized children would be able to make meaning of art, history, math, music, science, technology, liberating their passions and creativity, without first having to prove that they can use standardized features of language.

Diane Larsen-Freeman:

Meaning emerges in the interaction between speaker/signer and listener/interpreter or reader and writer adapting the code to a particular social and material environment. In other words, it is co-constructed in use. Moreover, language learners/users have the capacity to create their own patterns and to expand the meaning-making potential of a given language, not just conform to a ready-made system. In this way, new meanings are constantly being generated. Meaning-making operates at many levels and timescales and in the interstices between (an) agent(s) and the social and material environment. In order to make meaning, a variety of resources are drawn upon beyond the language code, including gestures, posture, visage, voice prosodies, images, music, art and artifacts in the environment. Meaning-making also entails interpreting and negotiating the meaning of others. In this regard, it is important to note that speakers/signers have goals that go beyond communicating a message intelligibly, including establishing their identity. For this reason, the context of use with its immanent routines is indispensable in constraining interpretive possibilities.

(3) How do humans communicate?

Jan Blommaert:

Hymes gave us the answer a long time ago: 'use all there is to be used'. There is hardly a limit to the resources that can be turned into signs, and the range of resources thus made useful is continuously changing. This could suggest infinite creativity. I must qualify that: there is infinite creativity within sets of very strict constraints. There is the constraint of accessibility/availability of resources – not everyone has access to possibly the 'best' resources for specific forms of communication – and there is the constraint of communicability, i.e. interactionally established recognizability of signs as valid, or, if you wish, the inevitable genre-requirement of any form of communication. The latter involves uptake, and here is the most crucial constraint: we need others for us to be communicating beings.

Gunther Kress:

Human communication is an instance of social interaction; the latter is an instance of the former. Like all *action*, inter*action* is *semiotic work*, achieved by means of using tools: the (always individual version of the) semiotic resources of a community, as *signs* and *sign-complexes*, in social settings. The fundamental principle of human sign-making is that the *signifier* (a material element) is an apt means of making the *signified* (an element of significance for the sign-maker) materially evident. That is, signs are *motivated* conjunctions of *signifier* and *signified*. That principle is understood by those who interact with a sign. It enables those who engage with the sign to hypothesize about the meaning of the sign in making their new sign. Meanings made in interaction are always hypotheses; communication is always 'interpretation'. The material realization of signs depends on the social characteristics of the occasion of interaction; in another part it depends on physiological/biological factors (the senses, for instance) interacting with the materials used in sign-making. Both social and physiological factors shape what materials can and will be used in the making of new semiotic resources as signs, and hence for communication. The principles of sign-making apply to all modes, leading to a move away from the concept of 'language' as a quasi portmanteau term. 'Language' gives way to the concept of 'mode': as a socially shaped semiotic resource based on the 'affordances' of specific material means, elaborated to give expression to the community's (and with that the individual's) social-semiotic requirements – more or less developed.

   (As an aside: The principle of sign-making used here is likely to be shared by all mammalian species.)

Ofelia García:

Human communication always entails an interaction between speaker and hearer. Human beings select an assemblage of signs (linguistic and multimodal) that they believe give the hearers the best 'hints' of what is their intended meaning. These signs are sometimes linguistic (words, phonology, morphology) and sometimes multimodal (gestures, visuals, clothing, technology), and they often occur as an assemblage of signs. The intended hearer(s) of the message may or may not match the meaning of the message to that intended by the speaker. Sometimes, the listener works at making meaning because they are interested in what the speaker has to say. They ask for repetitions, other signs, other media, other tools. Other times, however, the listener simply does not want to listen to the message being given by the speaker because they hold the speaker in low regard because of the speakers' race, gender, socioeconomic status, country of origin, bilingualism and other social markers. In those cases, the speaker is often regarded as the culprit in the breakdown of communication, although it is the listener who creates it by assigning the body of the speaker negative characteristics that go beyond linguistic or multimodal signs.

Diane Larsen-Freeman:

CDST is a relational theory; it focuses on what goes on between and among components of a system and systems themselves. Interlocutors in an interaction are not autonomous, but are part of a larger, coupled system. In a coupled system, individuals do not function independently since each affects the other continuously linguistically, physically (e.g. kinesthetic mirroring), emotionally and ideationally as the interaction unfolds. This dynamic and reciprocal process is what CDST researchers call 'co-adaptation'. As interlocutors convergently or divergently adapt to one another while communicating, the semiotic resources of each are altered, and some novel shared meaning can be distributed in a way that may not be instituted with either alone. Thus, interlocutors come to an interaction with both shared and different ontogenetic histories and move on from the interaction changed in some way by participating in it. So, interlocutors and their semiotic resources both reflexively shape and are shaped by their communication.

(4) What is language?

Jan Blommaert:

It stands for just one of the many resources that can be deployed in social interaction. And of all these resources, it is the most overrated one. It is overrated because popular beliefs equate 'communication' and 'language', and so attribute way too much weight to the role of language (as 'correct' mapping of form over denotational content) in meaning-making. Which is why, for instance, we keep bumping into the idea that multilingualism might be detrimental to social cohesion because people 'can't communicate unless they share a language'. People have to share a mutually ratified set of communicative resources, and if no such resources are readily available, they will construct them *ad hoc*. How to change these views? By explaining (over and over again) to the people around you how they effectively communicate, here and now.

Gunther Kress:

'Language' is the (still) dominant English word to name – broadly and vaguely – the resources of *speech* and *writing* regarded as the two major means for dealing with meaning: in 'naming' and in (inter-)action. The word serves as a ubiquitous metaphor for many means, kinds and instances of communication, and for naming a wide range of such phenomena. In much academic work, the profound differences of *speech* and *writing* – whether in societies using an alphabet and particularly so in societies using different script systems – are not in focus. Without going far afield, *signing* raises the question of how it is to be regarded. Should the metaphor 'language' be used – as in 'sign language' – or should, given the entirely distinct materiality of *gesture*, and its instantiation both temporally and spatially, *signing* be treated as a distinct cultural/semiotic resource for representation and communication? The term 'mode' supplies an answer. 'Mode' encompasses all the semiotic features required to function as a full means of communication in a given society. This makes it possible to give 'recognition' to means of making meaning that have hitherto often been treated as marginal – as the 'extra-linguistic', the 'tacit', etc. That has profound political consequences, most immediately in educational settings. It also makes it unremarkable to deal with societies where speech and 'script' are not related in terms of the one providing a means of 'transcription' for the other. It does lead to the requirement to investigate the distinct and different affordances of each mode, and the means for the 'translation' of meaning across modes.

Ofelia García:

As I said before, language refers to the human capacity to make meaning and the deployment of those practices. It is a semiotic capacity that is widely distributed. It is a capacity that grows in the intimacy of family who want to communicate with an infant or child, in friendships and relationships that are developed for companionship, support and alliances.

Language is made up of what can be defined as linguistic signs – features (phonology, lexicon, morphology, syntax) developed in social interaction with others, thus, a practice. Language is also made up of other semiotic signs, such as gestures, clothing, the body itself, etc. It is the deployment of this semiotic system that enables communication.

The semiotic system that is language has been truncated in schools so that multimodal features are considered 'scaffold' or support. In school, the only system that matters is a restricted linguistic system that excludes all multimodal features and all linguistic features not considered as making up a 'standard academic language'. This means the rejection of all linguistic features that are not considered part of the 'named language(s)' of instruction.

Diane Larsen-Freeman:

Language is a complex adaptive system. It is complex in that novel patterns emerge from the iterative interactions of its users. It is adaptive because its speakers rely on past experiences and present contingencies to continually (re)shape their repertoires. Thus, language is both a heterogeneous social practice that is built bottom up from the interactions of its diverse users, while at the same time being entrained by its historical trajectory and present sociocultural norms. This combination results in a continuous cycle of activity, propelled by reciprocal causality and fractal recursivity. Without entrainment, mutual intelligibility would be impossible; nonetheless, local use of language remains fluid and adaptable to be molded in accordance with users' intentions. Adopting a complexity perspective requires us to take seriously the interconnectedness of system components within and across nested levels and scales, as well as how they interconnect with the system's context. Finally, language is autopoietic, and as such, complexity theorists have adopted the term 'languaging' from enactivism to refer to both the endogenous and exogenous dynamics of bringing forth meaning in continuous becoming.

(5) What value do you place on culture in your thinking?

Jan Blommaert:

What does 'culture' actually mean in this question? In my current thinking, 'culture' in any traditional understanding of it has very little place. It can be used to describe the specific sets of microhegemonies valid and operating within a community of people engaging in specific forms of social action. 'Culture', there, would just be shorthand for the stuff that makes such forms of action mutually and collectively understandable.

Gunther Kress:

In social semiotics, 'the social' is seen as the domain of *action* in fields of *power* by members of a social group. Their actions and interactions both rely on and produce *cultural/semiotic resources* as tools. These objects/ entities, values, practices are constantly produced and changed in action and interaction. As an interconnected whole, these resources can be treated as constituting 'culture', as the term for an encompassing resource whose elements are available for use in ceaseless social action and interaction. In this view, *culture* (with *its constituent elements*) is the product of social actions; it shows the *traces* of actors and their actions and the environments that shaped the resources. The socially made elements – objects, processes, phenomena and values – in their turn shape those who use them in ceaseless actions and interactions, in which the elements and hence 'the culture' are both shaped and transformed, in line with the interests, requirements, demands of those who are acting and interacting.

Ofelia García:

Anthropologists have long talked about cultural practices rather than simply culture as an autonomous and bounded concept. All cultures are a product of what the Cuban ethnologist in the 1940s called '*transculturación*'. The process of transculturación refers to the complex transformation of cultural practices that occurs through colonialism and nation-state formations. My interest in transculturación as process has much impacted my interest in translanguaging. Transculturación is transmitted through language – language transformed from an autonomous and bounded named language to the practices that people have that go *beyond* named languages and that are products of colonialism and nation-state formations. Thus, for me, it was the concept of transculturación that liberated me from traditional definitions of language and that led me to translanguaging.

Diane Larsen-Freeman:

As with language, cultural practices emerge from the interactions of members who co-orient within a shared spatial-temporal context, metaphoric or actual. However, despite the co-orientation, culture is neither homogeneous nor static, but is rather expressed through the lived experience of its diverse members. Furthermore, as with language, the emergence of new cultural practices is constrained by the existing levels in the ecosystem. Although it is natural to perceive the levels hierarchically, language and culture are enjoined in a heterarchical relationship, a languaculture (Agar, 1994), so that mutual influence and causal relations flow in all directions. In any case, moving within and from one level to another is not simply a matter of transfer because such movement always results in a transformation. Note also that CDS theorists speak of cultural practices, giving culture a more dynamic construal.

(6) How do you conceptualize power in your theory?

Jan Blommaert:

Every bit of online-offline research I have done or have been confronted with lately confirms the Foucaultian vision of power as normative and moralized, infinitely fractal, reflexive and visible only after having executed it. Foucault spoke of the care of the self, the fact that we subject ourselves to elaborate procedures of normative control and micro-regimentation. In the online world, this has now been complemented with the care of the selfie: infinitely detailed normative complexes (microhegemonies) are made available for the regimenting of almost every aspect of online self-presentation. Let it be said in this context that power, thus understood, is dialogical and operates, notably, through ratification by others.

Gunther Kress:

Social interaction takes place in environments marked by differences of many kinds: physical, social, cultural. All these differences can potentially be used as indicators of power. Every community has histories of valuations of such difference; they tend to become solidified and form the basis – at the least a consideration – to be potentials for action or to limit potentials for action. In social action and interaction such knowledge about possibilities for inhibitions on action informs all instances of sign-making. That means that in sign-making, as well as attending to the aptness of the relation of signified and signifier, sign-makers need to attend to indicating, in every sign, the power relations in instances of interaction as communication. These indicators index who interacts with whom, and under what conditions. Power is central everywhere in sign-making and therefore in (inter) action/communication.

Ofelia García:

Power is central to my understandings of language. Power is exerted by armies and navies, but also by authoritative bodies and texts such as academias, dictionaries and grammars, and institutions like schools. As a Latina, I am especially interested in making visible the role that language played in the process of colonization of Latin America, of the formation of Latin American republics, of the imperialism of the US in expanding its borders to the south and west, and of US capitalism that facilitates the emigration of Latinx workers while criminalizing it so that they remain docile bodies. Power is the meollo of the question for those of us who live as Latinx bilinguals in what José Martí, the Cuban writer and patriot, called 'el monstruo'. The power of English over Spanish, and of Spanish over the languages spoken by native Americans and enslaved Africans and Chinese immigrants in Latin America, and especially the power of English monolingualism or Spanish monolingualism over the bilingualism of all Americans (North and South) has been foremost in my work.

Diane Larsen-Freeman:

Power relates to choice. Having power is being able to make choices and accessing the resources to exercise them. Granting choices or denying them may stereotypically be seen as acts being imposed top-down, but in fact, in a complex system, power-wielding is not unidirectional. Thus, if one wanted to seek social change, one would need to recognize that any action is tied into a web of connections that can influence and constrain it. For example, deciding to implement a specific educational policy may not yield the anticipated results because the classroom is not insulated from the influence of the greater sociopolitical dynamics and inequities. Therefore, to effect change, a systems-level strategy is needed. Despite systems consisting of many levels, the point of leverage or control parameter to change them may be simple – the tipping point in CDST terms. Finally, with human interventions intent on redressing power imbalances, no matter how well-intentioned, CDST warns social change agents to be mindful of the indirect consequences of their actions, also known as the law of unintended consequences.

(7) What is the relationship of individual agency and society?

Jan Blommaert:

Individual agency is an 'accent', a small inflection, of largely formatted moralized behavioral templates. I combine several sources here: Foucault (the individual as an effect, an artifact of power), Mead (individuals as the residue of the totality of social interactions they were involved in) and Garfinkel (individuals as concretely configured outcomes of social action). The fact that agency is 'accent' implies that its range is small, but not that it is unimportant. In actual fact, we engage with others largely through formats, but the actual ways in which we engage with actual individuals is a factor of their specific 'accents' (which is why we like certain colleagues and dislike some others, while most of our lives are shared with them, engaging in pretty well-formatted actions).

Gunther Kress:

Culture provides the resources for acting and interacting in the social world. In 'use' there is the dual process of the resources shaping those who use them in a likeness of those who had produced the resources; *and* of the reshaping of resources in relation to the interests, purposes of the present user. 'Social' and 'individual' aspects are combined. Members of a 'society' produce the cultural/semiotic resources. The use of the resource happens in always new situations, with always new purposes arising from a user's assessment of what is to be done. In the always new environments of interaction the user, in reshaping the resources is constantly reshaping the social. Socially shaped individuals are ceaselessly agentive in reshaping the social.

Ofelia García:

Individual agency is important for all. But structural societal factors limit individual agency for some who are considered the Other – women, transgender people, black and brown people, colonized and poor people. The Other have been constructed as not human or subhuman or plain inferior. Granting them a sense of individual agency when society has limited their real opportunities only victimizes them further and exacerbates their sense of inadequacy and insecurity. Transformations can only occur when societal barriers are removed. Giving the Other a sense of self-worth is important. This gives the Other the agency to speak, to use language. But if the hearer is not ready to listen, then raising the voices of the Other just leads to an impasse, a wall that is not only seen, but also heard as a wall that is impenetrable.

Diane Larsen-Freeman:

The choices we make as individuals cannot help but be influenced by our social embeddedness. In reciprocal fashion, we can also initiate change in society. Agency is not inhered in individuals, but is rather contingent and interpellated from the dynamic interaction of multiple factors at micro, meso and macro levels of the complex sociocultural system. In a word, agency is emergent.

The sociocultural system clearly has an impact on how agents' lives unfold (e.g. the initial conditions of a system are very important in CDST); nevertheless, it is important to remember that because complex systems are open systems, they are not fully determined by extant conditions. Agents have the option to reframe their relationship to the sociocultural context. It is also possible for agents to go beyond reproducing initial conditions (which are continually being updated) and for the system to develop along alternate trajectories. Thus, while agency in a complex system might be constrained by its history, it is not fully determined by it.

(8) How might your thinking be used by teachers?

Jan Blommaert:

Much of what I now express as theory is actual common sense. In talking to teachers and other people who might benefit from these efforts, I often try to 'peel off' the layers of language-ideological beliefs, trying to get to a pretty simple bottom-line understanding of communicative practices online and offline, for which a handful of structuring terms and arguments can then be offered in reconstructing a more accurate understanding of what 'language' (the term they mostly use) actually is.

Gunther Kress:

Learning and teaching are instances of interaction/communication. The account set out here applies in every respect, everywhere in the social-cultural environments of learning and teaching. It provides both map and tools for a full understanding of the *semiotic work* of learning and teaching (that is, as another instance of communication/interaction). The insistence on *communication as interaction and as interpretation*, forces us into an acknowledgment of the semiotic work of the interpreter/ learner. The *recognition of the many modes* through and in which interpretation takes place, forces a *radical shift toward both recognition and valuation of the semiotic work of the learner*. The substitution of 'language' by the concept of 'mode' offers the possibility and *insists* on the recognition of all semiotic work with any and all semiotic resources used by learners in their semiotic work. It requires attending in absolute detail to the semiotic work done by them in canonical and noncanonical modes. This frame has the potential to make 'student-centred learning' a reality. It regards students as *serious, mindful, principled interpreters*. It requires teachers to be sensitive interpreters of the learner's principled interpretations. It asks teachers to see their pedagogical/semiotic work as designers of constantly redesigned, newly apt environments for learning.

Ofelia García:

Many of the teachers I have worked with have used my thinking to disrupt traditional concepts of language and bilingualism and to honor the ways of languaging of minoritized students. By denaturalizing the concept of a standardized named language and showing English–Spanish bilingual teachers how Spanish has been historically constructed as 'lengua del imperio' (Nebrija, 1492, the first grammar of the Spanish language), teachers understand language beyond categories of named languages and instead focus on student language practices. Teachers learn to appreciate bilingual students' *translanguaging*, their deployment of features from a single system that bilinguals maneuver depending on the audience. Teachers also learn to distinguish between *general language performances*, that is, students' ability to use language to tell a joke, find text-based evidence, infer, etc., and *language-specific performances* when those are called for, that is, students' deployment of signs from their linguistic system to complete appropriate tasks.

Diane Larsen-Freeman:

It is not my place to prescribe or proscribe practices to teachers; however, I will say that I have been concerned for a long time about the "inert knowledge problem," whereby students are unable to use for their own purposes that which they have been taught in the classroom. Some years ago, inspired by CDST, I came to see that grammar needed to be taught not only as a system, but also as a meaning-making process, which I called 'grammaring'. In grammaring instruction, teachers provide students opportunities for meaningful expression in iterative (as opposed to repetitive) activities. The iteration helps learners to notice and to practice the recurrent patterns in language use. It also identifies the need to teach students to adapt their language resources to the demands of a continually changing situation. This is especially pressing due to the increasingly common global exchanges among multilinguals. It is also important to understand that learners do not transfer their knowledge and ability from one situation to another; they transform it. Finally, recognizing and challenging harmful ideologies that impede learning is an essential undertaking in language education in order to resist deficit framings and stigmatization.

(9) What are the most crucial issues to be investigated today?

Jan Blommaert:

Inequality. By analytically expanding the range of communicative resources we intend to investigate, we necessarily find more objects of potential and effective inequality beyond 'language' in the sense used, e.g. in sociolinguistic work on minority languages. Think, for instance, of all that is required to successfully launch an online petition for the removal of a corrupt bureaucrat in the South of China: such a complex online action is only 'simple' and 'easy' for those who have full access to the totality of the resources required for it – including knowledge and experience. This is one of the reasons why I tend to attach great importance to online-offline sites as informal learning environments, where such resources are being made available, distributed, learned and practiced.

Gunther Kress:

The contemporary 'social' is marked by instability, provisionality and *fragmentation*. The effect of the contemporary (so-called 'social') media is to act as amplifiers of these current dis-integrative factors. For me, with aspirations to act as an intellectual, it seems essential to ask what I as an academic might do to act against tendencies that I see as deleterious and harmful to the vast majority. Qua academic, I can attempt to provide descriptive accounts of what seem to be emergent social configurations, new tasks and the new requirements. I can attempt to describe the contemporary social/semiotic landscape and its technologies: both in their relation to and as mirrors of the social. Qua intellectual, I attempt to provide new terminology, new 'namings' (whether in terms of disciplines or within disciplines), so as to get beyond current constraints for thinking. I attempt to move beyond former paradigms of response to unease with the social – as expressed in backward facing terms such as 'critique', moving rather to a prospective paradigm such as 'Design'. At the least, it suggests that I am able to give shape to my conceptions, and put them into the world as counters to current trends.

Ofelia García:

Language performances in schools are most often evaluated through assessments that measure, above all, features of a standardized named language. This means that students who language differently are always perceived as deficient. For me then, the most important issue right now is for researchers to document the ways in which judgments made with standardized assessments provide the basis for the exclusion of many from educational and societal opportunities. Consequential validity, how different groups fare in the assessment, must substitute for reliability as the most important measure of confidence in assessment. Transforming the sorting mechanism that schooling through language assessment has become is for me the most important challenge for language researchers today.

Diane Larsen-Freeman:

Given what I have just written in my answer to Question 8, I would say that a crucial issue is how to counter the widespread misunderstanding of languages and dialects today. I have in mind the monolingual bias, the standard language/dialect ideology, the individuation of languages and the belief that there is an endpoint to language and to language learning that coincides with native speaker norms and use. Such ideologies can have serious consequences for people's lives, disempowering individuals and groups, widening extant disparities, and can more generally undermine moves toward democracies.

(10) How do you imagine the others' bricolage fit with your thinking?

Jan Blommaert:

Let me make two preliminary points. (1) There are obvious and very deep similarities between what I argued and what my three interlocutors argued, for all three have tremendously influenced and inspired my own development. With Ofelia, I share the lifelong commitment to sociolinguistic inequality as a key issue in everything we do; with Diane, I share the awareness of the destabilizing effects of a complexity perspective, along with the commitment to turn them into a pedagogical tool with practical implications; from close collaboration with Gunther, I learned the overrated nature of 'language' as just one set of semiotic resources among many, as well as the emphasis of meaning as an effect of practice rather than as activated latent potential. (2) For the reader: the similarities between the different views are scattered over different answers. My answer to one question converges with my interlocutors' answers to different questions.

But the attentive reader will have soon sensed that all of us share a number of things: (a) most critically: an interaction-focused view of meaning-making, i.e. the view that meaning emerges out of social practices in which people draw on differentially (and unequally) distributed semiotic resources; (b) a clear awareness of how, as an effect of (a), power can never be elided from the analysis of meaning-making; (c) and neither can the complexity of actual meaning-making be reduced by invoking artefactualized notions of 'language' in its traditional sense. In fact, it is this ideological conception of 'language' that very often causes the forms of social inequality we all find extraordinarily important. Finally, (d) all of us share an acute awareness of profound social change affecting, fundamentally, our imagination of social life and inviting (or demanding) continual theoretical adjustment.

Gunther Kress:

The fundamental agreement about academic/political projects seems to me the most significant aspect here. The differences arise, I think, from different positions in the social/political and hence academic world, where different concerns are, inevitably, in focus. In terms of theories, there is broad agreement about the social as dynamic, as the site, inevitably of power, all of which requires theories to mirror that dynamism and the workings of power in their categories and relations.

As far as the book is concerned, and its possible future aims, this seems to me to provide a very good starting point for a – long and detailed – discussion, with the aim, perhaps of finding a way through the contemporary terminological morass.

Ofelia García:

In reading the bricolage, I am reminded that indeed there is no view from nowhere. My gaze over meaning and language stems from my positionality as a US Latina scholar. In the 1970s, as a young developing scholar, I was nurtured by two trends that I have held alongside each other in a perpetual heterarchy. As the magical realism of Latin American novelists lifted me from my particular circumstances, the struggles over civil rights kept me grounded. Educationally, I was immersed in semiotics to do literary analysis with one mentor, the Argentinean Angela Dellepiane, but I used semiotics to open up the descriptions of language in society inspired by my other mentor, the Yiddish-speaking Joshua A. Fishman. I have repeatedly taken up the ideas of Kress, Blommaert and Larsen-Freeman as I have explored and reformulated my own meanings, and as others take them up and transform them some more. Our understandings are nested, imbricated, provisional, emergent, but pointing differently. All point to a dynamism beyond borders, although even when all of us work across chronotopes and scales, the terrain is different. Kress' words in the bricolage focus on going beyond modes; Blommaert on going beyond the normative control of language; Larsen-Freeman on the complexity of language learning. I would say that mine reaches toward theirs, but is pulled by my work in schools, a normative institution that continues to ignore the reformulation of language, modes and language learners that make up the multiple meanings in this bricolage.

Diane Larsen-Freeman:

Although we come from different perspectives and employ different discourses, it seems to me that there are some common themes in our answers. We share a post-structural and social orientation to language and its use. We give importance to semiotic resources, multimodality, language practices and criticality. Two of us focus more on education, one on semiotics and the other of us more on sociolinguistics, but we all have in common calling for a departure from traditional views of language, and we share a commitment to social justice.

Threading Possible Readings, Imaging New Beginnings

Elisabetta Adami and Ari Sherris

As variously pointed out in all four answers to the last question, readers will easily see for themselves the many points of contact and commonalities among these four thinkers, each with their different language, points of departure, foci and interests. In what follows, we would like to offer some possible reading prompts for tracing sharedness among, through, within and behind/beyond differences in the bricolage.

Their languages are different, but similar concerns resound across the four voices: a concern for a time of profound social change, which requires new/further thinking; a concern for studying communicative phenomena (differently focused as semiosis, meaning-making, interaction, languaging and/or language learning) as deeply rooted in, reflecting and shaping society; a concern for finding new ways of theorizing, describing and explaining these phenomena as practices, beyond the fixities of previous frameworks and accounts; a concern for the complexities of human lives (in their profoundly relational, but also material and bodily nature), as well as a concern for where forms of social livings are heading today; which calls forth a concern for power and inequalities, and a concern for contributing intellectually to positive change.

Differences can be spotted too, in standpoints, trajectories, foci and interests. As an example, communication practices and resources can be conceived of in terms of 'use', of 'action' or of 'making'; language can be thought of as being multimodal itself (encompassing gestures and clothing, for example) or as one (overrated) semiotic resource out of many, or else as one artificial/ideological label for partially identifying/constraining meaning-making, out of all its possible realizations. Interests may lie (more) in observing social interaction as a means to understanding society/ies, or (more) in liberating language conceptions and teaching from ideologies that (re)produce inequalities. Terminological differences reveal different standpoints, in using 'systems' or 'relations'; 'actions' and 'effects' or 'meaning' and 'interpretation'; 'minoritized people', 'social groups' or 'communities', for example. Scattered throughout the answers, these different takes, directions and nuances seem to provide possibilities for opening a discussion. Dynamic openness does not seem to be only a key term in one perspective here, but also a shared intellectual stance, in what Diane terms as a 'common calling for a departure from traditional views', and a profound commitment to go 'beyond' (in Ofelia's words). Hence, differences sound to us as rather intriguing potentials for future stimuli, as they thread through a substantial political/ideal agreement for advancing thinking that needs to problematize common (mis)conceptions on language and communication, to adequately account for a time of change – and positively impact on it.

In gathering these four main theorists in linguistic ethnography, translanguaging, social semiotics and complex dynamic system theory in language, we have conceived this piece to be useful to make sense of the interconnections across different theoretical trajectories, terminologies and concepts, sensing a potential underlying sharedness beyond and behind differences, across traditional domains (sociolinguistics, applied linguistics, multimodality and language development/acquisition/learning), whose boundaries need to be crossed, as these four thinkers have shown in their theories and practices. A few keywords resound, which we find emerging across answers: complexity, dynamicity, social interaction, power, inequalities, resources for making meaning, practices, action and change. In line with what all the answers above seem to indicate, we are triggered by the idea that each of these terms/labels means something different for each of our four thinkers – and possibly has come to mean something further different after each one has met the other's thinking, at some point in their theorizing and, eventually, while contributing to this bricolage. Embracing the dynamics between situated meaning-making and 'recognizability' (in Jan's terms) involves accepting difference as coexisting with sharedness, engaging with this never linear dynamics and stemming from it to produce yet further meaning. In our thinking, this bricolage could provide readers (among which we include ourselves) with a canvass threaded with very much needed 'ways through' what at times may seem like a 'terminological morass' (in Gunther's words); this canvass will hopefully be generative of further readings, discussions and debates.

Here, we can suggest a few possible reading paths for the bricolage: as a most immediately pragmatic one, a reading path can look for a repertoire of definitions of fundamental concepts in each of the four thinkers' theories; the bricolage piece is indeed densely punctuated with definitions from each theoretical perspective. Another reading path can compare the four thinkers' positions thematically, as laid out together under each question, and generate a virtual dialogue among the four of them. A further one can instead follow one individual perspective through the 10 answers, and make sense of the unfolding of her/his thinking across some fundamental thematic pillars, which provide the milestones for a distilled version of the current theorizing of the four contributors. Yet another path could possibly (re)trace each of the four thinkers' theorizing into and across the empirical analyses of the other chapters in this volume, all of which, to different extents and in different ways, embody each of them, and their underlying stance for approaching the investigation of communication today. We would particularly like to add two other, more imaginative, reading paths, which from the space of the pages of this bricolage expand in(to) time. One reading path can ask how these answers – and emerging keywords – would have possibly differed had we asked them a few decades ago – and we suspect that differences would be quite a few; the answers above reserve very little or no room for concepts like 'code', 'proficiency', 'competence', 'grammar' or 'conventions' – to name only a few terms of traditional linguistics and semiotics – which, for us, signals a point in the four's theorizing that has reached far beyond the stage of critique, hence possibly beyond the 'post-' of structuralism. A second imaginative reading path can ask instead how these answers can lead to formulating new questions, and hopefully foster debate and further very much needed encounters in the future.

Finally, we would be remiss not to discuss the issues we link to education because the challenges for education, educators, educational policy makers, activists and researchers are deeply entangled issues of (1) equity (and a weightier lack thereof); (2) repressive restrictions on languages, creoles, language varieties, bi- and multilingualisms; (3) an unfair distribution of material wealth, access to that wealth and access to education worldwide; and (4) repression of a free, dynamic, creative, recognized and celebrated use of all semiotic modes for learning and for educational assessment. To be sure, traces of these challenges percolate beneath the surface of our readings of the bricolage, while even more explode from our embodied activism against repressive measures of nation states (see Heller & McElhinny, 2017 for a critical exposition). That is to say, if education – its practitioners and researchers – explored what Jan calls 'new forms of social imagination', what Diane says is the 'transformation' rather than the 'transfer' of knowledge, what Gunther calls a learner's 'principled interpretations' and if education explored the exclusionary language assessment practices with an eye to transform them into inclusive practices as Ofelia speaks of, the dynamics of teaching and learning would potentially resonate with a radical new mandate different than that which nation states construct as schooling and educational practice.

We imagine an advocacy for complex and dynamic ways of teaching and learning that might one day more fully embrace diverse semiotic repertoires, diverse ensembles of multimodality, equity and the free and creative emergence of those repertoires in ways that both address sociopolitical concerns moment-to-moment and across scaled levels and multiple discourses (Blommaert, 2010), imagined communities and deterritorialized, mobile and shifting educative spaces. At the same time, Diane reminds us that 'harmful ideologies' circulate in and through education as well as 'the inert knowledge problem', which concern us in that they lead us to think about the daily inequities that standards and norms and standardized tests construct (Ofelia's point) as they repress and erase varieties of human expression, delegitimize translanguaging and only provide spaces for a very limited multimodality in enactments of learning and their assessments. Or as Ofelia states, 'language has been truncated in schools', which is as untenable as the truncation of multimodal forms of expression, the negative impact of which is shown and evidenced in much of Gunther's work. Such enactments of learning that constrict creativity and focus on very structured and narrow ways to teach and assess language and knowledge are often, sadly, still generated by and for the benefit of an elite designing and supporting educational systems across rural and urban spaces, relentlessly driven by neoliberal forces that distribute and garner material wealth in expanding socially imbalanced ways, harming humanity, flora, fauna and the planet. To carry knowledge in 'perpetual heterarchy' as Ofelia engages us to consider, not only leads us to think about the conclusion of this volume, our Heterarchic Commentaries, but heterarchy as a subject positioning for knowledge, for meaning-making in school and out of school and the fluidity across these spaces. That fluidity is no less an indispensable dynamic in a social justice model of education, including the semiotics of human 'encounters and experiences' (Buber, 1923); for throughout the bricolage (as in all chapters of this volume), humanity is conceptualized as profoundly relational. Designing education so that it is first and foremost about the dynamic, emergent, open and nonlinear relationalities of and through existence and taking risks to think freely, as Jan, Ofelia, Gunther and Diane's thinking implies, is foundational to a radical education that struggles against narrowness, bigotry and economic inequalities.

Within the puzzling, and often worrying, fast-paced changes of today's world, education is only one field in need of such intellectual and active engagement. Adopting such a radical stance, we believe, would be beneficial not only for and within education, teaching and learning, but for and within all domains of social interaction and social life. Hence, we might even begin to re-imagine community and the commons (Amin & Howell, 2016) through a de-centering of humanity (Pennycook, 2018), not just the de-centering of language, which does not mean overshadowing the need to struggle for social justice; quite the opposite in fact, as Bateson (1972) clearly indicated nearly half a century ago. This would be the broadest move on the ecologically dynamic pathways that open before us, for they include epistemological and ontological questions about knowledge – and interaction – beyond the current faltering disciplines and hyphenated liminalities of cobbled together thinking, which Gunther challenges us to disturb, to rethink. Hence, as interpreters who disturb the status quo, we have continuously focused and refocused on what we know and do not know, how we know and knowing itself, which is – to our thinking – a promising futurity for dialogic exploration that we have only just begun.

References

Agar, M. (1994) *Language Shock: Understanding the Culture of Conversation*. New York: William Morrow.

Amin, A. and Howell, P. (2016) *Releasing the Commons: Rethinking the Futures of the Commons*. New York: Routledge.

Bateson, G. (1972) *Steps to an Ecology of Mind: Collected Essays in Anthropology, Psychiatry, Evolution, and Epistemology*. Chicago, IL: University of Chicago Press.

Blommaert, J. (2010) *The Sociolinguistics of Globalization*. Cambridge: Cambridge University Press.

Buber, M. (1923/1970) *I and Thou*. New York: Simon and Schuster.

Heller, M. and McElhinny, B. (2017) *Language, Capitalism, Colonialism: Toward a Critical History*. Toronto: University of Toronto Press.

Pennycook, A. (2018) *Posthumanist Applied Linguistics*. New York: Routledge.

Selected Readings

We asked each contributor to list five of their publications that they would recommend as further reading on their thinking for readers of this bricolage piece.

Jan Blommaert

Blommaert, J. (2005) *Discourse: A Critical Introduction*. Cambridge: Cambridge University Press.

Blommaert, J. (2008) *Grassroots Literacy: Writing, Identity and Voice in Central Africa*. Abingdon: Routledge.

Blommaert, J. (2010) *The Sociolinguistics of Globalization*. Cambridge: Cambridge University Press.

Blommaert, J. (2013) *Ethnography, Superdiversity and Linguistic Landscapes: Chronicles of Complexity*. Bristol: Multilingual Matters.

Blommaert, J. (2018) *Durkheim and the Internet: Sociolinguistics and the Sociological Imagination*. London: Bloomsbury.

Ofelia García

García, O. (2009) *Bilingual Education in the 21st Century: A Global Perspective*. Chichester: Wiley/Blackwell.

García, O. (2017) Problematizing linguistic integration of migrants: The role of translanguaging and language teachers. In J.-C. Beacco, H.-J. Krumm, D. Little and P.

Thagott (eds) *The Linguistic Integration of Adult Migrants/L'intégration linguistique des migrants adultes. Some Lessons from Research/Les enseignments de la recherche* (pp. 11–26). Berlin: De Gruyter Mouton. (Open access: https://www.degruyter.com/ downloadpdf/books/9783110477498/9783110477498-005/9783110477498-005.pdf. In cooperation with the Council of Europe.)

García, O. and Li Wei (2014) *Translanguaging: Language, Bilingualism and Education.* London: Palgrave Macmillan Pivot.

García, O., Flores, N. and Spotti, M. (2017). *The Oxford Handbook of Language and Society.* New York: Oxford University Press.

García, O., Johnson, S. and Seltzer, K. (2017) *The Translanguaging Classroom. Leveraging Student Bilingualism for Learning.* Philadelphia, PA: Caslon.

Otheguy, R., García, O. and Reid, W. (2018) A translanguaging view of the linguistic system of bilinguals. *Applied Linguistics Review.* doi: https://doi.org/10.1515/applirev-2018-0020.

Gunther Kress

Bezemer, J. and Kress, G. (2016) *Multimodality, Communication, Learning: A Social Semiotic Frame.* Abingdon: Routledge.

Hodge, B. and Kress, G. (1979/1993) *Language as Ideology.* London: Routledge.

Hodge, B. and Kress, G. (1989) *Social Semiotics.* London: Polity Press.

Kress, G. (2010) *Multimodality: A Social Semiotic Approach to Contemporary Communication.* Abingdon: Routledge.

Kress, G. and van Leeuwen, T. (1996/2006) *Reading Images: The Grammar of Visual Design.* Abingdon: Routledge.

Diane-Larsen Freeman

Ellis, N.C. and Larsen-Freeman, D. (eds) (2009) *Language as a Complex Adaptive System.* Chichester: Wiley-Blackwell.

Larsen-Freeman, D. (2011) A complexity theory approach to second language development/acquisition. In D. Atkinson (ed.) *Alternative Approaches to Second Language Acquisition* (pp. 48–72). New York: Routledge.

Larsen-Freeman, D. (2012) Complexity theory. In S. Gass and A. Mackey (eds) *Handbook of Second Language Acquisition* (pp. 73–87). New York: Routledge.

Larsen-Freeman, D. (2017) Complexity theory: The lessons continue. In L. Ortega and Z.-H. Han (eds) *Complexity Theory and Language Development: In Celebration of Diane Larsen-Freeman* (pp. 11–50). Amsterdam/Philadelphia, PA: John Benjamins.

Larsen-Freeman, D. and Cameron, L. (2008) *Complex Systems and Applied Linguistics.* Oxford: Oxford University Press.

3 Multimodal Sign-Making in Today's Diversity: The Case of Leeds Kirkgate Market

Elisabetta Adami

How do people use semiotic resources to communicate when they share little cultural and linguistic background? Works on language and super-diversity, translanguaging, polylanguaging and metrolingualism have increasingly acknowledged the multimodality of communication, while still retaining language as their predominant focus and interpretative lens onto communication; in turn, the field of multimodal research has not explicitly addressed issues of intercultural communication and sociocultural diversity. The chapter aims to bridge current research in languaging and (super) diversity with the field of social semiotic multimodality, by investigating contexts of sociocultural diversity (broadly conceived) through a social semiotic multimodal approach. It presents findings on sign-making practices in a butcher's shop, as part of a one-year ethnographic social semiotic study in Leeds Kirkgate Market (UK). Findings show the complex layering of the multimodal deployment in the shop, as a result of the butcher's design choices through time, to accommodate and respond to the communicative needs of an increasingly socioculturally and linguistically diverse demographics of customers. Discussion of findings highlights the potential of a social semiotic multimodal approach for understanding communication in today's diversity, and the implications of current theorising on superdiversity for research in multimodality, sketching a research agenda for an ethnographic social semiotics of communication.

Multimodality and (Super)diversity[1]

In a programmatic paper, Blommaert and Rampton (2016) discuss the implications of today's superdiversity (Vertovec, 2007, 2010) for the study of language practices. A world characterised by enhanced 'polycentricity', 'mobility' and 'complexity' (Blommaert, 2017: 33–34), resulting from the fast-changing transnational phenomena connected with migration, demands changed paradigms for the investigation of language and communication. Before sketching a research agenda, they trace a series of paradigm shifts in sociolinguistics derived by and responding to the enhanced transnational composition of today's communicative environments. One of the paradigm shifts they identify is multimodality. Humans make meaning through a multiplicity of semiotic resources (or modes), of which language is only a part.

In the last two decades, stemming from the work of Kress and van Leeuwen (1996), research in multimodality has increasingly questioned a logo-centric approach to communication and interaction. Multimodal theorising and empirical research (for a recent review, see Adami, 2017a) has refuted the assumption that language is the predominant (let alone the sole) resource defining communication, hence paradigmatic for understanding communication as a whole. Communication is multimodal; we normally combine different modes whenever we represent and interact, and each of these has specific affordances for making meaning. When combined in actual representations and interactions, modes have different functional loads. Hence, to describe and explain meaning in any instance of communication, we need to attend equally to the function played by each mode, and, chiefly, to the meaning made through the relations between modes co-occurring in a communicative event or artefact.

Research in sociolinguistics and applied linguistics is increasingly acknowledging the multimodality of communication (Canagarajah, 2017; García et al., 2017). The contribution of non-verbal resources to meaning-making is considered in most studies on language and superdiversity (Arnaut et al., 2016b), translanguaging (Creese & Blackledge, 2010; García, 2009; García & Wei, 2014), polylanguaging (Jørgensen, 2008) and metrolingualism (Pennycook & Otsuji, 2015), as well as in research on linguistic landscape (for a review, see Huebner, 2016), stemming from the pioneering work of Scollon and Scollon (2003), and further elaborated in Blommaert's (2013) ethnographic linguistic landscaping. Yet, works in these fields adopt an eminently linguistic perspective; they provide data and analyses that are mainly language based and language driven, with minor analytical detail to resources in other modes (for a 'semiotic turn' in these areas, see Hua et al. [2017] and Kusters et al. [2017]).

In using phrases such as 'multimodal translanguaging' (García & Kleyn, 2016: 167–169; García-Sánchez, 2017: 25–26; Melo-Pfeifer, 2015: 197) or 'multimodal languaging' (Busch, 2014: 40; Gynne, 2015: 513–523; Joutsenlahti & Kulju, 2017), some research implicitly ascribes multimodality to features of language, instead of considering speech and writing as part of the resources that concur to the multimodality of communication, *de facto* reproducing a power regime that considers language as a superordinate of all semiosis, and its processes and practices as inclusive of all sign-making.

Research in multimodality, in turn, has increasingly developed theories, methods and tools for a semiotic approach to meaning- and sign-making, allowing for a balanced fine-grained analysis of all resources used in communication (for different theoretical perspectives to multimodality, see Jewitt *et al.*, 2016). Yet, multimodal studies have not addressed issues of cross-, trans- and intercultural communication. Although Kusters' (2017) focus on gestures in deaf/hearing interaction indicates possibilities in this direction, no thorough attempt has been made to adopt a semiotic perspective to investigate how people communicate, interact and make meaning with all available resources in today's diverse contexts.

As flagged also in Adami (2017b) and Kusters *et al.* (2017), this is producing a two-faceted gap in research on communication and (super) diversity, which this chapter aims to address. On the one hand, while acknowledging multimodality as a phenomenon, yet still focusing primarily on language, linguistic research fails to embrace the potential paradigmatic shift that the notion of multimodality can bring to our understanding of communicative practices; this risks ultimately reproducing hegemonic discourses on language as paradigmatic to account for all communication, as in Parkin (2016):

> Our interest may indeed be in a general semiology, of which language is but one strand, possibly absent altogether in, say, silent rituals lacking verbal and textual comment. But, as a matter of heuristic choice rather than of theoretical stance, it can be argued that language normally provides an empirically convenient starting point for tracing out the other different visual and acoustic sign systems that accompany, substitute for, blend with, and shadow speech. (Parkin, 2016: 86)

On the other hand, by disregarding contexts of and research in (super) diversity, studies in multimodality are failing to (1) provide insights on communication (multimodally rather than linguistically conceived) in today's diversity, and (2) test and further develop their theoretical, methodological and analytical apparatus against a changed and fast-changing social scenario.

Yet, social semiotics (Hodge & Kress, 1988; Kress, 2010; van Leeuwen, 2005), one of the originating theoretical approaches of multimodal analysis, seems to reason well with the assumptions and perspectives of the latest research in language and (super)diversity, in that,

- it is interested in *socially situated semiotic practices*, with a focus on the *sign-maker's agency* and assuming the 'social' as prior to semiosis;
- it sees *meanings as fluid and contextual*;
- it conceives of *meaning- and sign-making as practices and processes*;
- *signs are never used*, they are always *newly made each time* a sign-maker chooses a semiotic resource and associates it with the meaning she/he wishes to make in actual representations;
- in labelling sign-making practices, it *does not use notions* such as *national codes, (non-)standard varieties*, let alone *(non-)nativeness* of sign-makers;
- it uses modes as heuristics; they are *not fixed or pre-given codes or systems* of ready-made signs and rules for their use; rather, they are *semiotic resources*, which have an ever-changing set of *meaning potentials* as derived from their materiality and previous uses, developed by specific social groups to fulfil specific functions;
- sign-makers draw on the *resources available* to them to make signs in socially situated contexts, in relation to their *interests*, their *communicative purposes* and their *assessment* of their audiences.

This sounds an apt basis for Parkin's 'general semiology' cited above. Research on language and (super)diversity is indeed questioning the ideological nature of national languages, as separate, bound and identifiable entities that speakers need to master to be fully proficient, and is instead interested in situated practices of 'languaging', and in how these reveal individuals' dynamic repertoires that draw on diverse linguistic resources, as needed to communicate in specific situations.

   In sum, in spite of the 'semiotic turn' of recent research on language and communication in today's diversity, no attempt has been made to adopt a social semiotic approach to investigate this, which this chapter aims to do. The next section presents the findings on an ethnographic social semiotic investigation in Leeds Kirkgate Market. Highlighting the potential of a social semiotic multimodal approach for the understanding of communication in (super)diversity, and the implications of current theorising on (super)diversity for research in multimodality, the concluding section advances a series of hypotheses and directions for future research.

Sign-Making Practices in Kirkgate Market

In 2015/2016, I was involved in the British Academy/Leverhulme-funded project Leeds Voices: Communicating Superdiversity in the Market (http://voices.leeds.ac.uk/), which combined different disciplinary perspectives for the investigation of superdiversity in Kirkgate Market, in the city centre of Leeds (Northern England, UK). I collected visual data, supported by extensive fieldwork observations and interviews, to understand how traders (British citizens and old and new migrants) used disembodied modes, such as writing, font, colour, images, objects and layout, to shape the identity of their activity and to address the increasingly diverse demographics of customers populating the market.

Leeds Kirkgate Market is said to be one of the oldest and largest still functioning indoor markets in the UK and Europe (http://www.leeds.gov.uk/leedsmarkets/Pages/Kirkgate-market.aspx). It hosts nearly 400 stalls and shops providing a wide range of generally low-budget goods and services, ranging from food, clothing, mobile accessories and second-best white goods, to beauty services, key cutters, shoe repair, takeaways and cafés. It is located in the city centre, in an area currently undergoing gentrification. Kirkgate Market itself, managed by the city council and traditionally attracting a low-budget population, has long been subject to plans for renovation (for the impact on traders' sign-making, see Adami, 2018).

The population of the market has changed considerably in recent years, with increasingly diverse demographics of traders and customers (Gonzalez & Waley, 2013). A survey conducted by Leeds Voices in 2016 has identified 25 different nationalities among traders (the survey involved only one person in each stall, hence the count for all staff is possibly higher). As emerged from interviews with 21 traders, the customer population encompasses all ethnic groups living in the city, including old and newly arrived migrants as well as British citizens (for census data on Leeds, see http://www.ukcensusdata.com/leeds-e08000035#sthash.1Zamo6F5.dpbs).

The following sections discuss the sign-making practices resulting from data collected in a butcher's shop in the market. Data were collected through observation, photos, fieldnotes and semi-structured interviews. While my data collection was specifically focused on sign-making, interviews conducted by Penny Rivlin of Leeds Voices were tailored to cover the broader aim of the project on issues of culture, language and communication in relation to the demographics of the market; they are used to support the analysis for insights into the motivation behind the trader's sign-making.

Indexing selves

In contrast to most other shops in the market, butchers frequently deploy the Union Jack (the flag of the United Kingdom). In Figure 3.1, the image of the flag on the top right of the banner below the butcher's window refers to the provenance of the activity and of the meat, i.e. 'this is a British butcher and we sell British meat', as the butcher also confirmed when asked for the motivation for the flag:

> Even though we are … sort of manipulating our stock to sort of provide for different cultures, and people from different countries, um, we are still priding ourselves on giving a different alternative but still keeping it, keep it as English meat.

Figure 3.1 B&J Callard butcher's shop window in Leeds Kirkgate Market

The flag indexes tradition, i.e. 'we've been here for generations' (the shop has been running its activity in the market for over 30 years). Tradition and permanence are further reinforced by the word 'traditional' in the stall's banner at the bottom and by the materiality of the stall's name, with 3D letters mounted on the wall at the top of the stall (other stalls in the market have more temporary signage, such as plastic-coated banners pinned to the stall's frame). On the top left, the banner also displays the symbol of Yorkshire (the city's county), functioning as an identity marker specialising further the cultural provenance of the activity, i.e. 'we are from here (and we're proud of it)'; it also ties cohesively with the 'locally sourced' writing below, which indexes ideas of 'terroir', feeding into current food consumption ideologies. National and county images, together with the writing in the banner and the font and materiality of the upper signage, multimodally construct a cohesive identity of the butcher's activity marked towards indigeneity. Yet, in the overall multimodal deployment of the shop, there are other signs serving other purposes that articulate further and fragment this primary cohesive identity, as discussed in the next section.

Addressing 'others'

A lucky cat is placed on a shelf facing the butcher's window (Figure 3.2). The butcher was asked about it at a point in the interview when he was discussing the shopping preferences of his many regular Chinese customers:

> The lucky cat, yeah, exactly, that's a perfect example. Why would an English butcher have a lucky cat in the window? [giggles]. That's purely because they love it, you know, the Chinese love anything to do with lucky cats! And it was just, it started off as a kind of novelty thing, we saw it in a shop one day, we thought we'd get one, and they love it, you know. The little Chinese kids, love waving to it.

In the butcher's explanation, the lucky cat is used as a sign functioning to befriend, welcome and attract Chinese customers. A multimodally marked Yorkshire-British trader has appropriated a sign that he perceives as coming from another culture, to reach out towards a new niche of migrant customers populating the market. It would be an exemplary case of 'translanguaging', yet no language is used to address a culture-specific customer group; what is used instead is an object-as-sign.

In a social semiotic perspective, a sign has been newly made by the butcher/sign-maker, who has associated the signifier (the object 'lucky

Figure 3.2   The right side of the butcher's window

cat') to a signified 'Chinese culture', motivated by its assumed provenance, because of his interest, i.e. to address Chinese customers. In making the sign, the butcher has made an 'educated guess' ('it started off as
a kind of novelty thing [...] and we thought we'd get one'). He 'gave
it a try' and then turned himself into an observer to check whether the
sign had the desired perlocutionary effect ('and they love it, you know.
The little Chinese kids love waving to it'). The butcher interpreted the
Chinese kids' waving to the lucky cat as a sign of appreciation and positive feedback for his guess, i.e. something like 'the lucky cat speaks well
to Chinese customers'; so he kept it on the window.

As Blommaert and Rampton argue (2016), in (super)diverse contexts, non-shared knowledge is the norm rather than the exception, and
metapragmatic reflexivity is crucial. This invests all semiotic resources.
A perspective that sees signs as newly made (rather than used) can better
account for the inherently tentative practice of sign-making in socioculturally diverse contexts (cf. also the always hypothetical nature of
meaning-making in Kress, Chapter 2, this volume).

In the visual multimodal deployment of the shop facade, the Union
Jack and Yorkshire images in the banner (further reinforced and articulated through 'traditional' and 'local' in the writing) and the lucky cat
are geo-culturally marked signs that point to different directions and
serve different functions. The images index the cultural provenance of

the activity; the object indexes the cultural specificity of the addressed customer audience. The relation between resources pointing to different cultural provenances reveals a multiplicity of meanings indexing the multilayered attempt at positioning the butcher's activity to respond to the complex needs of a socioculturally diverse environment.

On the shelf above the lucky cat, the butcher has plastic grapes (as shown in Figure 3.2). During an informal chat, he explained the reasons for placing the plastic grapes on the shelf. Following the closure for renovation of the fishmongers' aisle in the market, the fishmongers were temporarily relocated opposite the butchers. While butchers have traditionally a low-budget clientele, fishmongers in the market attract a higher-income population. As emerged in the interview and indexed also in the 'locally sourced' writing in his banner, this particular butcher is trying to position his activity at a higher quality and price level than the others. With the fishmongers' 'posh' clientele now walking by his window, the butcher has thought of decorating his shop. In the attempt to accommodate the design of his shop to the taste of a 'posh' clientele, he has chosen plastic fruit, which is instead a typically vernacular form of decoration (for the materiality of the resource, inexpensive and long-lasting compared to fresh fruit, a luxury item in households in the past). Traditional linguists would consider this a case of hyper-correction; in order to reach out to a 'higher' speech community, the butcher has intended to produce their register, yet drawing on his knowledge (and taste, in Bourdieu's [1986] sense) of what he believes that register to be.

A social semiotic analysis of the lucky cat and the plastic grapes as signs reveals in fact the same sign-making principle, which could be named 'trans-signing' (to avoid 'languaging' for practices that involve other modes). In both cases, the butcher has made a sign through an object to reach out towards a perceived 'other', either in nationality or in class. The specific resources in both signs have been chosen because the sign-maker has assumed that they belonged, and hence could 'speak', to that specific sociocultural 'other'.

Further ethnographic investigation among customers would be needed to see the extent to which the lucky cat and the plastic grapes are successful in communicating with their intended addressees. Yet, these signs 'speak' beyond their intended audiences. To me, as a migrant in the UK, who, after Brexit, has become increasingly aware of British citizens' xenophobic feelings, the exotic provenance of the lucky cat has served to exclude or mitigate a nationalist meaning of the British flag in the butcher's banner – something like 'yes, he marks his Britishness, as the flag says, but he is also open to other cultures, given that he has a lucky cat; so I, as a migrant, may be welcome in his shop'. High taste customers are unlikely to interpret the plastic grapes as an index of high taste; yet they may appreciate the plastic grapes as signs of vernacular authenticity, i.e. exotic in class rather than in nationality, quite paradoxically against the butcher/sign-maker's motivations.

Through a social semiotic perspective, it is immediately manifest that the lucky cat and the plastic grapes are signs made with an overarching common purpose, that is, to address socioculturally perceived 'others'. They may be equally (un)successful and/or mis- and reinterpreted.

In times when political agendas are fuelling nationalism hinging on racist discourses, and low-income citizens are motivated to associate with and elect billionaires to 'take their country back' from migrants, a semiotic perspective on diversity seems particularly necessary. In revealing the same semiotic processes at work to bridge cultural gaps that are potentially equally wide across all demographic dimensions within society, it can unveil the ideological nature of assumed hierarchies of differences (with nationality and ethnicity as weighing more for cultural 'otherness' than class and lifestyle, for example). People make the effort to accommodate their sign-making practices to reach out to 'others'; these 'others' may well be linguistically, ethnically and legally identified as part of the same community, as native speakers, white British and co-citizens (rather than non-native speakers, Chinese and migrants); yet, sign-making can hinge equally on non-shared knowledge (as for the plastic grapes) and can reveal equally non-coinciding repertoires.

Focusing attention

Multimodal analysis not only considers individual signs or their co-presence, but also meaning in relations produced through the resource of layout, i.e. relative positioning of signifying elements in space, which invites specific semantic and pragmatic relations; in this it can provide an even finer-grained analysis of sign-making practices.

After a series of topic changes, the interview with the butcher proceeds on how communication works with customers who speak little English. After mentioning resources such as pointing and eye contact, the butcher highlights the value of experience in inferring buying preferences ('knowing what they'll probably want'). Referring again to Chinese customers as an example, he says, 'You know, they'll definitely want belly pork'. In his experience, only Chinese customers buy "belly pork" (more commonly known as "pork belly"); he has started to supply it in response to the needs of this customer segment. He would position the belly pork beside the lucky cat on Tuesday (the day when the photo in Figure 3.2 was taken), because in his experience Chinese customers come to shop for meat in larger numbers on that day. Hence, on a Tuesday, adjacent positioning of the belly pork and the lucky cat is used as a resource to signal Chinese customers that he sells that specific cut of meat.

Through positioning, a sign-complex is created between the lucky cat and the belly pork. The lucky cat has (1) an addressing function towards a specific audience (Chinese customers), and (2) a deictic function towards the intended focus of attention (the belly pork) – something like 'Chinese visitors of the market, look here: we sell belly pork'. Positioning in space is used as a focusing device, i.e. to direct a specific audience's attention to an aspect of reality that the sign-maker wants to make salient to them, because of his experience of what, in his shop, could interest that specific audience.

This is all done by using non-verbal resources. Writing in the butcher's shop is entirely in English, including the labels identifying the cuts of meat on sale. To direct Chinese customers' attention to the availability of belly pork on sale through language, the butcher would have to resort to someone who could write Chinese (that is, to translation). Instead, he could make that specific meaning through the use of semiotic resources available to him.

There is more. Using one mode or another always entails meaningful differences. Language is particularly loaded in terms of national ideologies (for attitudes of fixity towards language, see Otsuji & Pennycook, 2010); when we see or hear some written/spoken language that we perceive as foreign (in respect to the context), we immediately associate a national label with it (e.g. if I write *sémiologie* or *Bonjour* in a chapter written in academic English, it will immediately stand out as 'French'). A Chinese script in the butcher's shop could index more markedly his will to address Chinese customers (*only*), thus risking to exclude others (to those who cannot read it, a signage in a Chinese script means solely 'Chinese', see also Banda, Jimaima & Mokwena, this volume). Instead, in the age of globalisation, with enhanced transnational mobility of goods, the presence of 'exotic' objects in our everyday spaces is so common as to be unremarkable (for the semiotics of the transnational circulation of objects, see Archer & Bjorkvall, this volume).

The use of a diversified range of modes enables the butcher to address multiple audiences at once: a general one, through the use of English for writing, an unmarked resource for an activity in the UK, hence interpreted as addressing everybody; and a specific one, through an 'exotic' object, intended to address Chinese, but open to a series of other interpretations by others (such as mine, as a migrant customer, in the sense of 'this British butcher is not hostile to migrants').

Making meaning with 'others'

As emerges frequently from our data and interviews among traders, multimodal communication in both embodied and disembodied modes is used extensively to compensate for non-shared linguistic resources in the exchange of information. As for embodied resources, the butcher makes the following example of interactions with a customer:

> she won't speak a word of English, but we will get a product for her and she'll get what she wants. And there'll be no communication; it's purely pointing, eye contact, knowing what they'll probably want.

As observed by Blackledge *et al.* (2015) in exchanges in Birmingham Bull Ring Market, non-verbal communication is deployed extensively when linguistic resources are little shared. This calls for the need of video-recorded data collection for the multimodal analysis of face-to-face interaction, which cannot rely solely on tape-recording and fieldnotes, to avoid unbalanced analyses of speech vs other meaning-making resources.[2]

As for disembodied modes, two large posters representing beef and lamb cuts are attached to the left wall when entering the shop (Figure 3.3).

Figure 3.3 Image of beef and lamb cuts in the butcher's shop

When explaining how communication works with customers who have little English, the butcher added:

> we've got pictures on the back wall of the pigs and the lambs, um and the cows, so we always take them to the wall; can you pick it out on the picture? If not, we just take them around.

The posters are positioned at eye level, on the wall facing the customers' space in the shop, within easy reach of customers (other butchers in the market have the same posters attached instead to the wall behind the counter). Positioning is functional to facilitate exchange of information, as the butcher says, 'we always take them to the wall'.

By virtue of their pictorial elements, the posters serve as an aid for mutual learning, both for the specific communicative needs of the moment and for possible future uses. Identification of information using the posters may serve not only for the specific shopping activity, but also to expand the customer's linguistic resources for 'English meat cuts' to be used in future interactions with this or other butchers. It may also augment and refine the butcher's experience of individual customers' preferences in meat, further generalised into broader (stereo)typical cultural ones (e.g. Chinese customers are likely to want belly pork), which may then inform his supplies, and his guesses for interactions with other customers.

Significantly, non-shared linguistic knowledge is not only assumed (as in the tentative sign-making with the lucky cat), but also explicitly factored in, addressed and compensated by the butcher in his positioning of the posters. He has designed the multimodal deployment of his shop to facilitate communication, by choosing and positioning specific multimodal resources that will serve the purpose of exchanging information in the socioculturally diverse context where he operates.

Designing (super)diverse spaces

The butcher as sign-maker has made use of different modal resources in his stall to make a complex and layered set of meanings, aimed at fulfilling different functions responding to the needs of his specific (super) diverse context. The sign-maker's choice in different modal resources evidences his multiple interests; through the use of different modes, the shop is intended simultaneously to:

(1) Index values of
- national and local cultural provenance (image: Union Jack and Yorkshire);
- tradition and permanence of the activity (writing, font and materiality);

(2) Address multiple target customer audiences
- a culture-specific one (object: lucky cat);
- a lifestyle/income-specific one (object: plastic grapes; writing: locally sourced);
- a generic one (unmarked writing: English);

(3) Foreground specific aspects of reality to specific addressees (positioning: lucky cat+belly pork);

(4) Exchange information (drawing+photo+writing: posters and their positioning), used as a support for face-to-face communication involving embodied resources such as pointing, gaze and body movement.

The multimodal deployment of the butcher shop has been designed through time,[3] by adding signs in multiple layers, following changes in customer groups, through tentative guesses on how to accommodate them and by supporting guesses through interpreted feedback.

Through multiple choices among available resources, he has visually shaped the public space he manages, to fulfil his multiple communicative needs, which include interpersonal functions (such as projecting his identity and addressing specific sociocultural niches of customers) as well as ideational (such as exchanging information) and textual ones (such as focusing attention on specific aspects for specific addressees), all designed to the needs of the specific diverse environment of the market where he operates.

Conclusions: Towards a Research Agenda

The multimodal deployment of the butcher's shop, along with his sign-making in face-to-face interactions with customers, can be considered the result of complex hetero-semiotic vernacular practices, to adapt Parkin's (2016: 79) notion of 'heteroglossic urban vernaculars' to the whole semiosis. These practices, of which we know very little, are being developed to serve the specificities and complexities of communication in a socioculturally diverse context such as Kirkgate Market.

All the writing in the butcher's shop is in English. The butcher is a white British man from Yorkshire operating in Leeds. The butcher's shop would have hardly been selected as a case study in translanguaging and linguistic landscape research. His sign-making accommodating to the specificities of a socioculturally diverse environment would have escaped any linguistic analysis. This evidences the need and potential of adopting a fully semiotic perspective onto communication in today's diverse contexts; the present study has shown the aptness of a social semiotic approach for its investigation.

From the evidence on the butcher's shop, we can formulate the following working hypotheses on multimodal communication in today's diverse environments:

- non-verbal resources are readily available and particularly apt for sign- and meaning-making in contexts where language is little shared;
- sign-making relies on semiotic resources for a wide and articulated range of functions: to exchange information, to index identity, to focus and frame and to address particular sociocultural groups;
- multimodal composition enables the simultaneous display of nuanced, multifaceted and multilayered meanings, through the fulfilling of multiple functions pointing to different interlocutors at once (e.g. English writing paired with the 'Chinese' object), best apt for the diversified communicative needs of socioculturally diverse environments.

A series of theoretical and methodological insights can be derived:

- Analysis needs to pay equal fine-grained attention to all meaning-making resources, to aim for the kind of 'more holistic understanding of how people communicate with each other' called forth in (the language-focused study of) Goodchild and Weidl (this volume).
- Analysis of non-verbal resources (less subject to national codification) rules out from the start artificial separations between the traditional domains of 'diversity' and 'intersectionality'. Non-shared repertoires and equal distances can exist as much among citizens of the same ethnicity as with people crossing national borders. A semiotic stance to communication can therefore shed a different light onto sociocultural diversity, and reveal the ideological nature of common (neonativist) preconceptions.
- Anything can be potentially meaningful; anything can be made into a sign (not only what is printed onto a signage, as considered in linguistic landscape analysis, but also 'unremarkable' objects such as plastic grapes). This is a main methodological challenge for multimodal analysis, which is often time consuming and necessarily fine-grained; yet it is an inescapable task, if we want to account for the whole semiosis of communication in today's diverse environments. To address the challenge, the use of modes as analytical heuristics can serve as a navigational aid in the mapping of potential resources of a semiotic space. Pinpointing disembodied modes (such as colour, font, image, writing, objects, layout, clothing, music and sounds) and embodied modes (such as speech, gesture, gaze, face expression, proxemics and

body movement) can help to scan communicative environments for resources potentially made into signs.

- A traditional multimodal analysis cannot alone account for the actual and intended uses of artefacts-as-signs (as in the case of the butcher's posters), which only an ethnographic approach to social semiotics can reveal.

In their programmatic paper, Blommaert and Rampton (2016) sketch a research agenda for the investigation of 'language and communication' in superdiversity. This chapter has brought evidence for the need to broaden the agenda through a social semiotic take and analytical focus. A full understanding of communication in all its meaning-making possibilities calls for a *social semiotic ethnography* or *ethnographic social semiotics* of communicative practices in today's diverse times (see also Bradley & Moore, this volume).

A research agenda on the social semiotics of today's diversity needs to carry out investigation in at least three intertwined *areas of semiosis*:

- face-to-face interactions, where data collection needs necessarily include video-recording, to capture all visual and auditory resources, instead of only speech;
- online interactions and representations in digital environments, which afford enhanced transnational circulation of semiotic resources and discourses;
- sign-making in the built-environment, as evidenced in the butcher's shop.

While the present chapter has focused only on visual disembodied *resources*, investigation should widen to auditory ones (such as sound, music and speech), as well as meaningful resources perceived through other senses (like smell and touch, for example); these are not only a particularly salient part of the semiotic landscape of a multisensory environment such as a market, but of all our sensible and meaningful experience of the world more generally.

Markets have been widely shown to be privileged places to observe diversity (e.g. Hiebert *et al.*, 2015); yet research should broaden the *sites of observation* to include contexts that have a more private and intimate character, as well as for more ludic and interpersonal, less transactional purposes, up to more formal and official contexts (both online and offline). Broadening the contexts of social semiotic investigation of diverse communication could provide in-depth mapping of multimodal use of resources for a wider *range of communicative func-tions*, like expression of feelings, beliefs and stances, as well as projection, co-construction and negotiation of identity for example (as pointed out for language in Sherris, Schaefer & Mango, this volume).

When refocused towards today's sociocultural complexity, a social semiotic perspective on signs being newly made (rather than used) high-lights the multifaceted, fluid and fragmented nature of meaning-making practices, and the transnational and trans-sectional character of semi-otic resources that we use to communicate. This shows the potential of (1) paying attention to resources other than language, which have a wider transnational circulation, have been less subject to national codification, and even when originated locally, are not subject to translation; and (2) an ethnographic stance to semiotic research to grasp adequately the nuances and intricacies of today's social complexity.

Notes

(1) Other concepts have been proposed along with superdiversity (for a discussion, see Arnaut *et al.*, 2016a). The chapter does not delve into the debate on the notion in rela-tion to others (for a criticism, cf. Pavlenko, 2016); it aims to pinpoint the potential of multimodality to advance understanding of communicative practices in light of the sociocultural complexity of our times. It uses a bracketed '(super)diversity' label as an umbrella term, to contribute, through a semiotic perspective, to the most promising applied and sociolinguistic research in the field.

(2) Video-recording is an essential method of data collection in all multimodal studies focused on face-to-face interaction (e.g. Jewitt *et al.*, 2016; Mondada, 2014; Norris, 2004; see also Perera, this volume), yet not systematically used in linguistic ethno-graphic work, even when focusing on resources other than speech (e.g. Blackledge & Creese, 2017); for a thorough discussion on video as a research method, see Jewitt (2012).

(3) Although a longer ethnographic observation would be needed to trace the punctual semiotic changes in time, from the butcher's interview and broader events investing the place, it is apparent that the making of given signs occurred at different times, in relation and as a response to specific changed conditions in the market, i.e. the lucky cat as a response to the increasing Chinese clientele of the market, the plastic grapes after fishmongers were moved to the butchers' aisle in 2015, when their dedicated aisle was closed for renovation.

References

Adami, E. (2017a) Multimodality. In O. García, N. Flores and M. Spotti (eds) *Oxford Handbook of Language and Society* (pp. 451–472). Oxford: Oxford University Press.

Adami, E. (2017b) Multimodality and superdiversity: Evidence for a research agenda. *Tilburg Papers in Culture Studies* 177. See https://www.tilburguniversity.edu/upload/0677a845-216b-4fc1-828d-1ec041bfd333_TPCS_177_Adami.pdf. Accessed 26 July 2017.

Adami, E. (2018) Shaping the social through the aesthetics of public places: The renovation of Leeds Kirkgate Market. In F. Forsgren and E.S. Tønnessen (eds) *Multimodality and Aesthetics* (pp. 89-112). London/New York: Routledge.

Arnaut, K., Blommaert, J., Rampton, B. and Spotti, M. (2016a) Introduction: Superdiversity and sociolinguistics. In K. Arnaut, J. Blommaert, B. Rampton and M. Spotti (eds) *Language and Superdiversity* (pp. 1–18). London/New York: Routledge.

Arnaut, K., Blommaert, J., Rampton, B. and Spotti, M. (2016b) *Language and Superdiversity*. London/New York: Routledge.

Blackledge, A. and Creese, A. (2017) Translanguaging and the body. *International Journal of Multilingualism* 14 (3), 250–268.

Blackledge, A., Creese, A. and Hu, R. (2015) Voice and social relations in a city market. *Working Papers in Translanguaging and Translation* 2, 1–118.

Blommaert, J. (2013) *Ethnography, Superdiversity and Linguistic Landscapes: Chronicles of Complexity*. Bristol: Multilingual Matters.

Blommaert, J. (2017) Durkheim and the Internet: On sociolinguistics and the sociological imagination. *Tilburg Papers in Cultural Studies* 173 (January).

Blommaert, J. and Rampton, B. (2016) Language and superdiversity. In K. Arnaut, J. Blommaert, B. Rampton and M. Spotti (eds) *Language and Superdiversity* (pp. 1–18). London/New York: Routledge.

Bourdieu, P. (1986) *Distinction: A Social Critique of the Judgement of Taste*. London/New York: Routledge.

Busch, B. (2014) Building on heteroglossia and heterogeneity: The experience of a multilingual classroom. In A. Blackledge and A. Creese (eds) *Heteroglossia as Practice and Pedagogy* (pp. 21–40). Dordrecht: Springer.

Canagarajah, S. (2017) The nexus of migration and language. The emergence of a disciplinary space. In S. Canagarajah (ed.) *The Routledge Handbook of Migration and Language* (pp. 1–28). London/New York: Routledge.

Creese, A. and Blackledge, A. (2010) Translanguaging in a bilingual classroom: A pedagogy for learning and teaching? *Modern Language Journal* 94 (1), 103–115.

García-Sánchez, I.M. (2017) Friendship, participation, and multimodality in Moroccan immigrant girls' peer groups. In M.A. Theobald (ed.) *Friendship and Peer Culture in Multilingual Settings. Sociological Studies of Children and Youth* (pp. 1–31). London: Emerald Group Publishing Limited.

García, O. (2009) Education, multilingualism and translanguaging in the 21st century. In A. Mohanty, M. Panda, R. Phillipson and T. Skutnabb-Kangas (eds) *Multilingual Education for Social Justice: Globalising the Local* (pp. 140–158). New Dehli: Orient Blackswan.

García, O. and Wei, L. (2014) *Translanguaging: Language, Bilingualism and Education*. New York: Palgrave Macmillan.

García, O. and Kleyn, T. (2016) *Translanguaging with Multilingual Students: Learning from Classroom Moments*. London/New York: Routledge.

García, O., Flores, N. and Spotti, M. (2017) Conclusion: Moving the study of language and society into the future. In O. García, N. Flores and M. Spotti (eds) *The Oxford Handbook of Language and Society* (pp. 545–552). Oxford/New York: Oxford University Press.

Gonzalez, S. and Waley, P. (2013) Traditional retail markets: The new gentrification frontier? *Antipode* 45 (4), 965–983.

Gynne, A. (2015) Languaging in the twenty-first century: Exploring varieties and modalities in literacies inside and outside learning spaces. *Language and Education* 29 (6), 509–526.

Hiebert, D., Rath, J. and Vertovec, S. (2015) Urban markets and diversity: Towards a research agenda. *Ethnic and Racial Studies* 38 (1), 5–21.

Hodge, R. and Kress, G. (1988) *Social Semiotics*. Cambridge: Polity.

Hua, Z., Otsuji, E. and Pennycook, A. (eds) (2017) Multilingual, multisensory and multimodal repertoires in corner shops, streets and markets. Special Issue. *Social Semiotics* 27 (4), 383–393.

Huebner, T. (2016) Linguistic landscape: History, trajectory and pedagogy. *Manusya: Journal of Humanities* 22, 1–11.

Jewitt, C. (2012) An introduction to using video for research. *NCRM Working Paper.* NCRM. See http://eprints.ncrm.ac.uk/2259/. Accessed 15 July 2017.

Jewitt, C., Bezemer, J. and O'Halloran, K. (2016) *Introducing Multimodality*. London/New York: Routledge.

Jørgensen, J.N. (2008) Polylingual languaging around and among children and adolescents. *International Journal of Multilingualism* 5 (3), 161–176.

Joutsenlahti, J. and Kulju, P. (2017) Multimodal languaging as a pedagogical model: A case study of the concept of division in school mathematics. *Education Sciences* 7 (1), 1–9.

Kress, G. (2010) *Multimodality. A Social Semiotic Approach to Contemporary Communication*. London: Routledge.

Kress, G. and van Leeuwen, T. (1996) *Reading Images. The Grammar of Visual Design*. London: Routledge.

Kusters, A. (2017) Gesture-based customer interactions: Deaf and hearing Mumbaikars' multimodal and metrolingual practices. *International Journal of Multilingualism* 14 (3), 283–302.

Kusters, A., Spotti, M., Swanwick, R. and Tapio, E. (eds) (2017) Beyond languages, beyond modalities: Transforming the study of semiotic repertoires. *International Journal of Multilingualism* 14 (3), 219–232.

Melo-Pfeifer, S. (2015) Multilingual awareness and heritage language education: Children's multimodal representations of their multilingualism. *Language Awareness* 24 (3), 197–215.

Mondada, L. (2014) The local constitution of multimodal resources for social interaction. *Journal of Pragmatics* 65, 137–156.

Norris, S. (2004) *Analyzing Multimodal Interaction: A Methodological Framework*. London/New York: Routledge.

Otsuji, E. and Pennycook, A. (2010) Metrolingualism: Fixity, fluidity and language in flux. *International Journal of Multilingualism* 7 (3), 240–254.

Parkin, D. (2016) From multilingual classification to translingual ontology. A turning point. In K. Arnaut, J. Blommaert, B. Rampton and M. Spotti (eds) *Language and Superdiversity* (pp. 71–88). London/New York: Routledge.

Pavlenko, A. (2016) Superdiversity and why it isn't: Reflections on terminological innovation and academic branding. In S. Breidbach, L. Kuster and B. Schmenk (eds) *Sloganizations in Language Education Discourse* (1689–1699). Bristol: Multilingual Matters.

Pennycook, A. and Otsuji, E. (2015) *Metrolingualism. Language in the City*. London/New York: Routledge.

Scollon, R. and Scollon, S.W. (2003) *Discourse in Place: Language in the Material World*. London: Routledge.

van Leeuwen, T. (2005) *Introducing Social Semiotics*. London: Routledge.

Vertovec, S. (2007) Super-diversity and its implications. *Ethnic and Racial Studies* 30 (6), 1024–1054.

Vertovec, S. (2010) Towards post-multiculturalism? Changing communities, conditions and contexts of diversity. *International Social Science Journal* 61 (199), 83–95.

4 Material Sign-Making in Diverse Contexts: 'Upcycled' Artefacts as Refracting Global/ Local Discourses

Arlene Archer and Anders Björkvall

Adami (2017: 1) claims that the potential of a social semiotic multimodal approach for understanding communication in 'superdiversity' has not yet been adequately explored and neither has the concept of 'superdiversity' been addressed in multimodal research. While the focus of this chapter is not on superdiversity as such (Blommaert, chapter 2 this volume), it does look at mobility and communication from a social semiotic perspective in order to explore global/local discourses instantiated in and circulating around 'upcycled' artefacts, particularly plastic bottles. The chapter looks at *semiotic resources*, *discourses* and *narratives* that are drawn on when upcycled artefacts are used to make meaning locally and globally.[1]

By upcycling, we mean the process of converting waste, used, thrown-out, found and repurposed elements into new products for different consumer markets. In developing countries, where new raw materials can be expensive, upcycling is commonly practiced. Objects that already have some other defined purpose are used and transformed into 'art' or into objects with another function. For instance, upcycled candy wrappers are converted into consumer products such as handbags or laptop sleeves. Globally, upcycling as a phenomenon has been on the increase due to marketability, the lowered cost of reused materials and fashion trends.

In recycling, materials and products are reused to create other products, for instance, when plastic bags are turned into plastic bottles. New value is not necessarily added, even though 'sustainability' is always part of the processes of recycling (think of 'downcycling' through which value is decreased when a material is used for a new purpose). However, there is always value adding in the processes of upcycling and the creation of 'trashion'. Here, both professional designers and laypeople take what artefacts they can find in flea markets, weekend car-boot sales, garage sales, even rubbish dumps and transform them into something fashionable that they can use themselves or sell. Such upcycled products tend to gain not only economic value in the process of being transformed from used, old things, but also an ethical value through being created out of a responsibility for the environment and resistance towards mass consumerism (Archer & Björkvall, 2018).

The aesthetic and functional values that are added in upcycling address the demands of different local and global markets. When people do upcycling, they draw on different discourses. The main focus of this chapter is how discourses *in* and *around* an upcycled artefact make it possible for the artefact to move between cultural and geographical places and spaces, and in that process both maintain and transform the meaning potential of the artefact. Upcycled artefacts can refract racial, gendered, classed and countercultural identities, and can mobilise social and cultural difference for profit. To this end, this chapter examines discourses in and around upcycled artefacts made from plastic bottles. By 'in' we mean the discourses that are suggested by the materials and the design of the artefact; discourses 'around' the artefact are the ones that are not explicitly present in the artefact but in other texts or practices that contribute to the realisation of the key meaning potentials of the artefact.

Bottles are one of the most common containers in society, which also makes them an easily available material to be used in upcycling. For instance, the material could be foregrounded in an upcycled artefact (in this chapter we look at plastic), or the shape of the bottle. Both the material and the shape are *semiotic resources*, as well as colour and texture. Discourses around an object are located in practices and multimodal texts that are historically, geographically or culturally related to the object. This chapter explores how semiotic resources in upcycled South African artefacts realise discourses that allow the artefact to 'travel' (circulate as a finished product), but also how such artefacts often need complementary discourses and narratives to make that mobility possible.

Authenticity and Mobility of Artefacts in Global/Local Discourses

Pietikäinen and Kelly-Holmes (2011) examine the labelling of tourist artefacts in the context of global and local tourism, focusing specifically on Sámi souvenirs in Inari in Northern Finland. They explore the tensions between *authenticity* and *mobility*. Drawing on these notions, we explore the resources used to construct authenticity in and around the upcycled artefact, as well as the resources used to ensure the mobility of the artefact in global/local locations and discourses. Along with Pietikäinen and Kelly-Holmes (2011: 326), we see authenticity as 'discursively constructed, always situated in a particular communicative event and subject to alterations and interpretations'. Mobility refers to the extent to which other semiotic resources can be used to make objects mobile across places, domains and practices (Blommaert *et al.*, 2005; Pietikäinen & Kelly-Holmes, 2011: 326). This links to Budach *et al.*'s (2015) notion of 'boundary' objects. These are seen as flexible and able to adopt different meanings in different contexts, or as Kell (2009) puts it, they have 'trans-contextual potential' in that they are able to move physically across contexts and can carry meaning potential across spatial distances, domains and contextual boundaries (cf. Adami, this volume). This is as opposed to 'bonding objects', namely objects that flow freely across contexts and 'display a remarkable stability of meaning' (Budach *et al.*, 2015: 394), and 'bounded objects', which have limited mobility and are often part of specific and scripted spaces.

It should be noted that we do not regard the differences between 'boundary', 'bound' and 'bounded' objects as absolute – it is rather a matter of degree. Further, one could easily argue that all artefacts are more or less 'bounded' objects since meanings always change according to context. However, the point is that some upcycled artefacts tend to have the potential to 'travel' between geographical locations, say, South Africa and Sweden, and still maintain their main meaning potentials. In such cases, the 'mobility' properties of an object tend to dominate over its communicated geographical and cultural 'authenticity'. One example would be artefacts that connect to discourses and practices in the international art scene. This is different from 'bounded objects' such as, for instance, tools used in specific, local crafts practices that only become meaningful to people who recognise them as such. Most upcycled artefacts that have the potential to 'travel' globally tend to be of the 'boundary' type. Their marketability depends on their capacity to communicate a *provenance* (see below) in both rubbish and contexts in the developing world, but at the same time be functionally, aesthetically and commercially relevant in the culturally and geographically distant location.

Discourses in and around signifies a two-way movement; as well as refracting discourses circulating in society, artefacts can also 'prompt' discourses. Latour (1996) talks about artefacts as having agency. However, from a social semiotic perspective, objects are seen as powerful prompts rather than non-human agents. What is the artefact doing in relation to discourse? We understand discourses to be 'socially constructed knowledges of (some aspect of) reality which give expression to the meanings and values of an institution or social grouping' (Kress & Van Leeuwen, 2001: 4). The terms 'instantiation of discourse' and 'refracting' discourse can be problematised as can the notion of 'materialisation' of discourse. While analysing upcycled artefacts, there is the danger of presupposing the existence of a 'discourse'. In doing this, the notion of discourse is reified and taken for granted, as being 'out there'. In order to avoid a circular and deterministic analysis, it may be useful to think about *fragments* of discourses. In this way, we can think of the artefact as having provenance in a range of discourses, domains and practices. Artefacts as texts reflect and refract fragments of discourses, and semiotic resources always carry traces of the work of others. They are 'made, produced, remade, "transformed", as a result of social work' (Kress, 2010: 14).

Methodology for Analysing 'Fragments of Discourses' in and around Artefacts

The study aims to address the tension between detailed analysis of material artefacts and that of circulating discourses and texts around the artefact as well as upcycling in general. An important methodological question for looking at upcycled artefacts and how they refract fragments of discourse is: what kind of (socially and culturally shaped) 'background knowledge' do we need? More specifically, our research questions are: (i) how do we identify discourses suggested by the *recontextualised materials* and the *design* of the artefact; (ii) how do we identify discourses 'around' the artefact that contribute to the realisation of meanings (in changing local and global contexts)? Kopytoff (1986) also reminds us that the meaning of an artefact varies in time and space, and between individual social actors. Our study is thus located at the intersection of artefacts, communication, materiality and practice.

Social semiotic multimodal analysis (Jewitt, 2014; Jewitt & Oyama, 2001; Kress & Van Leeuwen, 2006) is used as the main method of data analysis to investigate artefacts and practices. A social semiotic analysis focuses on 'the relationship among texts, social contexts, and the social practices [...] modes realise' (Stein, 2000: 334). Social semiotics provides a way of thinking about meaning making as a motivated, social activity in which humans always draw on the semiotic resources that they consider most relevant or apt (Kress, 2010). The term 'semiotic resource' is a key term in social semiotics and it refers to the resources that we use to make meaning, ranging from colours to shapes, words to grammar, sounds to letters. We look at how these semiotic resources are used and recontextualised in upcycled objects, and how this refracts instances and fragments of discourse. We specifically use the term 'refracts' rather than a term like 'reflect' that signals a somewhat simplistic relationship between artefact and circulating discourses.

When people do upcycling they draw on different discourses. These discourses provide much of the 'value adding' that is the key feature of upcycling, or what Pietikäinen and Kelly-Holmes (2011) call the 'authenticity' of the artefact. We look at discourses *in* an artefact as instantiated through explicit semiotic resources, focusing specifically on material, shape and colour. Multimodal theorists assert that materiality matters, as it contributes to the meaning potential of texts. Björkvall and Karlsson (2011: 141) argue that 'materiality in itself contributes to meaning-making'. They provide the example of Post-it notes that have material semiotic resources, including surface, size, format, adhesiveness, mobility and colour. Material can also have 'texture' (cf. Djonov & van Leeuwen, 2011). The material of wood, for example, could evoke the 'natural' as a material, but the texture (whether it is smooth and shiny or rough) could recall different values to those evoked by the 'natural' or could have provenance in different styles, such as 'rustic' for example. Materials used to construct artefacts can communicate various ideas such as 'nostalgia', 'durability', 'environmentally conscious' and so forth.

Discourses *around* an artefact are located in practices, other artefacts or texts. Here we focus on the provenance (cf. Adami, 2015; Djonov & van Leeuwen, 2011; Kress & van Leeuwen, 2001) of semiotic resources. Björkvall (2017) describes the concept of provenance as multimodal in the sense that its main analytical and explanatory value is located at a level of abstraction above specific features of, for instance, written texts, images or colours. Originally defined by Kress and van Leeuwen (2001: 72) as how '"mythical" signifieds are "imported" from some other domain (some other place, time, social group, culture) to signify a complex of ideas and values which are associated with that "other" domain by those who do the importing', its application in this chapter is somewhat broader. Here, provenance refers to the historical or contemporary origins of any given feature of an artefact or text in, for example, a type of design, a genre, discourse or the practices of specific social groups or professionals. Björkvall (2018) points to how provenance is concerned with *connotational* meanings that require specific cultural knowledge in order to be recognised, even as these meanings may change over time. The connection to concepts such as 'intertextuality', 'interdiscursivity', but also to 'resemiotisation' (cf. Bradley & More, this volume), is obvious. However, the main argument for using and partially redefining provenance is to turn the analysis not only in the direction of 'origins' in other types of texts and discourses, but also towards broader semiotic practices, artefacts and material designs.

This data was part of a larger corpus for a study investigating the 'semiotics of value' in upcycling, including the movement of artefacts between South Africa and Sweden (cf. Archer & Björkvall, 2018). In relation to the use of ethnographic methods and tools in other chapters in this volume (e.g. Banda *et al.*; Sherris *et al.*), this study is more semiotic and design and artefact oriented than ethnographic. We look primarily at the design of the artefacts as such, and their local contexts and global trajectories. However, with a few exceptions the artefacts were documented where they were actually sold and/or displayed. For instance, we have visited several shops and street vendors in both South Africa and Sweden, and also art schools, universities and other commercial buildings where upcycled artefacts were displayed. During many of these visits, we have engaged in informal conversations with salespersons as well as artists and designers. We have also visited websites that are sometimes connected to artefacts on display and for sale. Through these conversations and through looking at related texts, a number of narratives surrounding the artefacts have been identified.

The data analysed in this chapter includes a doorway curtain made from discarded plastic bottles and bottle tops; an installation in a shopping centre made from the bottles of a washing liquid; large light fittings made from recycled milk bottles; jewellery made from plastic water bottles; and animal trophy heads made from discarded oil containers and bottle tops. We selected these artefacts for analysis in this chapter based on two main criteria. Firstly, in exploring the discourses instantiated in artefacts, it was deemed important to work with the same material substance. All of these artefacts were made from different kinds of waste plastic bottles. Plastic bottles can be seen as a global resource that is used to package food, cleaning materials and other liquids such as motor oil and pesticides. Secondly, although global products, the upcycled bottles in all of the artefacts are mixed with local resources to reflect particular local contexts. These artefacts utilise three dominant resources, namely material, colour and shape, which point to a provenance in different discourses. The fragments of discourses explored in and around these artefacts include social upliftment, branding and advertising, global environmental design discourses (ethical consumerism), as well as critical discourses that include elements of parody. We will now look at each in turn.

Discourses of social upliftment

The artefact in Figure 4.1 is made from cut up plastic bottles, which are strung on twine to make a curtain to hang across a doorway. The curtain was displayed in a shop in Stockholm, hanging against a glass wall. The plastic curtain communicates a certain 'authenticity of origin', but it is also an example of an artefact that needs a narrative to reach its full 'authenticity' potential. An elaborate narrative was provided by the salesperson in the shop. It was claimed that unemployed women collected the plastic bottles as rubbish discarded on the beaches of Cape Town. The same women then produced this artefact, which moved from a local to a global market. The authenticating narrative that accompanies this artefact is thus built on environmental ethical discourses, discourses of women's empowerment, poverty prevention and social upliftment in Africa. However, the 'authenticity' of the artefact is somewhat undermined by the limited wear and tear on the upcycled bottles that one might expect if they had been exposed to the natural elements on the beach.

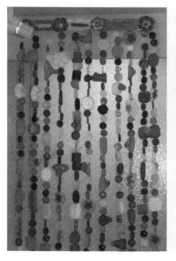

Figure 4.1 Doorway curtain made out of plastic bottles

The colours in the curtain are primary and gaudy. The pattern of the curtain reflects some kind of symmetry. This is similar to the type of aestheticisation that Adami (2015) has identified in food blogs. Shape, colour and size are resources used in the pattern. Big and small bottle tops are mixed to form a sequence of one big, followed by three small. The shapes of the bottom of the bottles are cut to look like plastic flowers. Colour and shape contribute to the pattern through regular repetition of the yellow bottoms of bottles. The plastic bottles that form the substance of the curtain have largely had their logos removed, except the bottle tops of 'Minute Maid' and 'Coca-Cola', so the branding is not primarily achieved through the recontextualisation of trademarks. Instead, the branding of the curtain as upcycled is mostly realised through the semiotic resource of shape, the materiality of the plastic and the aesthetic use of patterning. Shapes of the fragments of the bottles remain recognisable, so we are able to discern the highly mundane function of the objects in other contexts, such as the long curved necks of the toilet cleaner bottles and the lift-up nozzles of the cooldrink bottles. Arguably, the curtain is a good example of an upcycled artefact as a 'boundary object' that connects both to contexts in the developing world (e.g. poverty, pollution and the need for women to find independent ways of making money) and to functional, ethical and commercial relevance in another place, in this case Sweden. The provenance of the upcycled curtain in environmental ethical discourses thus relies on the recognition of the functional and material properties of the plastic parts that make up the curtain. The accompanying narrative also serves as a guarantee of the authenticity of the artefact, within the discourses of social upliftment and poverty reduction in South Africa.

Branding and advertising discourses

The second constellation of artefacts that we look at instantiates discourses of branding. Figure 4.2 shows a 'Skip' washing liquid installation at an affluent shopping precinct in Cape Town, 'The Waterfront'. The title of the installation is: 'Introducing the new skip liquid: the evolution of washing' and the aim is to promote a commercial washing powder (Behance, n.d.). The installation comprises an oversized washing machine surrounded by upcycled fish and birds made from the plastic bottles for the washing liquid. The fish are placed along the ground, the evolving fish are suspended midway between floor and ceiling, and the birds are held by thread from the ceiling in order to appear to be flying. This conveys the notion of 'evolution' over time, and is represented in a circular

Figure 4.2 The 'evolution of washing' installation

way, with the fish moving towards the left, and up and over towards the right. The evolution ends with the birds, which have the 'Skip' logo firmly displayed. The dominant colour is white. Commercial branding is instantiated in the semiotic resources of colour: whiteness and light feed into notions of freedom and cleanliness. The installation attests to the old adage 'cleanliness is next to godliness' and is another temple to consumption located within the shopping mall, the ultimate temple. These are not ethical discourses operating here, but consumer-driven discourses that feed into the notion that consumption can make you a better person and enable you to self-actualise, 'evolve' and reach your potential'.

The construction of the fish from the liquid bottle is delicate and innovative (see Figure 4.3). Here the material, the plastic, is foregrounded, rather than the shape of the bottle. This is not crass consumerism by any means. The message is one of beauty, delicacy, freedom, flight and artistry. Even the upcycled birds that maintain the 'Skip' logo are beautifully crafted and subtle (see Figure 4.4). The emphasis here is on evolution, transformation and renewal.

Contrary to the plastic curtain example examined earlier, the upcycling that happens here has not been justified for environmental reasons. In other words, the advertising/branding campaign does not draw on environmental discourses or notions of ethical consumerism. Neither does it make reference to a specific South African 'authenticity of origin'. Instead, the 'whiteness', 'lightness' and 'smoothness' of the designed fish and birds point to a provenance in middle-class practices connected to,

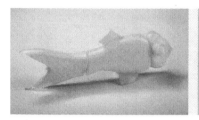

Figure 4.3 Detail of fish made from washing liquid bottle (logo removed)

Figure 4.4 A flock of birds made from washing liquid bottles, with the logo still visible

for instance, the functional and modern home in the Western world. The particular artistry of the bird design connects more to the international art scene than to local, African practices. So, the mobility potential of the upcycled birds in Figures 4.2 through 4.4 stems from their connection to the global market of advertising and art rather than from connections to semiotic practices in the African context. In the terminology of Budach *et al.* (2015), the mobility of the birds makes them 'bonding' objects: their semiotic potentials are assumed to be more constant across global contexts – at least in those in which middle-class consumption and advertising are well known phenomena.

Global environmental design discourses/ discourses of ethical consumerism

Another set of discourses circulating around upcycled artefacts is that of global design taking into consideration environmental concerns. Consumerism here is packaged as both 'trendy' and ethical. These have the character of designed 'boundary objects' with a high degree of mobility from local to global locations. In thinking about global environmental design discourse, we focus on two different types of artefacts: a functional but aesthetic artefact (a light fitting) and artefacts used for adornment (jewellery). Figure 4.5 shows milk bottles that South African artist, Heath Nash, refashioned into large light fittings. These lights are used in both institutional and domestic spaces. As in the 'art of washing' installation, the colour 'white' is a resource and only the white plastic from the milk bottles is used for construction. This allows a large amount of light to shine through, but also contributes to the ethereal quality of the lights. The artist, Heath Nash (n.d.), talks about 'translucency' as a resource, which is slightly different to colour as it is interlinked to light: 'I also began to encounter all the translucencies available – that occur when the plastic is blown into the mould'. In the lights shown in Figure 4.5, the light shines through the plastic, transforming the white into a warm yellow glow interspersed with grey less-translucent patches, adding texture and depth to the artefact. The lights comprise a constellation of many flowers made into a 'flower ball' that suggests life, light and growth. The materiality of the milk bottles, such as the embossed brands' logos, the date stamp on the milk bottles and the varied textures and thicknesses of different bottles primarily function as markers of 'authenticity' with provenance in mundane household practices.

These upcycled milk bottles have been used to produce functional yet aesthetic objects to be used in particular spaces. Plastic bottles have also

Figure 4.5 Recycled milk bottle lights

been used in far more personal artefacts, such as in jewellery. A jewellery designer in South Africa, Mikhela Hawker, produced jewellery from plastic water bottles, including rings (Figure 4.6), bangles (Figure 4.7) and earrings. Here, the material of the artefact, namely plastic, is of utmost importance in realising the discourse of ethical consumerism. Plastic water bottles are rife globally and are a scourge on the environment. Something natural (such as water) is a scarce resource in some global contexts, and has become fashionably commodified into a branded product for consumption in others. The 'natural' has become packaged in such a

Figure 4.6 Plastic bottles, cold enamel and sterling silver rings. Mikhela Hawker (Miky Rose)

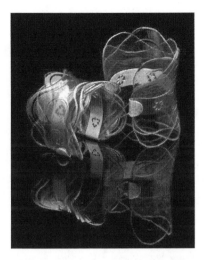

Figure 4.7 Plastic water bottle and sterling silver bangles. Mikhela Hawker (Miky Rose)

way as to work against nature. In the jewellery, the colour 'blue' is foregrounded, keeping the resonances of both the plastic bottle and the water it contained. The shapes of the rings and the bangles are also resonant of water and flow. In the bangles shown in Figure 4.7, the plastic and the silver weave together like ripples in water, creating a sense of movement and transparency, and perhaps the 'translucency' of the material to which Nash (n.d.) draws attention.

Even though the provenance of the plastic bottles is important for the 'ethical' meaning potentials of the light fittings and jewellery, the delicacy and sophistication of these upcycled products connect them to 'fine arts' practices rather than to, for instance, practices of trying to make a living out of redesigning rubbish. In fact, the level of artistic sophistication of the objects in Figures 4.5 through 4.7 makes it hard to recognise the used and repurposed material from which they are made. Complimentary narratives such as that provided by Nash are required in order to realise the discourses of ethical consumerism that, in turn, become sales arguments both locally in South Africa and globally.

Critical Discourses

In thinking about the ways in which artefacts can open up critique, the question is not only how the social world is constructed and represented through upcycled artefacts, but also how it is and can be contested through these artefacts. It is often difficult to decide whether we are confronting a reverent use of a revered work or concept or a more familiar, even parodic playing with it. According to Bakhtin (1981: 75), it is 'the nature of every parody to transpose the values of the parodied style, to highlight certain elements while leaving others in the shade'. Thus, 'every parody is an intentional dialogized hybrid'. Within parody, styles 'actively and mutually illuminate one another' (Bakhtin, 1981: 76). The use of the material (plastic) can be seen as parodic in the curtain (in Figure 4.1), for example. Plastic is the material of 'chemistry, not of nature' (Barthes, 1972: 54) and it is detrimental to the environment. Plastic is also the preferred material of mass production and modernity. In the design of the curtain, we see a play with these connotations. We see a mixture of irony, humour and irreverence that encourages us to critically reflect on overconsumption of plastic. There is humour in the choice of bottles, including the choice of toilet cleaners. The most down-to-earth and practical, cheap plastic objects, described by Barthes (1972: 54) as 'at once gross and hygienic', have been upcycled for aesthetic purposes.

According to Kress (1989), argument is a cultural textual form that produces difference rather than closure and can as a result produce 'change'. Brenner and Archer (2014) claim that argument in art can take the form of instantiating negotiation with existing and entrenched conventions of the various genres. This would seem to be the case in the upcycled animal trophy head in Figure 4.8. By creating a juxtaposition between the traditional genre (the slaughtered and stuffed real animal head) and the revised genre (the upcycled plastic animal head with demure eyelashes), 'difference' is produced and certain cultural values and knowledge questioned.

The animal trophy head made out of plastic waste passes critical commentary on a number of social issues, including the practice of hunting for status and the display of killing prowess placed above the mantelpiece as an indicator of bravery and often masculinity. It passes critical commentary on consuming as 'collecting', just as the hunter collects its prey, and with a different kind of attendant violence. The head is made out of a container used for holding oil, which could also point to socioeconomic issues around oil, including wealth, consumption and power. The snout is made from the cut off top of a bottle. The horns are made out of bottle tops strung together, with the apex of the horn, the suction nozzle on drinking bottles (with connotations of the infantilising of the user). The horns use the *affordance* of the shape of the nozzle, and also exploit the humour in shape, in the same way that the recognisable shapes of the toilet cleaners were used humorously in the plastic curtain.

Figure 4.8   Animal trophy head in Stockholm

Most noticeable are the eyelashes, which are segments of a bottle cut into strips and curled, softening the face of the animal trophy as it 'bats' its eyelashes at the viewer/consumer.

The critical discourse here is also complexified by the local/global configurations around the object. These trophy heads were made in South Africa and were photographed in a shop in Stockholm. The quarrel with the genre of animal trophy heads has currency in contemporary South African design and popular culture. There are different kinds of trophy heads made out of a variety of materials, such as wire, beads, gold ceramic and so forth (see Figure 4.9). The upcycled plastic bottle trophy heads are firmly located within this local genre. The relocalisation and thus recontextualisation of the artefact in a Swedish shop that sells African and Mexican crafts serves to provide a metalevel critique on the 'authentic' or, rather, what might be regarded as 'authentic' African or 'authentic' indigenous in this context. Even the high price tag (on something made from discarded plastic bottles) could be regarded as something of a joke on the consumer.

Perhaps here it is worth reflecting on how these artefacts as 'signs' travel, in terms of what is shared meaning potential, but also what is situated, more individual and specific to the context. The question of interest

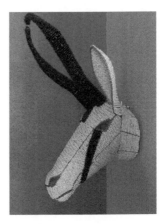

Figure 4.9 The trophy head 'genre' (Antelope head made from beads and wire)

to us is how they would change their meanings or meaning potentials to work in different contexts through shared transnationally circulating resources. Although a South African might find the high price tag in the Swedish shop amusing, in that context it may not be interpreted as a critique on consumerism, but rather may appeal to a certain segment of society, for instance Scandinavian environmentalists who are against exploited cheap labour in 'less-developed countries'. It could also appeal to those for whom handmade, unique artefacts that require time, creativity and labour in their production are valued (see discussion below about ethnographic tools to identify and analyse individuals' interpretations of the artefacts). So, what may be refracting critical discourses in one context, may be exploiting a certain sensitivity and taste or cultural capital in another geo-political context.

However, what seems clear is that the discourses around the animal trophy head are located in certain global and local practices, including trophy hunting, which would lead to the conclusion that we are dealing with a typical, upcycled 'boundary object'. The semiotic resources utilised in this artefact (including material, shape and colour) realise discourses that allow the artefact to travel from one context to another, including a critical discourse that parodies both the practices signified by the artefact and the consumer of the artefact.

Here it is worth pointing to some of the methodological limitations of the type of social semiotic multimodal analysis that has been employed and presented in this chapter. We have illustrated how an analysis of fragments of discourses and semiotic resources in an artefact as well as the discourses, narratives and practices around it can provide us with a number of insights regarding local authenticity, global mobility and other meaning potentials of upcycled objects. But we have not provided an account of what happens when actual buyers and users of the artefacts in Sweden and South Africa (and in other places around the world) interact with and interpret them. Turning to more ethnographically oriented methods, such as interviewing buyers and producers of the upcycled artefacts and documenting their uses in the homes of the buyers (cf. Björkvall, 2014; Björkvall & Karlsson, 2011) would to some extent challenge the results presented above. As an example, individual consumers in Sweden may totally disregard the critical aspects of the animal trophy head that we have described as key features and instead connect their design to colourful and playful (plastic) design practices of 1970s Scandinavia. Such ethnographic insights can be useful for sharpening and challenging the results of social semiotic analysis, both in terms of what is to be found *in* an artefact and the connections that people make to discourses, texts and practices *around* it.

Conclusion

This chapter has explored how to identify fragments of discourses in and around an upcycled artefact. A social semiotic approach has worked well in this endeavour as its conception of meaning-making as both fluid and situated has enabled an interrogation of the ways in which objects instantiate varying discourses across global/local contexts, which are often characterised by (super)diversity. In thinking about discourses in an upcycled artefact, we have primarily discussed colour, shape and material. In thinking about discourses 'around', we have applied Pietikäinen and Kelly-Holmes' (2011) notions of authenticity and mobility, and Budach *et al.*'s (2015) 'boundary' and 'bonding' objects. We have also used the concept of provenance to discuss how upcycled artefacts relate to other artefacts, texts, semiotic domains and practices. This has helped us to highlight the diverse and multifaceted nature of meaning making through upcycling, and the ways in which artefacts draw on such varied phenomena as environmentalism, poverty reduction, Western functionalism and trophy hunting.

All the artefacts examined here are produced from plastic post-consumer waste and are aimed at potential customers. 'Re-use as a design tool ... has so much potential – both as a source of raw material and as a beautiful limitation' (Nash, n.d.). This notion of creativity within limitations or constraints echoes Bell's (2016) work.

The constraints of the plastic bottle enable a sharper look at the object, in terms of available resources for making a new artefact, such as shape, size, colour, translucency, texture and material. What all of the artefacts have in common is an investment of 'time' in their making. This notion of 'time' as a value-adding resource is captured in Nash's (n.d.) words: 'There are literally hours invested in every single part of everything we make, and this invested time and energy is what makes the product beautiful and inherently valuable'. Here, value is defined primarily aesthetically, but also in terms of economic value. We have also shown how value is added by drawing on and refracting circulating discourses in the social world. More specifically, the chapter has pointed to global processes of 'value-adding-through-upcycling'. These practices may in many ways be environmentally and socially responsible, and upcycled artefacts can actually be empowering as a creative means for critical comment on various social issues. Nonetheless, they depend on access to both local and global consumer markets, which, at best, is to be regarded as contradictory to the intentions of those concerned with upcycling as a way to deal with issues around mass consumerism.

Note

(1) The research presented in this chapter was performed within the lager project Multimodal Texts and Pedagogies in Higher Education, funded by the Swedish Foundation for International Cooperation in Research and Higher Education (STINT) and the National Research Foundation in South Africa (2015–2018).

References

Adami, E. (2015) Aesthetics in digital texts beyond writing: A social semiotic multimodal framework. In A. Archer and E. Breuer (eds) *Multimodality in Writing: The State of the Art in Theory, Methodology and Pedagogy* (pp. 43–62). Leiden/Boston, MA: Brill.

Adami, E. (2017) Multimodality and superdiversity: Evidence for a research agenda. *Tilburg Papers in Cultural Studies* Paper 177. See http://www.tilburguniversity.edu/upload/0677a845-216b-4fc1-828d-1ec041bfd333_TPCS_177_Adami.pdf (accessed 5 May 2017).

Archer, A. and Björkvall, A. (2018) The 'semiotics of value' in upcycling. In S. Zhao, A. Björkvall, M. Boeriis and E. Djonov (eds) *Advancing Multimodal and Critical Discourse Studies: Interdisciplinary Research Inspired by Theo Van Leeuwen's Social Semiotics* (pp. 165–180). London/New York: Routledge.

Bakhtin, M. (1981) *The Dialogic Imagination: Four Essays.* Austin, TX: University of Texas Press.

Barthes, R. (1972) Toys. In R. Barthes (ed.) *Mythologies* (pp. 53–55). London: Vintage.

Behance (n.d.) The Evolution of Washing. See https://www.behance.net/gallery/The-Evolution-of-Washing/2250264 (accessed 17 March 2017).

Bell, S. (2016) Writing against formal constraints in art and design: Making words count. In A. Archer and E. Breuer (eds) *Multimodality in Higher Education. Studies in Writing* (vol. 33; pp. 136–166). Leiden: Brill.

Björkvall, A. (2014) Practical function and meaning: A case study of Ikea tables. In C. Jewitt (ed.) *The Routledge Handbook of Multimodal Analysis* (2nd rev. edn; pp. 342–353). London/New York: Routledge.

Björkvall, A. (2018) Critical genre analysis of management texts in the public sector: Towards a theoretical and methodological framework. In C. Seiler Brylla, G. Westberg and D. Wojahn (eds) *Kritiska textanalyser* (Södertörn Discourse Studies 6) (pp. 57–79). Huddinge: Södertörns högskola.

Björkvall, A. and Karlsson, A.-M. (2011) The materiality of discourses and the semiotics of materials. A social perspective on the meaning potentials of written texts and furniture. *Semiotica* 187, 141–165.

Blommaert, J., Collins, J. and Slembrouk, S. (2005) Spaces of multilingualism. *Language and Communication* 25, 197–216.

Brenner, J. and Archer, A. 2014. Arguing Art. In A. Archer and D. Newfield (eds) *Multimodal approaches to research and pedagogy: Recognition, resources and access* (pp. 57–70). Oxon and New York: Routledge.

Budach, G., Kell, C. and Patrick, D. (2015) Objects and language in trans-contextual communication. *Social Semiotics* 25 (4), 387–400.

Djonov, E. and van Leeuwen, T. (2011) The semiotics of texture: From tactile to visual. *Visual Communication* 10 (4), 542–564.

Jewitt, C. (ed.) (2014) *The Routledge Handbook of Multimodal Analysis* (2nd rev. edn). London/New York: Routledge.

Jewitt, C. and Oyama, R. (2001) Visual meaning: A social semiotic approach. In T. Van Leeuwen and C. Jewitt (eds) *Handbook of Visual Analysis* (pp. 134–156). London: Sage.

Kell, C. 2009. Literacy practices, text/s and meaning making across time and space. M. Baynham and M. Prinsloo (eds.) *The future of literacy studies* (pp. 75–99). Hampshire: Palgrave MacMillan.

Kell, C. and Patrick, D. (2015) Objects and language in trans-contextual communication. *Social Semiotics* 25 (4), 387–400.

Kopytoff, I. (1986) The cultural biography of things: Commoditization as process. In A. Appadurai (ed.) *The Social Life of Things: Commodities in Cultural Perspective* (pp. 64–91). Cambridge: Cambridge University Press.

Kress, G. (1989) Texture and meaning. In R. Andrews (ed.) *Narrative and Argument* (pp. 9–21). Milton Keynes: Open University Press.

Kress, G. (2010) *A Social Semiotic Approach to Contemporary Communication*. London/New York: Routledge.

Kress, G. and Van Leeuwen, T. (2001) *Multimodal Discourse: The Modes and Media of Contemporary Communication*. London: Arnold.

Kress, G. and Van Leeuwen, T. (2006) *Reading Images. The Grammar of Visual Design*. London: Routledge.

Latour, B. (1996) On interobjectivity. *Mind, Culture and Activity* 3 (4), 228–245.

Nash, H. (n.d.) Heath Nash makes cool things. See http://heathnash.com (accessed 24 March 2017).

Pietikäinen, S. and Kelly-Holmes, H. (2011) The local political economy of languages in a Sámi tourism destination: Authenticity and mobility in the labelling of souvenirs. *Journal of Sociolinguistics* 15 (3), 323–346.

Stein, P. (2000) Rethinking resources: Multimodal pedagogies in the ESL classroom. *TESOL Quarterly* 34 (2), 333–336.

5 Semiotic Remediation of Chinese Signage in the Linguistic Landscapes of Two Rural Areas of Zambia

Felix Banda, Hambaba Jimaima
and Lorato Mokwena

We introduce the notion of semiotic remediation emphasising repurposing to underscore agency in sign-making and consumption, and as a tool in social semiotic approaches to multimodal discourse analysis in linguistic landscapes (LL) studies. Using data from observations, interviews and images of LL in Chinese from two rural sites in Zambia, we highlight the agency of social actors in the re-imagination and re-invention of the Chinese signage for new meanings and new purposes in narrations of place. We show how the social actors appropriate authorship of the signage from the Chinese originators, through (oral) re-narrations that infuse Chinese signage with new local meanings and purposes. Reflecting that local people do not necessarily 'read' and (re)cognise the signs as Chinese sign-makers envisioned, we discuss the layered materialisation of 'authorship' and the duality of sign and object and the resulting contrasting interests and intended meanings in the dynamic interactions of sign, people and place. We highlight the need for LL studies to theorise sign production and consumption that counterbalances the interests of the sign-maker with those of local social agents who impose their own through subjective remediations. We conclude that as the Chinese signs become part of the local repertoire of signs for place making, there is simultaneous connection and disconnection between local and faraway Chinese lifeworlds and the transformation of the local and global contexts of sign-making and consumption.

Locating the Rural in Linguistic Landscapes

The dominant narrative in LL studies has been about urbanised spaces, conventional signage and upmarket configuration in which computerised monitors and signboards (Jaworski & Thurlow, 2013) are used for place description and general meaning-making enterprise. Upmarket signage refers to high-end signage as opposed to low budget shop signage, whose low budget materiality and design, for example, may be seen to index the low standing of the text producers and consumers in society's socio-economic structure.

This is reminiscent of Stroud and Mpendukana's (2009) characterisation of sites of luxury and sites of necessity, respectively. In their discussion of the social structuring of signage, Stroud and Mpendukana (2009) categorise grammatically edited, professionally done and expensive signage in the sites of luxury, and unedited and usually handmade signage with low-quality material in the sites of necessity. However, the bias towards urban areas is apparent in the seminal definition of LL, in which Landry and Bourhis (1997: 25) refer to LL as '[t]he language of public road signs, advertising billboards, street names, place names, commercial shop signs, and public signs on government buildings [which] combines to form the linguistic landscape of a given territory, region, or urban agglomeration'. The urbanscapes orientation of LL studies led Zabrodskaja and Milani (2014) to lament the apparent dearth of studies that have looked at LL in rural areas.

On the other hand, Lyons (2017) and Malinowski (2009) lament that LL studies have not made the analysis of human agency and authorship a priority. Malinowski's (2009: 108), in his discussion on authorship in LL, describes landscapes as sites of continuous, intense and varied human activity that produce multiple meanings. Not denying the role of a sign-maker in designing and producing a sign, Malinowski (2009) outlines the complex and agentive ways in which people engage with the landscapes. He proposes the view of the 'author of signs as a complex, dispersed entity who is somewhat in control of the meanings that are read from his or her written "utterances"'. Drawing on Peirce's (1955) tripartite components of a sign as the *representamen*: the form of the signs or 'sign vehicle'; an *interpretant*: what *senses* are made of the sign; and the *object*: the *referent*, what the sign stands for, Lyons (2017: 5) notes that the majority of LL studies have been primarily indexical by concentrating on 'the Representamen and the processes... by which these signs denote their Object'. Lyons (2017: 1) argues that LL studies need to focus on the senses made of the sign (*interpretant*) as a consequence and to account for selective and subjective meanings local people as producers, consumers or passers-by draw from the signs. In describing the 'critical turn in LL' and outlining new methodologies and areas of research, Barni and Bagna (2015: 7) single out 'the role of people in the linguistic landscape, and their awareness of being part of it, as authors and as actors, [as] constitut[ing] new layers of LL research'. Scollon and Scollon (2003) define social agent or actor as the instigator of action.

Exploring social actors as/and authors in the production and consumption of signage in LL entails 'balancing [the] significance of producers' intention and knowledge with potential viewer uptake and reaction' (Lyons, 2017: 3; Adami, this volume). Considering the proposal for multiple authorships, the chapter explores the role of social actors in sign-making and consumption as a way to theorise and characterise the materiality of the duality of sign and object in the LL. The chapter also considers the extent social actors 'read' and re-cognize signs as per the (original) producer's intentions. This is one area that still needs to be addressed in LL studies (cf. Banda & Jimaima, 2015; Lyons, 2017).

However, considering that the signage used in our study was emplaced by the Chinese, and is mostly in Chinese script, with little or no translation into English or local Zambian languages both of which use the Roman alphabet, we highlight the senses and meanings local social actors produce and consume from the physical attributes of the Chinese signs in the narrations of place. In this regard, we introduce the notion of semiotic remediation as repurposing to contribute to social semiotic theory of multimodality and to account for the transformation of semiotic material and discursive regimes during narration of place.

Although the discourse practice of repurposing can be found in urban areas, we decided to use two sites in rural areas of Zambia as studies have shown that there is a dearth of studies exploring the production and consumption of signage in LL in rural areas. We determined that the limited number of emplaced signs, the absence of streets and street names and planned built environments in the selected rural areas, would highlight better the kinds of remediation and transformation of semiotic material in the signage for meaning-making in narrations of place.

Translocality and Glocal Cultural Flows

We use the notion of translocation to account for the localised nature of sign consumption and meaning-making in spite of where the sign was originally produced. Translocality has been defined as 'the dynamic between localized lifeworlds in faraway sites' (Ma, 2002: 133).

Translocation not only refers to the movement of people but it also involves the movement of cultural objects such as food, language, scripts and clothing within and across national boundaries. Translocated people and cultural objects are multilocally located, creating nodes of connected lifeworlds in far places (Ma, 2002). Appadurai (1996) talks about cultural flows in which ideas, cultural symbols and knowledge circulate across regional and national boundaries, often to be used for new meanings and purposes in diversified localities. Global cultural flows do not just end up in the cities of Africa; they find their way to rural localities as well.

For instance, Chinese signs indicating their various investments and, for example, the American presence through Coca-Cola signage are found not only in urban areas but also in rural areas of Africa. Although the signage can be said to connect faraway places (China and America, for example) with various localities in Africa, local people draw their own meanings in the local contexts of consumption of the translocated cultural material. In this conceptualisation, translocal mobility can be said to forge 'an ever changing relationship between sociocultural happenings of one locality with that of another locality producing blurred and flattened boundaries' (Oakes & Schein, 2006: xiii), and that the people of the localities in which the material culture is transported are not passive receivers of regional, national or global cultural flows (Hedberg & Carmo, 2012).

The receiving localities are 'spaces of imagination and spaces of representation' (Bridge & Watson, 2008: 7), as they 'are involved and connected on their own accounts' (Hedberg & Carmo, 2012: 1). Our interest in the notion of translocal spatiality is that it helps to account for the appropriation of global and local semiotic material in the construction of localised spatialities, that is, localised narratives of place (Ma, 2002; Pennycook, 2010).

Remediation of Semiotic Material

Related to the foregoing is Kress' (2010) argument that signs are always newly made in sociocultural contexts. In his conceptualisation of a social semiotic approach to multimodality, Kress (2010) opines that each time a semiotic resource is remade it implies a different signification. A sign thus becomes a social semiotic resource with multiple meaning potentials actualised in social contexts of communication. In addition to emphasising sociocultural factors in sign-making, Kress (2010: 10) says that signs are an expression of the interests of the sign-maker to realise meaning 'using culturally available semiotic resources, which have been shaped by practices of members of social groups and their cultures'.

Closer to the notion of remediation as used in the chapter is Kress' (2010: 53) argument on representation: that signs people make are in some way a remaking of previous signs so that sign-making is 'constantly transformative' and 'a constant remaking'. Also of interest is Kress' proposal that signs 'are *motivated* not *arbitrary* relations of meaning and form; the motivated relation of a *form* and a *meaning* is based on and arises out of the interests of makers of signs'. Sign-making is thus conceived as generative and agentive, while the signifiers deployed in sign-making 'are *made* in social interaction and become part of the semiotic resources of a culture' (Kress, 2010: 55; italics in original). This will be important to understand how the uncommon/unfamiliar Chinese signs are not only reshaped for meanings in narrations of place, but they also become part of everyday semiotic resources for sign-making for local communities.

This brings us to the notion of remediation focusing on repurposing. Irvine (2010) and Vandenbussche (2003) suggest that the notion of remediation has been understood and used in different ways. This includes recontextualisation and transformation of say an oral report into a written one, where the meaning of the content is not necessarily different. What has changed is the medium or mode of meaning-making. Resemiotisation refers to the adaptation and transformation of semiotic material to suit different communication contexts and practices (Bradley & Moore, this volume). However, in foregrounding repurposing in our use of remediation, we aim to highlight the agentive nature of the production and consumption of signs and of the human–sign–environment interaction (and hence on the) 'ever-emergent social relations, and on the ways semiotic forms can serve as resources for social agents' (Irvine, 2010: 236), to deploy multiple meanings and purposes. Scollon and Scollon (2003) define the social agent or actor as the instigator of action. Semiotic remediation focusing on repurposing as used in this chapter is not about mediating *a-new* (Prior & Hengst, 2010) or recycling the content of one media into another; it is about the re-invention and infusion of new meanings and purposes into semiotic material in the *now* leading to the creation of new contexts for future references, 'responses and acts' (Prior & Hengst, 2010: 7). Thus, the social actor assumes responsibility for the action taken. This means social actors who *repurpose* semiotic material become the agents of the new consequences of the repurposed material.

In repurposing, old signs, objects (Archer and Björkvall, this volume), events and media may be visible or not visible but they acquire new meanings and purposes to which they are newly redeployed (Prior & Hengst, 2010). There is thus a shift in focus in terms of analysis from looking at change of meaning resulting from the mobility of texts, objects and other semiotic material from one context to another, to accounting for the creative processes that go into the transformation of texts, objects and other semiotic material for new meanings and purposes. In this conceptualisation, it is not just the new contexts but also the kinds of new meanings and new purposes for the repurposed texts, objects and other semiotic material, that is the focus of study.

Although it can be said that repurposing is a human activity prevalent in urban areas, the dearth of emplaced signage in the LL of rural areas makes the study of remediation in the latter spaces potentially more interesting and productive. In urban areas, social actors can refer to streets and street names, for example, a luxury not available to those in rural areas. The limitations imposed by material conditions (Stroud & Mpendukana, 2009) also means that the repurposing of signage in as far as narration of place is concerned, is much more a matter of necessity in rural areas than in urban areas where it can be said to be a matter of choice.

Methodological Issues

We draw on Stroud and Jegels' (2014) walking approach, a conflation of walk, talk, gaze and photography. Walking brings researchers within the mundane of the daily life of rural dwellers; talk generates extended narratives out of which the semiotic potential of signs referred to in the narration of place acquires dynamic meanings. While the gaze undercuts the range of signs available in the semiotic environment, photography freezes a fleeting moment in which time and space get conflated. The methodology focused on the social actors' agency in the production and consumption of signs. Stroud and Jegels (2014) underscore the importance of observing human social action as it is intricately linked to the eventual production and consumption of locality. In fact, Stroud and Jegels (2014: 180) remind us that locality is 'organised, narrated, and interactively accomplished by means of – direct or indirect – engagement with situated material semiotic artefacts'. The idea therefore is to capture the 'habitual' way local people engage and make meanings out of the signs in place. LL studies are amenable to 'walking' methodology as they often involve walking (or driving) to capture images of semiotic materials in place for analysis. Walking interviews enable the capturing of local consumers' construction and sense of place. Rather than disembodied extrapolation of meanings, in walking interviews the scholar taps into the local people's lived experiences of place first hand, and the different meanings they attach to the different objects in place. The dynamic interactions of walk, talk, gaze and photography enable the building of social theories bottom-up, that is, develop social theories that are socially and community engaged, as local interviewees become co-researchers in the construction of situated, relational and material-based theories.

The data used in this chapter was collected as part of an ongoing larger research project on the semiotic ecology of the material culture of multilingualism/multiculturalism in the LL of urban and rural areas in Zambia, Botswana, Malawi and South Africa. We have collected more than 8000 images using cameras, and more than 10 'talk' interviews and 10 walking interviews were conducted in each country using digital audio recorders. The images captured the different kinds of LL in place, ranging from shop signage, street signage, official and private signage on buildings, especially in urban areas, to natural objects, faded and blank signage and so on, used as signage for narration of place in rural areas in particular.

A purposive sampling procedure was used targeting those known to have knowledge of the place under study. The data for this chapter were extracted from that collected by one of the researchers who spent seven months in the rural spaces of Zambia (rural spaces of Livingstone [Zimba and Kazungula] and Lusaka rural area [Chongwe, which is east of the capital city]). The months were spaced as follows: June–September 2014 and November 2014–January 2015. He took notes, made observations of social actors involved in sign-making and consumption practices and took images of signs, as he 'walked' with the interviewees.

While some interviews were done while walking, others were at the convenience of the respondents. Questions were mostly unstructured such as 'How do I get from point A to B [past a Chinese sign]?' 'Can you tell me what the sign on that signpost means?' The kinds of questions changed with the kinds of observed semiotic material and objects used for sign-making. The respondents were at least bilingual speaking at least two of the following languages: Nyanja, Bemba, Tonga, Toka-Leya, Lozi and English. Since the researcher is multilingual and speaks all these languages, the language or languages used depended on the respondents' preferences. The interviewees ranged from primary schoolchildren, not so formally educated adults, to formally educated retired or working civil servants in government and private organisations. Introducing himself as a researcher on sign-making in rural areas, and new to the rural area, it was convenient for the researcher to ask about how to get to this or that area. It was also not uncommon for some rural folk to volunteer to walk with him to the place he was asking, or orally narrate the place. With permission, he would then record and ask questions about specific landscapes and the few emplaced signs/objects in place, and their meanings or how they are used for meaning-making.

Consuming Chinese Characters in Rural Spaces

In most LL studies that focus on the production and consumption of signage in public spaces, focus has been on the readability of the inscribed messages on signposts. Normally, the graphemes are consumed for their semiotic potential. As will be illustrated below, the semiotic potential of graphemes (and Chinese characters) goes beyond their meanings in Chinese when remediated for new meanings in English or Zambian languages in narrations of place. The font types and sizes, colours, shapes and so on add different dimensions to meaning-making. It is often assumed that social actors should be able to read and understand the message on the signs as long as the language used is accessible to them.

However, the case of Chinese signage in the rural spaces of Zambia provides an interesting semiotic pattern of consumption in which consumers refer to the language used in the signage rather than the message in the sign. Posing as a newcomer to these rural spaces, one of the researchers would ask for directions from rural dwellers to find out the kinds of signage referred to. This kind of enquiry yielded interesting narration of space. Consider the interview with a respondent on the Livingstone and Zimba road in rural southern Zambia.

Researcher: How do I get to the next village?
Respondent 1: You'll see a signpost with the writing in Chinese.

Without reference to the message or what is written on the sign (cf. Figure 5.2), the response provides an extended semiotic potential of Chinese signage. Rather than limiting the signage to the purpose for which it is emplaced, the social actors repurpose it; that is, reuse it for something else in the narration of space. In this case, the Chinese sign has been used beyond its semiotic functionality intended by its original producer. It does not often matter that the sign also has English words written in the familiar Roman script. It is now being used to locate a next village, which is not named on the sign. Considering that villages have no streets and emplaced signs are often limited to local schools, the presence of Chinese signage is a bane for villagers who use them to signpost oral language-mediated messages (cf. Banda & Jimaima, 2015).

There are many private Chinese companies and Chinese government-to-government projects in Zambia. Wherever they are, it could be argued, the Chinese mark their 'territories' with Chinese signage, whose messages the local people cannot read, as they are not usually translated into English or an indigenous Zambian language. Since Zambians generally do not read the Chinese writing system, it can be assumed that the originator's intended message is not directed at local people. Figure 5.1 is one of many Chinese signs that do not have English and indigenous Zambian language translations.

This can be taken as indexical that the Chinese sign-maker's intended message is not directed at Zambians. This in contrast with the other two signs: one in English pointing the direction to a bureau de change intended for tourists, as there are some game parks dotted around the rural areas of the Victoria Falls outside Livingstone City. However, we want to argue that having a sign in a language people read and understand does not guarantee its visibility in narrations of place. In relation to narrations of place, Figure 5.1 for example, respondents would draw attention to the Chinese script, whose meaning they cannot decipher, and not the two English ones in the familiar Roman alphabet.

We want to propose that the Chinese script can be said to be marked for distinctiveness, as it is not as common as the Roman alphabet used in the adjacent two signage in English. In addition, familiarity with a language in an emplaced signage and the sign-maker's intended message does not guarantee that social actors will use it as intended or for narration of place. It seems the question of whether respondents are able to read Chinese or English is less important in narrations of place in these environments than what is *seen* and *observable* in the signage (Jaworski & Thurlow, 2013). We develop this argument further in the rest of the discussion.

Figure 5.1 Untranslated Chinese sign

The following interaction took place in Chongwe, a rural area east of Lusaka City. Some social actors see the presence of signs in Chinese as a transgression of their semiotic environment, or as representing/meaning a new colonisation, after the British, of the country and its languages and cultures by the Chinese. The following discussion, which started with the interviewer saying that he did not understand and did not care what the sign meant in Chinese, shifted to the proliferation of Chinese signage and the 'infiltration' of Chinese language into Zambia's sociolinguistic situation.

Researcher: [Do you mean] … is Chinese now part of our Zambian languages as is English?

Respondent 2:   Chinese now qualifies to be a tribe in Zambia. There were 40,000 seven years ago according to records at Statistics Office. You see them everywhere. Our children are learning Mandarin... it is a threat to smaller languages. Zambia is a melting pot of Chinese.

Researcher: Do you see Chinese signs?

Respondent 2:   They are everywhere.

Researcher: Can you distinguish between Chinese characters and those of Japanese?

Respondent 2:   Even if it is Indian, Japanese or Korean, it is all Chinese … most people refer to any writing in characters as Chinese. If you say Japanese most people would be lost. Just say Chinese signage.

The idea that Chinese has become a Zambian language is interesting, and that Zambian children are now learning the Chinese language and endangering indigenous languages in the process can be said to be an exaggeration. However, the respondent's argument is not merely a matter of 'illiteracy' or 'village ignorance', it is evident that he is educated and is well read, as seen from his citing statistics from the national census data. He shows sociocultural consciousness around minority languages. The significance of the response that Zambia is the melting pot of Chinese becomes apparent later: any signage written in 'unfamiliar' characters is characterised as Chinese. This effectively inflates the number of 'Chinese' signage; at the same time it magnifies the threat of 'extinction' to local languages, which cannot compete for space, especially if one adds English signage to the mix.

Thus, the response shifts the locus of repurposing yet further by re-materialising to 'Chinese' any code whose writing system is not in the familiar and commonly used Roman alphabet. The re-signification of non-Roman writing systems as 'Chinese' illustrates further the agency of social actors to (re-)assign different meanings and purposes to these signs, leading to the (re-)production of signage in narrations of place. No wonder Mitchell (2005) argues 'depictions have lives and that these lives are only partly controlled by those who gave them birth'. Evidently, the Chinese sign-makers have no control over what purposes and meanings the social actors reuse the signage.

Figure 5.2 is a sign located on the stretch between Livingstone City and a rural outpost called Zimba in southern Zambia. It clearly shows 'Zimba Farm' and 'China Geo' in capital letters. But asked about how to get to Zimba, what was salient to respondents was the Chinese inscription. This is despite the presence of 'readable' English graphemes on the signpost.

China Geo is the short form for China Geo-Engineering Corporation whose business includes road and bridge construction, irrigation and hydropower, mining and landscaping. The company constructed the road from the city of Livingstone to the rural outpost called Zimba. The inclusion of English in the sign can be taken to indicate the sign-maker's attempt to communicate with local people, who may or may not read English, especially as the place is a rural area.

However, the writing in English is too brief and confusing, especially when taken together with the Chinese script and the bush surrounding the sign. The sign is in an isolated area with no villages or farms in the vicinity. Thus, the arrow pointing to empty space and the surrounding bush, taken together with the words 'ZIMBA FARM' and, particularly 'THE RESULTANT ENTRY', makes the entire signage difficult to decipher. It is also difficult to figure out the intended message and who it was

Figure 5.2 China Geo

designed for. There is nothing in the emplaced sign indicating the businesses the company is known to do. In this case, respondents focusing on the Chinese script as a point of reference in narrations of place is justified.

The Chinese owner of Pumuna Inn put up the sign shown in Figure 5.3 to locate the place for travellers wishing to spend time on their way to the urban cities of Lusaka in the north or Zambia's tourist capital, Livingstone, in the south.

The Chinese owner translated the Chinese lexemes as 'A feeling of going back home in the "inn" or "family-like inn"'. Pumuna in Tonga means 'rest', thus, 'Rest Inn' in translanguaged Tonga/English. The meaning and message as given in Chinese do not exactly tally with that indexed in the Tonga-English text. The interviewees can be excused for not knowing what exactly the Chinese texts mean.

The respondents know what 'Pumuna' means in Tonga and they assumed that is what it meant in Chinese. The disparity in meaning and information value between the Chinese texts and the translanguaged Tonga/English translation illustrates the problem of translating messages across cultures and languages, as observed by Kress (2010). However, it is worth noting that for the respondents it is the 'visuality' of the Chinese writing that constructs the space (Jaworski & Thurlow, 2013), that is, the uncommon Chinese script redirects and refocuses social actors' gaze, which becomes the basis of situated action and meanings in their narrations of place using local languages.

In the local discourses of communities around the inn, the place is reframed 'Chinese Inn' or they semiotically remediate it as 'PamaChinese'.

Figure 5.3 Pumuna Inn

This translates into 'The Chinese Place/Home' (literally 'On the Chinese'). Pa- is a locative morpheme and ma- is a plural morpheme in Tonga, Nyanja and many Bantu languages. Bantu languages are agglutinative so that affixing morphemes to roots forms words and even sentences.

In their account of semiotic remediation as discourse practice, Prior and Hengst (2010: 6) argue the need to focus 'on the situated and mediated character of activity, and that recognizes the deep integration of semiotic mediation with the practices of everyday sociocultural life'. The Chinese signs in Figures 5.1 through 5.3 above, can be said to have been translocated and incorporated into local ways of sign-making and consumption.

The semiotic remediation of the Chinese texts to 'PamaChinese' reflects the localisation and situated nature of place narration activities. The signs have become semiotic material with which local social actors routinely locate and represent places bordering the inn in oral narrations, as well as to 'routinely navigate multiple representational worlds or indexical fields on the one hand, and ... situated interactions' (Prior & Hengst, 2010: 6) in their sociocultural worlds. For instance, in narration of place interactions, the Chinese signage is a point of reference and is repurposed to indicate the location of nearby villages and farms, as illustrated in the response: 'You will see a sign in Chinese. Forget the arrow, go the opposite direction'.

This illustrates the performative nature of remediation conceptualised in the chapter as shown by social actors taking semiotic material at hand and, 'putting them to present use, and thereby producing altered conditions for future action' (Prior & Hengst, 2010: 1). Similarly, located on the rural Lusaka–Chongwe stretch, the building in Figure 5.4 is referred to by locals as a Chinese space ('PamaChinese' = Chinese Place) despite the writings in English.

Officially opened in 2011, it was built with funding from the Chinese government as a demonstration centre and to train small-scale and subsistence rural farmers in modern methods of farming, including the use of technology as a way to transition them to commercial farming.

The site of the centre is Liempe Farm owned by the University of Zambia, in a rural area east of Lusaka city centre. Zambian agriculture experts from the University of Zambia often work with their Chinese counterparts in the training programmes. However, the discourses of local people surrounding the area, ownership of the land as well as participation by Zambian experts have been erased by the apparent focus on Chinese characters in the re-narration of place. The reference to the place as 'Chinese' provides further illustration that the meanings local

Figure 5.4 China Aid Zambia Agricultural Technology Demonstration Center

people attach to the Chinese words are not what the original sign-maker intended but what the local social actors reuse them for in situated discourse practices.

Discussion and Conclusion

In their description of the dynamics of how, when and what is seen at airports, Jaworski and Thurlow (2013: 155) highlight the importance of '"visuality" – the ways in which our seeing (our "vision") is constructed: "how we see, how we are able, allowed, or made to see, and how we see this seeing and the unseeing therein". We want to argue that the uncommon, and hence marked Chinese writing scripts push to the periphery the visibility of other signs written in the common and unmarked Roman scripts in the locally situated narrations of place. Whatever the signs mean in Chinese is of little or no consequence as social actors repurpose and *re-sign* the Chinese signage for novel meanings quite unlike originally meant in localised ways of sign-making and consumption.

The social actors rework the Chinese signage and deploy their own messages, often using the Chinese script 'visuality' rather than the content in the script as a point of departure. The social actors assume authorship of the signage in three ways: first, the Chinese signs do not have any translations or have inadequate translations into English or indigenous languages. Second, rural areas have very few signs emplaced; the few signs are thus vulnerable to repurposing in which social actors infuse their own oral messages on the signs. Third, for the local communities, reworking and re-ordering semiotic material and cultural objects for sign-making appear to be integral to routine everyday discourse practices. In this regard, semiotic remediation enables us to account for the agency of social actors in the reproduction and consumption of signage. This puts into spotlight the role of the original Chinese sign-maker, perhaps residing in China, and social agents who usurp authorship and project their own interests and intentions on the remediated signs. Drawing from Kress (2010), we want to argue that the social agents are dependent on the signs made in China but by reshaping the signs for new meanings and purposes the social agents may claim a 'fresh start'. But, both the Chinese sign-maker and the social agents are connected and integrated into a 'ceaseless chain of semiosis' (Kress, 2010: 53). However, the connection is simultaneously a disconnection as social actors act on signs for local meanings and purposes.

In this regard, the chapter drew insights from Ma's (2002) and Pennycook's (2010) conceptualisation of translocation in narratives of place to show that the relationship between the sign-maker and the recipient, and between different cultures and localities is not a matter of cut-and-paste transaction. Rather, the recipient individuals and cultures of translocated cultural objects in different localities are actively engaged in reshaping the signs in place for different meanings and messages, some of which are unlike those intended by the originator of the sign in the case of emplaced LL. Thus, although the Chinese scripts we analysed can be said to link the signage to China, there is a simultaneous divorce, as seen from social actors infusing and *re-signing* emplaced semiotic material for new meanings and purposes in locally situated contexts. In essence, the local social agent's voice is now layered above the original sign-maker's. This is transformative of both local and global (Chinese) ways of sign-making and consumption as translocated Chinese semiotic material becomes part of the extended repertoire of signs.

This resonates with recent studies which maintain that translocal meanings are made in localised contexts by people who draw on localised shared sociocultural knowledge and history of meaning-making (Kress, 2010; Ma, 2002; Pennycook, 2010). The meanings of signs as semiotic resources are not fixed; the transfiguration of global and local forms of semiosis takes place in the local contexts of consumption of meaning, which suggests the local becomes the main arena in meaning-making.

It is not surprising therefore that Kress (2010), Ma (2002) and Pennycook (2010) conclude that it is the people who make signs in local contexts for shared social meanings. This resonates with Irvine's (2010) argument that semiotic forms can serve as semiotic material for social agents to layer their own multiple meanings and purposes. Thus, although local people do not read, speak or understand Chinese, they recognise the Chinese characters as language around which they create different meanings including narrations of place using local languages for content. Whether the local people understand the content in Chinese is immaterial as a local language is used to express the content, whose meaning and effect is locally determined in time and place by interacting social actors, not by the Chinese sign-maker. The disparity in meaning between the Chinese text and the Tonga translation in Figure 5.3 illustrates the different materialisation of 'authorship', indexicalities and meanings in the same signage. From a social semiotic perspective, LL studies need to consider that indexicalities and meanings in signage are not necessarily fixed as to the original sign-maker's intentions. These are determined in the dynamic localised and socially negotiated interactions using local languages and local ways of meaning-making, hence the unboundedness of the link between the form, language of content and place, especially in language contact contexts as described in this chapter. This further gives impetus to arguments about the important roles social actors play in giving different meanings and interpretations to signs in LL, often quite different from that intended by the original creator of the sign. 'Authorship' is now claimed by social actors who use local languages for content and to impose their own meanings on the signage. Remediation focusing on repurposing enables us to account for social agents' appropriation of Chinese signage for new meanings and purposes, and to show that the translocated signs not only acquire localised meanings, but they also become part of the extended semiotic resources for sign-making and consumption. In terms of social semiotic theory, the notion of remediation as repurposing is an addition to the analytical tools of multimodality.

References

Appadurai, A. (1996) *Modernity at Large: Cultural Dimensions of Globalization*. Minneapolis, MI: University of Minnesota Press.

Banda, F. and Jimaima, H. (2015) The semiotic ecology of linguistic landscapes in rural Zambia. *Journal of Sociolinguistics* 19 (5), 643–670.

Barni, M. and Bagna, C. (2015) The critical turn in LL: New methodologies and new items in LL. *Linguistic Landscape* 1 (1–2), 6–18.

Bridge, B. and Watson, S. (2008) City imaginaries. In G. Bridge and S. Watson (eds) *Companion to the City* (pp. 7–17). London: Blackwell.

Hedberg, C. and Carmo, R.M.D. (2012) Introduction: Translocal ruralism: Mobility and connectivity in European rural spaces. In C. Hedberg and R.M.D. Carmon (eds) *Translocal Ruralism: Mobility and Connectivity in European Rural Spaces* (pp. 1–12). London: Springer.

Irvine, J. (2010) Semiotic remediation: Afterword. In P.A. Prior and J.A. Hengst (eds) *Exploring Semiotic Remediation as Discourse Practice* (pp. 235–242). New York: Palgrave.

Jaworski, A. and Thurlow, C. (2013) The (de-)centering spaces of airports: Framing mobility and multilingualism. In S. Pietikäinen and H. Kelly-Holmes (eds) *Multilingualism and the Periphery* (pp. 154–198). New York: Oxford University Press.

Kress, G. (2010) *Multimodality: A Social Semiotic Approach to Contemporary Communication.* New York: Routledge.

Landry, R. and Bourhis, R.Y. (1997) Linguistic landscape and ethnolinguistic vitality: An empirical study. *Journal of Language and Social Psychology* 16 (1), 23–49.

Lyons, K. (2017) #mysanfrancisco: Social Media and the Conceptual Linguistic Landscape. See https://osf.io/pmknm/ (accessed 14 February 2018).

Ma, E. (2002) Translocal spatiality. *International Journal of Cultural Studies* 5 (2), 131–152.

Malinowski, D. (2009) Authorship in the linguistic landscape: A multimodal-performance view. In E. Shohamy and D. Gorter (eds) *Linguistic Landscape: Expanding the Scenery* (pp. 107–125). New York: Routledge.

Mitchell, W.T. (2005) *What do Pictures Want? The Lives and Loves of Images.* Chicago, IL: University of Chicago Press.

Oakes, T. and Schein, L. (2006) *Translocal China: Linkages, Identities and the Reimagining of Space.* London: Routledge.

Peirce, C.S. (1955) *Philosophical Writings of Peirce.* New York: Dover Publications.

Pennycook, A. (2010) Spatial narrations. In A. Jaworski and C. Thurlow (eds) *Semiotic Landscapes: Language, Image, Space* (pp. 137–150). London: Continuum.

Prior, P.A. and Hengst, J.A. (2010) Introduction. In P.A. Prior and J.A. Hengst (eds) *Exploring Semiotic Remediation as Discourse Practice* (pp. 1–23). New York: Palgrave Macmillan.

Scollon, R. and Scollon, S.W. (2003) *Discourses in Place: Language in the Material World.* London: Routledge.

Stroud, C. and Mpendukana, S. (2009) Towards a material ethnography of linguistic landscape: Multilingualism, mobility and space in a South African township. *Journal of Sociolinguistics* 13 (3), 363–386.

Stroud, C. and Jegels, D. (2014) Semiotic landscapes and mobile narrations of place: Performing the local. *International Journal of the Sociology of Language* 228, 179–199.

Vandenbussche, B. (2003) Remediation as Medial Transformation: Case Studies of Two Dance Performances by 'Commerce'. See http://www.imageandnarrative.be/inarchive/mediumtheory/bertvandenbussche.htm (accessed 4 October 2015).

Zabrodskaja, A. and Milani, T.M (2014) Signs in context: Multilingual and multimodal texts in semiotic space. *International Journal of the Sociology of Language* 228, 1–6.

6 Resemiotisation and Creative Production: Extending the Translanguaging Lens

Jessica Bradley and Emilee Moore

Introduction

This chapter uses linguistic ethnography (Copland & Creese, 2015) video as a data source, and translanguaging (García & Li Wei, 2014) to explore resemiotisation in two linguistically and culturally diverse creative productions. The first involves street puppetry performers in Slovenia, and the second spoken-word poets in the UK.

Translanguaging provides an ontological lens for understanding fluid combinations of resources in and beyond languages. The foregrounding of multimodality and resemiotisation (Iedema, 2001, 2003; Scollon & Scollon, 2004) extends translanguaging's epistemological and methodological foundation. We trace meaning built and transformed across time, space and modes (e.g. spoken, written, visual, musical, gestural, spatial), shifting the focus from the linguistic repertoire to semiosis in performance poetry from the page to the stage, and in a puppetry performance from a studio to a street.

Translanguaging, Multimodality and Resemiotisation

'Translanguaging' is one of many terms available to account for an ontological change in conceptualising language and knowledge. Similar notions such as polylanguaging (Jørgensen, 2008), plurilingual practices (Lüdi & Py, 2009), metrolingualism (Pennycook & Otsuji, 2010) and codemeshing (Canagarajah, 2011) also shift traditional understandings of languages as monolithic constructs to *languaging* (Becker, 1995) as social action. 'Translanguaging', or 'the deployment of a speaker's full linguistic repertoire without regard for watchful adherence to the socially and politically defined boundaries of named (and usually national and state) languages' (Otheguy *et al.*, 2015: 283), is a term gaining acceptance by researchers from across disciplines with interests that include but also extend beyond how people use named languages. These include scholars from across the creative arts (Domokos, 2013; Eschenauer, 2014; Lee, 2015), whose perspectives are central to our research with street artists and poets. While translanguaging invites us to consider communicative practices that take place beyond named languages, until recently most previous research on translanguaging has foregrounded linguistic practices, and ignored additional semiotic resources and processes of meaning-making.

There is, however, a multimodal turn in translanguaging (Adami; Perera, this volume). Kusters *et al.* (2017), as well as Archer and Björkvall (this volume), foreground the concept of 'semiotic repertoires' in attending to the multilingual and the multimodal, while Blackledge and Creese (2017) extend the translanguaging lens to gesture (Perera, this volume). We take a holistic, repertoire approach to communication (e.g. Archer & Björkvall, this volume; Busch, 2012; Rymes, 2014), demonstrating translanguaging 'beyond' (i.e. across semiotic modes), with the 'trans' prefix referring in the main to transformation. Hence, we focus on a multimodality and semiotic changes extending the possibilities of translanguaging as a concept for researching communication, accepting the challenge put forward by García and Li Wei (2014: 29) for a multimodal approach to translanguaging grounded in social semiotics.

Drawing on Scollon and Scollon's (2004) mediated discourse approach, translanguaging might be considered in terms of communicative action leading to semiotic transformation (Archer & Björkvall, this volume). Indeed, in considering the transformational affordances of translanguaging, García and Li Wei suggest that as communicative actions move across modes in a process of resemiotisation, new meanings arise. To use Iedema's (2003: 41) definition, resemiotisation concerns how 'meaning making shifts from context to context, from practice to practice, or from one stage of practice to the next'. Iedema (2001: 23–24) describes the movement of 'meaning-making' from the 'temporal' (e.g. talk and gesture) to the 'durable' (in the case of the construction project he describes, these are written reports, architectural designs and buildings). Challenges encountered along the way, as meanings are abstracted (often verbally), are either woven into more 'resistant materialities' (Iedema, 2001: 24) (recontextualised), or disappear across the process (Kell, 2009). Applied to and considered in conjunction with translanguaging, the notion of resemiotisation provides a conceptual lens for understanding how semiotic transformations emerge with and beyond linguistic practices, and for focusing on the semiotic processes leading to them. It opens opportunities for shifting our analytical aims and methods, thus broadening the empirical possibilities of translanguaging for understanding how communication happens in contexts of linguistic and cultural diversity.

Citing Scollon and Scollon (2004: 170), García and Li Wei (2014: 29) suggest we ask of our data, 'is the action under examination a point at which resemiotisation or semiotic transformation occur?'. To this end, we identify moments at which resemiotisation occurs throughout the trajectories of two texts (Kell, 2009, 2015) – a Slovenian folk story and a British teenager's poem – and the historical bodies, discourses and cultural tools (Hult, 2016; Scollon & Scollon, 2004) embedded in and leading to their transformations. We draw on notions from Nexus Analysis, in particular the idea of mapping semiotic cycles at key points in the processes under investigation, following Scollon and Scollon's (2004: 104) work that traces different semiotic cycles and discourses converging in beadwork workshops with indigenous Alaskans. This approach is like the analytical framework emerging within translanguaging research of moment analysis (Li Wei, 2011; Li Wei & Zhu Hua, 2013), which enables the identification of what Li Wei (2011: 1222) describes as 'semiotically highly significant' actions, and seeks to identify which factors, or discourses, are converging at particular points in time. The chapter also considers how multimodality in social interaction (e.g. Goodwin, 2000; Mondada, 2014; Norris, 2003; Perera, this volume) has developed robust transcription systems for managing analytical concerns of different types, including plurilingual and multimodal practices, although the focus has mainly been on integrating verbal, spatial, gestural, kinesic and visual elements. We argue that additional transdisciplinary approaches for representing and interpreting translanguaging data are necessary.

From Studio to Street

The research presented in this section was conducted over a period of five months during the production processes of a collaborative multilingual street theatre production for an international street arts festival in Ljubljana, Slovenia. Taking translanguaging as a conceptual lens, the investigation sought to understand how performers made meaning across languages, cultures and practices. The production, devised by aspiring street arts performers, toured across Slovenia during the summer of the same year. Bev, a UK-based street puppetry practitioner, led the project as part of a longer-term collaboration with the Ljubljana-based street arts company.

Over the course of the production process, a performance (titled 'How Much Is Enough?') based on the traditional Slovene folk story of the Zlatorog, or golden-horned goat (Copeland, 1933), was devised. The Zlatorog is a well-known story to Slovenians and visitors to Slovenia. Motifs and images of the Zlatorog are commonplace, and found in the branding of 'Zlatorog' beer, on statues and in books sketching out mountain walks. Following Scollon and Scollon (2004), the story represents a nexus with the coming together of overt and covert discourses. The tale is one of travel: a cautionary tale in which a series of interactions and subsequent actions leads to the destruction of the Alpine mountain paradise.

The stages of the production process

The researcher identified four broad stages within the street arts production process that categorised the activities under investigation: conceptualisation, making, devising and performing. The stages also provide a frame for the multiple, layered and overlapping resemiotisations of the Zlatorog story in its trajectory across this process. They are overt and covert, embodying different time frames and scales. The linguistic and visual data in this chapter are taken from across the four stages, summarised below.

Conceptualisation (March 2015): During this first stage, the group work together for the first time during a three-day puppetry workshop. English dominates plenary sessions, although plurilingual spaces open spontaneously throughout the programme. Midway through, the students begin to sketch initial ideas for the production, introducing a series of folk stories. The story of the Zlatorog is told by Lyder, who is from the same region as the story, and he intertextually draws his own narrative into that of the story (for an analysis of this, see Bradley, 2017).

Making (May 2015): This second stage occurs over a long weekend. Between stages of conceptualisation and devising, the initial story is developed; Jimmy, puppet-maker, is contracted to design and make puppets, costumes and props.

Devising (June 2015): During this third stage, the performers work together to devise the production, playing with puppets, costume and props. During a process of experimentation, the production emerges as it will be performed during the festival.

Performing (July 2015): The group perform the production across cities and towns in Slovenia. The street arts festival takes over empty shop units in which props and puppets are stored in bags and boxes. The production unfolds at timetabled intervals at different times of the day and different sites.

A time- and place-bound structuring device, the above enable the categorisation and initial analysis of the data, while also providing a frame for the production activities. Yet, as with the beadwork workshops described by Scollon and Scollon (2004: 105), the discourses interacting within and across each stage circulate through this process and through the historical bodies of the participants. The activities are not bounded within the stages, instead they bleed across borders. Making happens in the conceptualisation stage as the story is explored. Devising commences in the making stage. Making (and fixing) continues in the devising stage. During the performing stage, props and costumes are fixed and adapted. The performance is redevised and changes are made. Costumes are removed and masks are discarded on the pavement. Everything is then gathered together and stored in an empty shop.

The resemiotisation of the story across the processes of making, devising and performing the ephemeral production disrupts the planning and architectural processes analysed by Iedema (2001: 36) as having 'increasingly durable and resistant materiality', a disruption also highlighted by Kell (2009). But equally, in another sense, the performance simply occupies a different cycle (Scollon & Scollon, 2004: 105) and a different time scale – its durability and resistance relative to the cycles, time scales and spaces to which it is bound and connected. Here, following Lefebvre's (1991) trialectics of space, it occupies a third space (Bhabha, 1994), one that is both liminal and fleeting. The materiality of the production is created and performed by the performers and embodies the historical bodies of those involved in the process.

Points of resemiotisation

The story travels and is decontextualised (Iedema, 2003: 42) across different and multiple semiotic modes in its trajectory across the four production stages. Here, we focus on a series of images (Figures 6.1 through 6.4) tracing the development of the costume of the story's main character, the Zlatorog.

The first set of visual data, taken from the conceptualisation stage, shows the performers exploring the story's goat imagery (the Zlatorog) through crafting with newspaper. The newspaper puppets are led through the city to interact with the public. Resemiotisation occurs as the story, originally narrated orally to the group in the previous workshop, forms the focus of a group activity extracting imagery from the story and making junk puppets that travel outside from the studio and into the streets. The resultant Zlatorog puppet must be manipulated by the performers as

Figure 6.1 Exploration of Zlatorog imagery through newspaper puppetry

it travels; its transformation is necessarily aided by them as they move its limbs and assist its embodied communication with onlookers. Interaction from body to puppet to street is integral to the successful excursion and the Zlatorog's new modal representation offers opportunities and challenges for its abilities to represent the text.

In between the first two stages, the story, as well as the experiences and discourses represented by the newspaper in material form (although by now discarded), is drafted into a synopsis by Bev, the workshop leader (Figure 6.2), and sent by email to the street arts education coordinator in Slovenia. Here, the text communicates a pitch around a named and scheduled performance for the festival. The story shifts its conceptual framework to that of the environment, with the 'Alpine paradise lost' as caused by greed and want foregrounded, developing a thread to the 'junk puppetry' work carried out historically by the UK-based arts organisation.

The third set of images (Figure 6.3) shows the development of the Zlatorog's head, as made by the puppet-maker, Jimmy, during the making stage of the production. This is constructed from a yoga mat, ping-pong balls and a series of found objects, spray-painted black and with a golden horn made of foam, wound up with wire. The gradual and deliberate development of the head and costume represents a convergence of discourses: those of Bev who is responsible for the production;

I hope you had a lovely weekend. It was gloriously sunny in England.

Below is a few lines of about the show.

And then I have a series of questions. It would be great if you can answer by email so that we have notes, but maybe we can have a skype conversation to discuss them? I am available today and Thursday at 11am if that's any good.

Promo: This is just a couple of lines at the moment as our ideas are still formulating. I hope this translates well. I have copied in Jess, who will be interested in the language. The synopsis and outline design ideas are just for you to understand our thinking so far.

How Much is Enough?

A tragic story of love, greed and our relationship with the natural world.

Based on a traditional Slovenian folk tale and using puppets made from the objects we have discarded, How Much is Enough is a fun, thought provoking visual street performance suitable for the whole family

Figure 6.2   Draft synopsis

those of Jimmy, responsible for the making; and the devised text itself. The Zlatorog head is supersized representing Jimmy's experience and expertise in 'gegant' and opera-based puppetry. The scale is larger than conceived in the original production design, and historical bodies in the form of different puppetry training, experience and practices are embodied within its production.

Figure 6.4 shows the Zlatorog head and the costume, worn by the actor, in the final stages of production. The scale affects the choice of actor who must be strong enough to carry the mask on her head and wear the costume to perform in July heat. The developing stages of resemiotisation and the authority in the crafting shift the communicative affordances of the street arts production itself. The Zlatorog's accompanying puppets are larger than planned and can therefore only promenade – not 'act'. This necessitates the introduction of dialogue to the devised production, originally devised to be non-verbal. The discourses and practices embodied by the Zlatorog and the puppets contribute to the transformation of the text, and the inclusion of verbal language.

Figure 6.3 The Zlatorog head in progress

Figure 6.4 The Zlatorog head and costume in progress

Returning to the focus of this chapter – the extension of translanguaging towards the multimodal – the Zlatorog production develops across, through and beyond two 'bounded' languages, Slovene and English (Fragment 1). The design and making of the puppets, props and costumes lead to the reintroduction of verbal dialogue to the performance itself, which evolves from a 'visual' production to a 'visual and verbal' production.

FRAGMENT 1: FIELDNOTES, 1 JUNE 2017

After some warm up exercises, Bev starts to introduce the production and her ideas for how it will go. They discuss whether to have a single voice or multiple voices to narrate the production. Bev feels that some narration (which language tbc) is necessary in order to be able to make the complexity understood to the audience in the street. 'A' volunteers to be the narrator with the English script. The group translate Bev's text into Slovene. There's quite a heated discussion about how it should be.

Focusing on the continuing and multilayered resemiotisations of a story, the insufficiencies and the consequent changes caused by these insufficiencies enable moments of semiotic transformation. These transformations embody ways in which the performers draw on their communicative and creative repertoires across production processes. These processes enact a transformation of the group's repertoire and the repertoire materially embodied within the final production.

From Page to Stage

The second research project involves teenagers and adult mentors in a youth spoken-word (YSW) poetry organisation, Leeds Young Authors, based in Leeds, UK. YSW is a particularly interesting practice for studying semiosis and translanguaging – as van Leeuwen (1999: 5) writes: '[...] things work differently. No hard and fast rules exist. Any bit of language you might lay your hands on could come in handy for the semiotic job at hand, whether it is grammatical or not, whether it represents a standard variety of English or not'.

This section focuses on part of the trajectory of one poem, titled 'To Him' (also known as 'Gospel' within the group), by Bekkie. She is a 17-year-old French–English bilingual poet and singer. The data was collected over eight days in May 2016 during after-school workshops. The poet was preparing to compete with a team for the 'Brave New Voices' international youth poetry slam in the United States.

The birth of a poem

'To Him' was conceived during an informal workshop, which was videotaped, involving four poets, one of their mentors and the researcher. Figure 6.5 depicts the poem's first five stanzas, which were quietly sketched out in a corner of the room. The first stanza is shown, with the original text included on the left and a transliteration on the right.

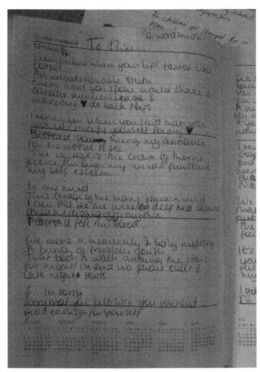

Transliteration of the first stanza:

I remember when your
lips tasted like
Gospel
An unquestionable truth
Every word you spoke
would shake &
awake my membrane &
make my ♥ do backflips

Figure 6.5 The handwritten draft poem

Only observations relevant to the whole analysis are highlighted. The poem was written in a recycled weekly agenda. Lines differ in length, and while some break at a syntactically logical point (e.g. 'An unquestionable truth), others break at an available space on the page (e.g. 'I remember when your lips tasted like'). Symbols – the ampersand (&) and the heart (♥) – are reminiscent of non-standard uses in digital discourse. The use of these resources may be a feature of the text's ephemerality, as one likely to become orally performed, consistent with the practice of YSW. The historical body of the poem is a love story intertextually linked to the poet's active religious life, through references to the 'gospel' and 'an unquestionable truth'.

Transformation across modes

The following day, a plenary workshop was held. The poet read her draft to the group, and said it lacked flow. She and her mentor agreed that she should sing the introduction to the poem rather than speak it. For them, speech and music were integrated and equally available, rather than pertaining to separate codes (van Leeuwen, 1999: 4). The poet had problems, however, singing the poem as she had it written in her notebook. She said it was hard to add a beat with lines that were not well separated. She typed the piece up using her phone. One of her adult mentors helped her edit the first stanza and find a tune for it. The photograph of her screen in Figure 6.6 is the result of this process.

From the handwritten to the digital version of the first stanza, lines have been altered and now tend to start and end with a natural break for a breath or for punctuation (e.g. a full stop or a comma). The stanza includes textual references to the change of mode, through repetitions ('like Gospel, like Gospel, like Gospel', 'Oh just for you x3'). The ampersand (&) and the heart (❤) have disappeared completely. Although this resemiotisation might point to standardisation of the teenager's language use, instigated by the adult mentor, observations do not corroborate this. Rather, given that the poet had difficulty performing her text as it was originally written, it is likely that the transformations were oriented to producing a text to be performed orally (e.g. the symbols might cause hesitation).

The remainder of this analysis will focus on the how the first stanza continues to transform across modes as it is performed orally. Few researchers have tackled the integration of music and speech, resources that intersect for the young poet and her mentor. Some exceptions to this are Erickson's (1982: 169) work on improvisation in classroom interaction, proposing a transcription system in which speech was represented using what he calls 'quasi-musical notation'. Van Leeuwen (1999) put forward an integrated theory of speech, music and sound. More recently, Falthin (2011, in Falthin, 2013) used musical score to represent the data of pupils in lower secondary school giving presentations while playing an instrument and/or singing. While not suggesting an analytical approach to multimodal data, Fernández-Toro (2016: slide 3) proposed the notion of musilingualism to account for 'a condition in which language and music are both involved in a practice, a skill, a process or a product'. Within translanguaging research, we are not aware of other analytical attempts to integrate musical resources in the study of how people mobilise their communicative repertoires. In the research presented in this section, a combination of multimodal representational systems (e.g. image, interactional transcription, musical notation) is both useful and necessary to symbolise the complexity of the poet's semiotic process.

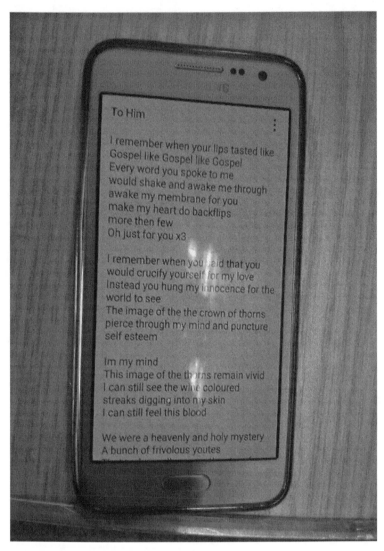

Figure 6.6 The edited poem on the poet's phone

Fragment 2 begins with the young author of 'To Him', referred to in the transcript as Bekkie, seated with her knees on the chair (see Figure 6.7). She reads the lyrics to the poem on her mobile phone (Figure 6.6) and sings them quietly, although within earshot of the other participants in the workshop.

Figure 6.7   The poet, Bekkie, positioned at start of Fragment 2, Line 1

FRAGMENT 2: BE: BEKKIE, THE POET, AI: AOIFE, ANOTHER YOUNG POET, SA: SAJU, ADULT MENTOR

1. BE ((singing) i: remember whe:n (.) your lips tasted like gospe:l (.) an
2.   unquestionable truth (.) every word you spoke would shake (.) me-)
3.   (0.1)
4. BE no.=
5. SA =yes. ((singing) shake [me throu:gh)]
6. BE   [((singing) me throu:gh)]
7.   (0.1)
8. BE ((humming same tune that she sang in lines 1-2))
9. AI it's [xxxxx]
10. SA   [don't be scared to play with it.]
11. SA you lot'll just be like erm: [xx]
12. AI   [it needs] to (move up?) i think like
13. BE ((humming))
14. BE it's just the beat you wrote works so well (.) °it's just i don't
15.   remember it.°
16.   (1.3)

```
17.   AI it needs to be like the first line you went too quickly this time i
18.       think. (.) cause it was too sho[:rt?]
19.   SA                               [ex]actly.
20.   AI so go back to how you did it before a little longer
21.       (0.3)
22.   SA who who who're you thinking of when you sing.
23.       (0.9)
24.   SA do me a lauryn.
25.   BE °who:?°
26.       (.)
27.   SA lauryn hill sweety.
```

Bekkie's singing has been represented with a comment in the interactional transcript, which follows basic conversation analysis conventions (Jefferson, 2004; Perera, this volume). Figure 6.8 shows the musical score produced by the researcher with the assistance of a musician of the lyrics sung by Bekkie in Lines 1–2, as well as in unison with Saju (an adult mentor) in Lines 5–6 on 'me through', and offers a multitude of interesting analytical information in just two lines. Reading music might be daunting for those not trained in the basics of notation; however, as van Leeuwen (1999: 94) suggests, even the non-musically inclined can follow the ups and downs of the dots, representing changes in pitch. They can also appreciate the metre marked at the beginning of the score –in this case 3/4, meaning that there are three beats within each section (measure) between parallel lines. Different types of dots represent the length or value of each note. Hollow dots with a stem are half notes (so 1.5 beats in 3/4 time), solid dots with stems are quarter notes and solid dots with stems and tails are eighth notes. Other symbols (e.g. the one that looks like a '7' in Figure 6.8, or those resembling squiggles or solid rectangles) represent rests or silences of different lengths. The musical notation of Bekkie's singing in Fragment 2 will be returned to in the section titled 'Transformation within a Mode'.

Returning to the interaction that takes place after Bekkie's singing in Fragment 2, as Bekkie continues to hum the tune to herself, from Line 9, another young poet, Aoife, and the mentor, Saju, give her advice on how to improve the poem. Saju encourages her to play with it, while Aoife suggests she move the pitch up (Lines 10–12). The same poet

Figure 6.8   The poem as sung by Bekkie in Lines 1–6 of Fragment 2

also suggests that the first 'line' of the song is being sung too quickly (Lines 17, 18 and 20), which Saju agrees with. Presumably, they are referring to 'I remember when', as a rest occurs after that word when Bekkie sings. This 'line' does not correspond to the first line of the written version, which would be 'I remember when your lips tasted like'. In Lines 14–15, Bekkie makes an interesting statement, saying that she does not remember the beat that Saju and she had 'written'. No beat markings were included on the version on Bekkie's phone – the beat that was 'written' was in fact sung by her and Saju. Both Bekkie's and the other young poet's use of words in Lines 14 and 17–18 is fascinating as it suggests that for them, the boundaries between what is written, said and sung are indeed blurred, as is the dependence or autonomy of the different texts. In Lines 24–27, Saju introduces the presumably shared cultural tool (concept) of 'a Lauryn' to mediate the transformation of Bekkie's performance, in reference to singer, songwriter and rapper Lauryn Hill's lyrical style.

Transformation within a mode

This final section of the analysis presents two more musical scores (Figures 6.10 and 6.12). The first was filmed on the same day as the interaction in Fragment 2, shortly after the previous exchange took place. The recording started slightly after the poet began to sing. The second was filmed one week later at another whole-group workshop. Figures 6.9 and 6.11 represent the poet's embodied disposition.

The following observations can be made about the performances. Firstly, the duration of the sung part of the poem is notably longer in the version in Figure 6.10 than it is in the other two versions. In the version in Figure 6.8, the entire stanza was not sung. In the version in Figure 6.10, the entire stanza was sung twice. In the version in Figure 6.12, the stanza was sung just once, and the final repetition of 'oh just for you' was omitted. Another notable transformation that takes place from the versions in Figures 6.8 through 6.10, then maintained in the version in

Figure 6.9   The poet, Bekkie, positioned at start of Figure 6.10 (Saju also in view)

Figure 6.10   The second version of the first stanza

Figure 6.11 The poet, Bekkie, positioned at start of Figure 16

Figure 6.12, concerns the metre. In Figure 6.8, the metre is 3/4, which is changed to 4/4 in the later rehearsals, meaning there is a change in overall rhythm. Between the first two versions and the third, there is also a drop in the key, from C-major (the default key) into B-flat major, meaning that it is sung at a slightly different pitch. All of these transformations, which are indicative of a translanguaging process concerning resources beyond Bekkie's linguistic repertoire, were mediated by the poet's interaction with her mentor and peers and by the different cultural tools (objects such as the pen, the recycled agenda and the mobile phone, and concepts such as 'a Lauryn') emerging therein, as well as by her independent rehearsing.

In order to take a closer comparative look at the data, we might focus on just the third and fourth lines, according to the poem written out on the mobile phone (i.e. 'Every word that you spoke to me, would shake and awake me through'), as it is sung across the three performed versions. Significant transformations take place at the micro level of the poem's words and lines. For example, there are changes in rhythm, with notes of different values used when singing the same words and rests (silences) introduced (e.g. after 'through' in Figures 6.10 and 6.12). The notes themselves are also different, illustrating micro alterations of pitch. For example, in Figure 6.8, the three syllables for 'every word' are sung with the notes D-D-D, in Figure 6.10 with E-G-A and in Figure 6.12 with D-F-G.

In terms of the poet's embodiment and use of space, in her first rehearsal of the poem (pictured in Figure 6.7) she was seated and clearly not in performance mode, in Figures 6.9 and 6.11 she stands before her peers, still reading from her phone as she sings. In Figure 6.9, she accompanies her singing with clicking on every second beat, which she does not do in Figure 6.11, possibly because she no longer needs help keeping the beat, or potentially because she feels more inhibited.

Figure 6.12   The poet, Bekkie, positioned at start of Figure 6.12

Translanguaging might be considered in this project, therefore, firstly in terms of Bekkie's own repertoire use, including different resources and transformations across written and spoken modes, embodiment and also her musilingualism. Secondly, translanguaging might be understood in terms of an analytical process, in which the transformation of the data beyond a linguistic representation (i.e. the production of musical transcriptions) was necessary in order to engage with the complexity of how Bekkie uses this repertoire to create meaning.

Conclusion

By tracing text trajectories in order to pinpoint semiotic transformations that we conceptualise in terms of translanguaging, it becomes clear that linguistic methods for analysis alone would be entirely insufficient. In the case of the poem 'To Him', while movements across spoken and written modes are observed, it is also in the intermingling of spoken and written language with other modes, including musical and embodied ones, in which resemiotisation takes place. In the case of the Zlatorog production, the objects themselves or verbal communication in isolation are insufficient for the communicative possibilities of the performance, as Iedema (2001: 33) states, representing the insufficiencies of certain modes and the necessity for multiple, co-existing resemiotisations of the story. Multiple, layered and concurrent resemiotisations across modes and through and beyond linguistic repertoires enable the development of new multimodal practices across the process of production and within the performance. This leads us to argue that semiotic transformation is not only a conceptual lens for pushing translanguaging research forward, broadening its multimodal possibilities, but also a highly necessary analytical process, in the sense that data sometimes needs representing in new ways to gauge the complexity of the meaning-making process. By taking a broad semiotic perspective, our chapter thus contributes to one of the major remits of this volume, which is to question the role of the linguistic repertoire as central in and paradigmatic to communication, and to translanguaging in particular.

Acknowledgements

Thanks are due to the street arts performers from the UK and Slovenia and to the poets, as well as to the creative organisations we work with: Faceless Arts and Leeds Young Authors. Real names are used in the text when requested as such by our participants. We would like to thank musician Angela Moore for her expertise in producing the musical notations included in this chapter, and for her guidance in their analysis and the editors for their extremely valuable insights. This chapter draws partly on data from Jessica Bradley's doctoral research (2014–2017) which is funded by the UK Arts and Humanities Research Council (AH/L007096/1). It also draws partly on Emilee Moore's postdoctoral research supported by the Beatriu de Pinós scheme (2014 BP_A 00085) and a Serra Húnter fellowship (Catalonia, Spain).

References

Becker, A. (1995) *Beyond Translation: Essays Towards a Modern Philology*. Ann Arbor, MI: University of Michigan Press.
Bhabha, H. K. (1994) *The Location of Culture*. New York: Routledge.
Blackledge, A. and Creese, A. (2017) Translanguaging and the body. *International Journal of Multilingualism* 14 (3), 250–268.
Bradley, J. (2017, forthcoming) Liquid methodologies: Researching the ephemeral in multilingual street performance. In J. Conteh (ed.) *Researching Education in Multilingual Settings*. London: Bloomsbury.
Busch, B. (2012) The linguistic repertoire revisited. *Applied Linguistics* 33 (5), 503–523.
Canagarajah, S. (2011) Codemeshing in academic writing: Identifying teachable strategies of translanguaging. *The Modern Language Journal* 95 (3), 401–417.
Copeland, F. (1933) Slovene myths. *The Slavonic and East European Review* 11 (33), 631–651.
Copland, F. and Creese, A. (2015) *Linguistic Ethnography: Collecting, Analysing and Presenting Data*. Los Angeles, CA: Sage.
Domokos, J. (2013) Translanguaging Cia Rinne's Poetry. Paper presented at The Poetics of Multilingualism – La Poétique du plurilinguisme International Colloquium, Eötvös Loránd University, Budapest, 4–6 April.

Erickson, F. (1982) Classroom discourse as improvisation: Relationships between academic task structure and social participation structure in lessons. In L.C. Wilkinson (ed.) *Communicating in the Classroom* (pp. 153–181). New York: Academic Press.

Eschenauer, S. (2014) Faire corps avec ses langues. Théâtre et didactique: vers une définition de la translangageance. In J. Aden and A. Arleo (eds) *Actes du colloque Langues en mouvement, Languages in Motion.* Nantes: Revue en ligne E-Crini. See http:// www.crini.univ-nantes.fr/actes-de-colloque-langues-en-mouvement-didactique-des-langues-et-pratiques-artistiques--1145716.kjsp last accessed is 22 June 2018.

Falthin, A. (2011) *Musik som nav i skolredovisningar [Music as a Hub in School Presentations].* Stockholm: KMH-Förlaget & Falthin.

Falthin, A. (2013) Transcription bank: Annika Falthin. *MODE: Multimodal Methodologies.* See https://mode.ioe.ac.uk/2013/05/01/transcription-bank-annika-falthin/ accessed on 22 June 2018.

Fernández-Toro, M. (2016) Musilingual Practices and Intercultural Citizenship. Poster presented at the BAAL SIG Intercultural Communication 7th Annual Seminar, The Open University, London, UK, 19–20 May.

García, O. and Li, W. (2014) *Translanguaging. Language, Bilingualism and Education.* Basingstoke: Palgrave Macmillan.

Goodwin, C. (2000) Action and embodiment within situated human interaction. *Journal of Pragmatics* 32, 1489–1522.

Hult, F. (2016) Nexus analysis as scalar ethnography for educational linguistics. In M. Martin-Jones and D. Martin (eds) *Researching Multilingualism: Critical and Ethnographic Approaches* (pp. 89–104). Abingdon: Routledge.

Iedema, R. (2001) Resemiotization. *Semiotica* 37 (1/4), 23–40.

Iedema, R. (2003) Multimodality, resemiotization: Extending the analysis of discourse as multi-semiotic practice. *Visual Communication* 2 (1), 29–57.

Jefferson, G. (2004) Glossary of transcript symbols with an introduction. In G.H. Lerner (ed.) *Conversation Analysis: Studies from the First Generation* (pp. 13–23). Philadelphia, PA: John Benjamins. See https://doi.org/10.1075/pbns.125.02jef

Jørgensen, J.N. (2008) Polylingual languaging around and among children and adolescents. *International Journal of Multilingualism* 5 (3), 161–176.

Kell, C. (2009) Literacy practices, text/s and meaning making across time and space. In M. Baynham and M. Prinsloo (eds) *The Future of Literacy Studies* (pp. 75–99). Basingstoke/New York: Palgrave MacMillan.

Kell, C. (2015) Ariadne's thread: Literacy, scale and meaning making across time and space. In C. Stroud and M. Prinsloo (eds) *Language, Literacy and Diversity: Moving Words* (pp. 72–91). London/New York: Routledge.

Kusters, A., Spotti, M., Swanwick, R. and Tapio, E. (2017) Beyond languages, beyond modalities: Transforming the study of semiotic repertoires. *International Journal of Multilingualism* 3, 219–232.

Lee, T-K. (2015) Translanguaging and visuality: Translingual practices in literary art. *Applied Linguistics Review* 6 (4), 441–465.

Lefebvre, H. (1991) *The Production of Space.* Oxford: Blackwell.

Li, Wei (2011) Moment analysis and translanguaging space: Discursive construction of identities by multilingual Chinese youth in Britain. *Journal of Pragmatics* 43 (5), 1222–1235.

Li Wei and Zhu Hua (2013) Translanguaging identities: Creating transnational space through flexible multilingual practices amongst Chinese university students in the UK. *Applied Linguistics* 34 (5), 516–535.

Lüdi, G. and Py, B. (2009) To be or not to be ... a plurilingual speaker. *International Journal of Multilingualism* 6 (2), 154–167.

Mondada, L. (2014) *Conventions for Multimodal Transcription*. See https://mainly.sciencesconf.org/conference/mainly/pages/Mondada2013_conv_multimodality_copie.pdf accessed 22 June 2018.

Norris, S. (2004) Multimodal discourse analysis: A conceptual framework. In P. Levine and R. Scollon (eds) *Discourse and Technology: Multimodal Discourse Analysis* (pp. 101–115). Washington, DC: Georgetown University Press.

Otheguy, R., García, O. and Reid, W. (2015) Clarifying translanguaging and deconstructing named languages: A perspective from linguistics. *Applied Linguistics Review* 6 (3), 281–307.

Pennycook, A. and Otsuji, E. (2010) Metrolingualism: Fixity, fluidity and language in flux. *International Journal of Multilingualism* 7 (3), 240–254.

Rymes, B. (2014) *Communicating Beyond Language*. New York: Routledge.

Scollon, R. and Scollon, S.W. (2004) *Nexus Analysis: Discourse and the Emerging Internet*. London/New York: Routledge.

Van Leeuwen, T. (1999) *Speech, Music, Sound*. Basingstoke: Macmillan Press.

7 Gesture and Translanguaging at the Tamil Temple

Nirukshi Perera

The nexus between language and religion in a migrant setting was explored via an ethnographic study in a Tamil Hindu temple in Australia. In this chapter, transcripts of second-generation migrants' interactions are analysed to understand the multilingual and multimodal, or semiotic, repertoires employed by young people in their communication in the temple's religious school. Gesture's interplay with spoken translanguaging is investigated and this chapter reveals how both phenomena play specific and complementary functions in the way the Sri Lankan Tamil Hindu children convey meaning in their religious classroom. The findings raise questions about how various signs combine and layer to make meaning, as part of translanguaging, and whether verbal language should maintain its primacy when it comes to the analysis of translanguaging.

Introduction

The concept of translanguaging is continuously evolving through research on its extensive, normative use in many different settings. In this chapter, I aim to combine two key aspects of sociolinguistics with the study of translanguaging – in particular, the sociology of language and religion and the role of multimodality in communication.

The nexus between religion and language has been gaining attention in the last decade or so with the identification of a subfield of sociolinguistics called the 'sociology of language and religion' (Omoniyi & Fishman, 2006). As part of this, scholars are investigating the significant role that religion can play in heritage language maintenance, especially in migrant contexts. It has been found that religious (or ethnoreligious) communities of practice can create a space in which to use a particular 'migrant' language, seen to be critical to the expression of faith and not easily replicated in another, say, dominant local language (e.g. Perera, 2016; Woods, 2004). Therefore, when it comes to heritage language transmission to the next generation, religious activities become critical languaging acts. In immigrant settings, religious institutions are an ideal environment for the study of religion and heritage language maintenance, and in this chapter I present a case study from a Tamil Hindu temple, in an urban centre of Australia, with the pseudonym the Saiva Temple.

While multimodality has been studied in a variety of disciplines from anthropology to psychology (Payrató, 2002), it has yet to be fully incorporated into traditional linguistic inquiry (Kendon, 2014: 1). Furthermore, in the study of translanguaging, scholars recognise the need for more research on multimodality in multilingual contexts (Bradley & Moore, this volume; Kusters, 2017; Payrató, 2002) and superdiverse contexts (Adami, this volume). In defining translanguaging, García and Li Wei (2014: 40) posit that 'all translanguaging is multimodal' and signals a 'trans-semiotic system with many meaning-making signs, primarily linguistic ones that combine to make up a person's semiotic repertoire' (42). This conceptualisation of translanguaging moves away from terms like 'code-switching', which focus purely on linguistic means of communication rather than multimodal ones (e.g. Backus, 2005; MacSwan, 2005). Subsequent discussions on translanguaging (see Li Wei, 2016; Otheguy, García & Reid, 2015) have incorporated the idea of semiotic resources; however, more work is needed to look at how different modes (such as gaze, gesture, posture, dress, etc.) combine with diverse linguistic features to make meaning.

In this chapter, I will explore the multimodal aspect of communication in the Saiva Temple's religious school for children. I will show how translanguaging is the interactional norm and how the religious and cultural context influences the kinds of resources that are deployed by the second-generation interactants. Thus, this chapter aims to contribute to an understanding of multimodality in a translanguaging and multilingual migrant religious context.

The religious context

The Saiva Temple was founded by a group of first-generation Sri Lankan Tamil migrants in an Australian city in the 1990s. The temple abides by *Tamil Saivism*, a branch of Hinduism that places Shiva as the pre-eminent god, and is popular in South India and with Tamils in Sri Lanka. For Tamil Saivites in Sri Lanka, the Tamil language and Saiva religion are closely intertwined (Suseendirarajah, 1980) and represent a strong language–religion ideology (LRI) (Woods, 2004). Their liturgical practice is based on canonical Tamil literature and thus, Tamil is seen as the necessary language in which to practice the religion. This is in addition to the use of Sanskrit, found in the ancient Hindu Veda texts, which is almost exclusively used by the priests.

For a religion like Saivism, strongly rooted in South Asia but transplanted to a multicultural and multi-religious Western nation like Australia, a new sociocultural context calls for adaptation. As predicted by Fishman (2006: 18), the language of the religion is certainly affected and it is the generations growing up in the new country who provide evidence of the diachronic endurance of a strong LRI. Hence, my research in the Saiva Temple sought to investigate how an LRI transforms in a diaspora setting and how this is reflected in the languaging of second-generation migrants.

The Saiva Temple's religious school is a Tamil-medium, volunteer-operated school that runs for two hours every Sunday. Approximately 60 students are enrolled in the school and most of them also attend a much larger Tamil language school on Saturdays. The Saiva School's main goal is to educate children in the teachings and worshipping practices of Saivism via the Tamil language.

My ethnographic study included the collection of naturalistic linguistic data across three school terms in 2015, in the highest grade of the Saiva School, Year 9. The Year 9 class comprised five regular students (13–15 years old) and a first-generation teacher, all who identified as having Sri Lankan Tamil origins. All students were raised with Tamil as their first language and all, except one, were born in Australia. Approximately 12 hours of video data was collected in the classes. As mentioned elsewhere (Adami; Goodchild & Weidl, this volume), the necessity of video recording to capture multimodality in communication is evidenced in this chapter. Student–student and student–teacher interactions were transcribed and translated with the assistance of a Tamil interpreter. Classroom observations and experiences, recorded in fieldnotes, and interviews with the students and teacher allowed for data triangulation.

Multimodality, semiotic repertoires, gesture and translanguaging

My sociolinguistic study in the Year 9 Saiva class found that translanguaging was the norm for verbal communication, despite the Tamil-medium policy of the school, and that multimodality was an integral part of the participants' communicative repertoires in this multilingual setting. Kress and van Leeuwen define multimodality as:

the use of several semiotic modes in the design of a semiotic product or event, together with the particular way in which these modes are combined – they may for instance reinforce each other..., fulfil complementary roles... or be hierarchically ordered... (2001: 20)

As with Kress and van Leeuwen's (2001) definition, scholars of translanguaging are adopting a change in perspective, using the term 'semiotic' rather than 'linguistic' repertoires to acknowledge the inherent multimodality of communication (see Adami, 2017; Blackledge & Creese, 2017; Kusters *et al.*, 2017). Adami (2017) points out that 'semiotic repertoires' account for the fact that different signs or modes (language being one of them) can have different functional loads in each representation or combination, and it is in this combination that meaning is made.

Both Adami's (this volume) and Blackledge and Creese's (2017) research in markets in the UK show that multimodality in meaning-making is especially relevant to superdiverse situations where interlocutors have a fair amount of non-shared knowledge. The Year 9 Saiva class is different in this regard because the students and teacher share socially situated identifications and have a 'coincidence of repertoires' (Adami, 2017: 14) – there is a shared level of Tamil and English (to use bounded language names [as discussed in Goodchild & Weidl; Sherris *et al.*, this volume]) among the interactants. At the same time, there is a generational disparity in the migration context signifying some salient differences in religious, cultural and linguistic knowledge between the students and the teacher. Therefore, in the case of this Saiva class, the interactants use various shared signs and modes to communicate with each other and, in the words of Canagarajah (2013: 80), 'Sharedness is not a given, but achieved'.

Taking a multimodal approach to translanguaging means considering the layers and interrelations between different modal resources that co-occur (simultaneously or in sequence) in a communicative act (Adami, 2017: 4). My analysis in this chapter does not attempt to account for every mode at work in the interaction, but I focus mainly on the modes of speech and gesture, with the use of gaze discussed at pertinent points. While my analysis of communication is not holistic, this focus enables a closer look at the functional load carried by gesture in these translanguaging scenarios, and how speech, as a semiotic resource, is used in relation to gesture.

McNeill (2005: 5) labels the type of gesture under investigation in this chapter as a 'gesticulation', that is, the 'motion that embodies a meaning relatable to the accompanying speech'. From a psychological perspective, Goldin-Meadow and Alibali (2013: 157) point out that gestures can reflect or even change speakers', often unspoken, thoughts. While most scholars agree that speech and gesture are combined and integrated in communication, there are questions around its treatment as a separate mode to language or whether, because of its co-expressivity and synchronicity with language, it is in fact a component of language (see Kendon, 2014; McNeill, 2005 for further discussion). While such issues are not directly addressed in this chapter, I acknowledge them as critical questions and, in the analysis, will pay attention to where the timing of a gesture with the affiliated verbal language is significant to understanding its functional load.

Referring to the work of Kress (2010), contributors to this book (Adami; Archer & Björkvall; Banda et al., this volume) assert that signs are newly made each time they are deployed by sign-makers who, at that moment, choose what meaning they wish to represent through that sign. This is relevant to the temple classroom because students enact gestures according to the religious and cultural context in which they occur and to associate religious and culturally significant interpretations. Thus, by adopting signs for their own purposes, the students display agency in sign-making (as discussed in Banda et al., this volume).

Discussion

The two extracts presented in this section come from one particular Year 9 lesson on Saiva funeral rites, which was an engaging topic for the students as they were eager to understand the details of certain rituals they had experienced. In a context where students have witnessed certain rites but have not had the intricacies or meanings explained to them, in either English or Tamil, gestures take on a functional load in the recall and recounting of such rituals, as part of signifying a shared knowledge.

In my analysis of translanguaging, I use elements of conversation analysis and interactional sociolinguistics, drawing on my ethnography to explain the conditions in which such signs are produced (see Adami, this volume; Hutchins & Nomura, 2011). When it comes to the analysis of gesture, there are a number of methodological issues. Firstly, Kendon (2014: 3) writes that a generally accepted method for analysing visible bodily actions does not yet exist and furthermore, there is not a standard notation system for the description of such modes (Kendon, 2014; Payrató, 2002). In the tradition of the printed academic genre, it is difficult to effectively present the layering and combining of signs, required of a fine-grained communicative analysis (see Adami, this volume), within the confines of a page and associated word count.

The video recordings of the two excerpts were watched repeatedly by the author in order to annotate the nature, timing and placement of gestures and gaze alongside speech. Ideally, this video data would be featured here to supplement discussion; however, to preserve anonymity, such data cannot be made public. Instead, using computer software, video stills of key moments in the gestural phrases were turned into sketches in order to de-identify the research participants. These images are limited in how they depict movement (e.g. the issue of length and positioning of arrows to indicate motion could lead to different interpretations); however, they act as visual aids and display the perspective of the video camera, which is yet another consideration in how gestures are perceived by the analyst.

In the transcripts themselves, I followed Gullberg's (2011) practice (based on McNeill) of identifying three aspects of the gesture (phrase, stroke and hold) and using symbols to show their occurrence in relation to speech. This has also proved problematic when trying to adhere closely to the transcription conventions used in conversation analysis, as well as accommodate additional requirements to represent translanguaging in the transcripts. This is because certain symbols or formats (such as bold or capital letters) can overlap in what they signify according to speech, gesture, translation and Roman transliteration, thus leading to some potential ambiguity for the reader. Furthermore, the abundance of symbols to depict gesture and translanguaging can affect the readability of the transcript as a whole. In an attempt to simplify the transcript, some gestures not considered relevant to the discussion (especially the teacher's) have been excluded. Recognising such issues, Bradley and Moore (this volume) call for more transdisciplinary work on developing transcription systems that represent translanguaging and multimodal data, and account for the complexity of the meaning-making process.

Both gesture and speech are segmented into intonation units in the transcripts. The gestural phrase is bracketed by $ to indicate the length; the onset and completion of the gestural stroke is represented by < >; and the post-stroke gestural hold (if applicable) is indicated by ^ for start and completion. For verbal signs, Tamil linguistic features have been transliterated into Roman letters (see Perera [2017] for the transliteration system) and are presented in bold font with the English translation, in italics, beneath. English features are presented as normal (unbolded) font. A guide to the transcription symbols is provided at the end of the chapter. While all five students are present in these particular extracts, only one student, Chitran (C), and the teacher, Mrs Chandran (MrsC), are interacting. For the sake of simplification, the sketches show only the student (on the left) and teacher (on the right); the other students have been erased from the scenes.

Saiva funeral

In this extract, Mrs Chandran introduces the topic of Saiva funeral rites and elicits a response from students about their knowledge in this area.

Transcript 1: Saiva funeral

	14Jun15	Timecode: 00:08:19.041–00:08:44.600

1	MrsC:	yaaraavathu niingkaL
		have any of you seen
2		(2.0) ceththaviiTu
		a funeral
3		(1.0) antharaTTi
		the eighth day
4		(1.0) thuvacam
		one year death anniversary
5		ithukaL ellaam paaththirukkiRiingkaLaa.
		all of this have you seen?
6		en2n2a paaththu.
		what did you see?
7	C:	aa ceththaviiTu it's like
		yes funeral it's like
8		(0.5) they put it \$<in a <u>b</u>>ox?\$
9		and then they do **puucai**, they put \$<like>
		and then they do puja they put like
10		^(1.5)^\$ \$<**man**>jchaL on your ey:e^s
		turmeric on your eyes
11		and then^\$ \$<<u>civap</u>>^parici, and then they
		and then red rice and then they
12		(0.3) get like the^\$ \$<**peerpp**>\$iLLaikaL?
		get like the grandchildren
13		\$<to ho>^ld er=

14   MrsC: =oo
                Yes

15   C: (0.5)^$ $<like (0.5)[fire thing]>$

16   MrsC: [pantham <u>pantham</u>] en2Tu colluRathu
                fire stick fire stick that's what it's called

In the first turn, Lines 1–6, Mrs Chandran asks the students to recall what they have seen of a Saiva funeral, known as *ceththaviiTu*. She also refers to two of the main funeral rites: *antharaTTi* (the eighth day) and *thuvacam* (one-year death anniversary) in Lines 3 and 4.

In terms of language, Chitran gives his answer in Lines 7–14 with a predominantly English turn that contains some specific and strategically placed Tamil nouns. He uses *ceththaviiTu* for Saiva funeral in Line 7 followed by the English filler *it's like* and a pause indicating some cognitive processing in composing his speech. In Line 8, as he states *they put it* his forearms are resting on the table. He then moves his hands, palms open and facing each other, about 20 centimetres apart and perpendicular to the table (see Figure 7.1); raises them to chin level and then lowers them to the table as he says *in a box?*, constituting the gestural phrase. At the end of the gestural phrase, his hands come to rest on the table,

Figure 7.1 Transcript 1, Line 8: they put it in a box (timecode: 00:08:30.281). *Note:* In Figures 7.1 through 7.4 Mrs Chandran is holding a mug in her right hand

Figure 7.2 Transcript 1, Line 8: they put it in a box (timecode: 00:08:31.041)

maintaining the same distance as when they were lifted just prior (see Figure 7.2).

The final rising intonation on *box* indicates some uncertainty. It is also as he utters *box* that Chitran looks at the teacher. He appears to be referring to the placement of the corpse (the *it* in Line 8) in a coffin – either he is searching for a Tamil equivalent for 'coffin' or he has forgotten the English name so he uses *box* instead. At this point, the use of gesture helps him to convey the type of box he is talking about and to complete his mental process about that very object. This is a conventionalised use of gesture in that Chitran is aiming to show the object's properties and spatial relationships (Kendon, 2004). However, the object is depicted gesturally in very general and ambiguous terms – not reflecting the true size of a coffin. Gullberg's (2011) study of the gestures used by adult second language (L2) learners showed that similar gestures are used in the process of L2 lexical retrieval and as a way of holding the floor while the speaker tries to recall a word. Gullberg (2011) calls this kind of gesture a representational gesture that can be accompanied by a shift in gaze to their interlocutor to signal that suggestions or corrections are invited, as Chitran has done.

In Line 9, English features continue to dominate except for the insertion of *puucai* for puja (a ceremonial act of worship). As with the use of *ceththaviiTu* (Saiva funeral) in Line 7, we see the influence of religion

Figure 7.3 Transcript 1, Line 9: and then they do *puucai* they put like (timecode: 00:08:33.601)

and the strong LRI as specific Saiva concepts are more aptly expressed in Tamil and not English. After Chitran utters *they put*, he uses the filler *like* (Line 9) and lifts both hands close to the front of his face, hovering just below his eyes. He gazes into the distance as if he is searching for words or ideas, enacting what Gullberg (2011: 141) labels a 'thinking face' (see Figure 7.3). After a considerable pause in Line 10, he shifts his gaze and head down so that his eyes are now covered by his hands (with fingers curled to form a half-cupping shape) as he states *manjchaL* (turmeric) in Line 10. Then he shifts his gaze, with hands still in the same position, to face the teacher as he utters *on your eyes* (see Figure 7.4). This gesture of covering the eyes indicates the shape and size of the turmeric object that is placed on the deceased's eyes. While the vocal modality names the object as well as the relevant verb and location, the visual modality depicts the embodiment of the action, what the corpse and turmeric would look like.

Chitran's shift in gaze indicates that he has moved from the position of recalling the idea, in Line 9, to confirming it by looking directly at the teacher in Line 10. At the end of this intonation unit, Chitran moves his hands away from his eyes but they remain hovering at his chin with his fingers curled over. If we look at the timing of the gesture, we can see that Chitran's mind has moved to the idea of the turmeric on the eyes in Line 9 (before it is actually vocalised in Line 10) and the position of the hands

Figure 7.4   Transcript 1, Line 10: *manjchaL* on your eyes (timecode: 00:08:34.761)

gives a clue that the subsequent speech will refer to something relating to the face or head area. Thus, for his fellow students and teacher, the gesture is engaging them in his description even before the accompanying verbal features are uttered. McNeill (2005: 53–54) raises an important point about the function of gesture in this regard. He believes that every gesture is simultaneously for the speaker and for the listener. It performs an internal or cognitive function such as lexical retrieval or boosting fluency for the speaker, and for the listener, it can assist in communicating meaning. Krauss (1998: 55) conceptualises this as a process of 'cross-modal activation'. However, my analysis is that lexical retrieval is not the issue here. From time spent in the Saiva classroom, I was aware that *manjchaL* (turmeric) was a frequently employed resource and was known by Chitran. In this instance, it would be more challenging for Chitran to express the complete idea of the eye-covering monolingually in Tamil because it is not merely turmeric but turmeric that is mixed and pounded with other substances. Expressing this accurately in Tamil could present a grammatical rather than a lexical difficulty (see Gullberg, 2011). So while the gesture affiliates with Chitran's utterance of *manjchaL on your eyes*, it performs the extra (one could argue, grammatical) function of showing the shape of the turmeric concoction and the appearance of the deceased's eyes. It is the gesture that carries more functional load than the Tamil verbal feature, *manjchaL*.

Figure 7.5 Transcript 1, Line 11: and then *civapparici* and then they (timecode: 00:08:36.281)

In Line 11, Chitran continues the pattern of inserting Tamil lexical items for religious or cultural concepts, using *civapparici* (red rice) but without any accompanying verb phrase. As Chitran utters *civapparici*, he opens up his left palm, joins all his right fingers to form a point and places them in the centre of the left palm (see Figure 7.5). As he completes the gesture, the fingers of the left palm curl in slightly. In a Tamil cultural context, this gesture is iconic in representing feeding. Food is eaten with the fingers of the right hand, but if someone was to give a piece of food to another, it would be placed in the left palm first and fed to the recipient with the right fingers. The gesture of feeding refers to the placement of red rice inside the deceased's mouth by close relatives (Mahesan, 2003).

In this case, it is the gesture that provides the specifics of what happens with the red rice while the language is not so explicit. In terms of how verbal and gestural semantics interact, this is a case of 'an "additive" relationship in which the hand action performed as an object is named indicates an action on the object, which changes its state or condition' (Kendon, 2014: 12). The functional load is demarcated clearly here where language conveys the object (noun) and the gesture indicates the verb phrase, again performing a grammatical function. The combination of gesture and spoken translanguaging still falls short of conveying the complete message; nevertheless, meaning is enhanced through the addition of gesture. As Blackledge and Creese (2017) attest, historical knowledge is an essential part of one's semiotic repertoire – the shared interpretation of the gesture for eating and feeding assists communication and comprehension.

In Line 12, Chitran continues his description of a Saiva funeral. After a short pause, he utters *get like the peerpiLLaikaL* (grandchildren). Tamil kinship terms are more specific than English and were commonly used by the students in class to mark their cultural belonging. As Chitran utters *peerpiLLaikaL* (grandchildren), his hands move from the holding position in Line 11 down to the table. In Line 13, Chitran holds up his right fist as he says *to hold er* (see Figure 7.6). The use of the filler *er* is a clue of his attempt at Tamil lexical retrieval. The combination of his speech in Lines 12 and 13 and his action of raising his right fist as if he is holding something, are adequate to convey his meaning to the teacher. She interjects with *oo* (yes) in Line 14 to signal that she understands Chitran's inference.

In Line 15, Chitran pauses and utters the filler, *like*. This marks the onset of the gestural stroke. Chitran's gesture mimics a flame torch, using his left hand to act like a flame emanating from his right fist (see Figure 7.7 – the arrow indicates the movement of the left hand). This gesture is completed before Chitran even utters the words *fire thing*. The timing of the gesture reflects what Schegloff (1984: 275–276) observed about iconic gestures in relation to their lexical affiliates (that is, the word/s that most closely reflect the gesture). He wrote that iconic gestures tend

Figure 7.6 Transcript 1, Line 13: to hold er (timecode: 00:08:41.561)

Figure 7.7 Transcript 1, Line 15: like fire thing (timecode: 00:08:43.161)

to be positioned before the utterance of their lexical affiliates, rather than occur simultaneously. This is in accordance with the finding that gesture can signal the introduction of new meaning into the dialogue before it actually surfaces in speech (McNeill, 2005: 37). In fact, we see the lead-up to the gesture in Chitran's prior intonation unit when he lifts his right fist (in Line 13) (see Schegloff, 1984: 286).

As with the use of *er* in Line 13, the English filler *like* in Line 15 hints that Chitran is attempting Tamil lexical retrieval. By uttering *fire thing*, he indicates that he has been unable to retrieve the Tamil name for the object, so the use of gesture assists in portraying the object more accurately than its lexical affiliate. In this translanguaging setting, the gesture's functional load increases as it is an easily accessible semiotic resource when the Tamil linguistic feature is not instantly available.

Mrs Chandran provides the name for the 'fire thing', *pantham*, in Line 16. As part of the Saiva funeral, the grandchildren of the deceased would traditionally hold these fire sticks to assist the departed soul's path to enlightenment (Mahesan, 2003). While Chitran's gesture is iconic in representing some kind of fire torch, the sign has a particular meaning in this Tamil Saivite context, that is, a specific fire stick for funerals. This exemplifies the multiple meaning potential of gesture and how shared historical knowledge enhances comprehension. In addition, the layering of the gesture with the verbal English feature *fire thing* is an example of signs being newly made in combination, and according to the agency of the sign-maker.

Grinding versus pounding

The next extract, taken from the same lesson, transpires shortly after Transcript 1. Continuing with the topic of the turmeric that is placed on the deceased's eyes, the teacher asks a question to ensure students' comprehension of this aspect of the ritual.

Transcript 2: Grinding versus pounding

14Jun15	Timecode: 00:08:51.590–00:08:59.561
1 MrsC:	antha $manjchaL: *that turmeric*
2	\<pooTa: muthal en2n2a ceyvin2am>$ *before they put it what will they do?*
3 C:	$a\<a: araikkiRathu>$ *ah grinding*
4 MrsC:	cuNNam iTikkiRathu en2Tu colluRathu *lime pounding is what you say*
5	cuNNam iTikkiRathu *lime pounding*

In Lines 1 and 2 Mrs Chandran asks, in Tamil, what is done to the turmeric before it is placed on the eyes. Her accompanying gesture provides the students with a clue to the answer. She raises her right fist as she utters *manjchaL* (turmeric) in Line 1, and the stroke is synchronous with speech in Line 2 when she moves her fist up and down, in front of her chest four times, to indicate a pounding motion (see Figure 7.8). While the object, turmeric, is verbally expressed, the action done unto the turmeric is represented kinesically and is used to prompt the preferred response from the students.

In Line 3, Chitran indicates some mental processing with *aa* (ah) (which is a filler common to both Tamil and English) as he tries to recall the appropriate Tamil verb for this action. As he says this, he raises his right fist and mimics the teacher's gesture, enacting the pounding motion. He continues to pound his right fist into his left palm, three times in total, while saying *araikkiRathu* (grinding) (see Figure 7.9). Chitran's answer, his choice of verb, is dispreferred. However, from his gesture the teacher knows Chitran understands the concept. In Line 4, she supplies the appropriate verb *iTikkiRathu* (pounding) and explains that it is mixed with lime. She repeats the clause in Line 5 as part of repairing Chitran's lexical error. The teacher is referring to the substance lime (slaked

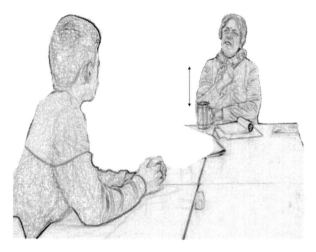

Figure 7.8 Transcript 2, Line 1: *antha manjchaL* (timecode: 00:08:53.721)

lime or calcium hydroxide powder), which is used to bind the turmeric together into a paste (as indicated by Chitran's eye-covering gesture in Transcript 1). The pounding of substances, like lime, to be placed on the eyes is seen as an integral part of Saiva funeral rites (Mahesan, 2003), and thus, it is important for the teacher to clarify with the students.

Figure 7.9 Transcript 2, Line 3: *aa araikkiRathu* (timecode: 00:08:55.561)

This particular extract demonstrates how gesture can assist in locating trouble sources in a translanguaging situation. In this scenario, the student's knowledge of Tamil is not as strong as that of the teacher, so when he makes a verbal error, the gesture takes on a functional load in clarifying his meaning to the teacher. From his gesture, Mrs Chandran deduces that Chitran has made an error in vocabulary (he has confused his lexical recall of *iTikkiRathu* [pounding] with *araikkiRathu* [grinding]) rather than misunderstanding the whole concept of making a turmeric paste. This combination of signs has been labelled a speech–gesture mismatch, when speech conveys one version of a situation and gesture a different one (McNeill, 2005: 137). But, by mimicking his teacher's gesture, Chitran is conveying his mutual understanding (McNeill, 2006: 65). Thus, in a multilingual classroom, gesture can assist the teacher in making an accurate assessment of the student's answer (Goldin-Meadow & Alibali, 2013: 274).

Conclusion

The Year 9 class in the Saiva School has provided a case study of multimodality and translanguaging in a multilingual, immigrant, religious education context. This chapter's perspective has drawn on studies from the sociology of language and religion, translanguaging and multimodality. The linguistic data from this religious setting has shown the influence of Tamil culture and the Tamil Saivite religion on the use of Tamil features by second-generation students. There is evidence that the strong language-religion ideology (LRI), brought to Australia with the first generation, has been transmitted to the next generation and that the temple is a space where this strong LRI can be practiced. Furthermore, we have seen how English and Tamil linguistic features, drawn from the students' semiotic repertoires, form an integrated system of communication. As alluded to in Sherris *et al.* (this volume), we see the potential for translanguaging, as a concept, to embrace a wider cross section of emergent Tamil speakers who can identify as Tamil even if they are not fully competent Tamil speakers.

Analysis of how multimodality interacts with translanguaging has been limited to gesture (and gaze to a lesser extent) in this chapter. The focus on only some aspects of multimodality is a shortcoming in presenting a holistic view of all that is at work in communication. However, narrowing analysis to particular modes has allowed for a closer inspection of how gesture is layered and combined with speech, and how it is temporally placed in relation to lexical affiliates. The combination of indicating gesture timing in the transcript, providing images to indicate the position of gestures and written descriptions of gesture, work to provide a presentation of the visuo-spatial actions that have occurred. The practical space constraints of academic publications and lack of universality in notation and analysis of signs mean that inspection is limited to very short transcripts and that presentation of the layering of all signs, in written form, is a challenge.

Having said that, this chapter has been able to interrogate how the functional load of gesture varies in translanguaging settings, especially when speakers need gesture to assist them in conveying meaning in their less-fluent language. A look at the timing of gesture in relation to its lexical affiliate has assisted in understanding its increased functional load. Analysis has shown how gesture assists in the student's Tamil lexical retrieval, in providing visual clues, in priming their interlocutors for meanings before they are uttered, in providing grammatical meaning, in confirming their mutual understanding of a concept conveyed by the teacher and in helping their teacher to locate trouble sources when there is a need for repair. In addition, shared understandings are created and reaffirmed through the use of gesture. The use of gaze by the student was also mentioned, and in this translanguaging situation, one could argue that gaze takes on a larger functional load when compared with non-translanguaging situations. There is a need to use gaze to seek the interactant's input, to signal 'thinking face' and to signal certainty when interlocutors have varying language competencies.

Just as we have seen the direct influence of religion and culture on the use of linguistic features (as part of the strong LRI), this is also evident in the visuo-spatial signs that have been presented in this chapter. The gestures in these extracts take on a primary role in communication since they pertain to the Tamil cultural concepts being discussed. For example, when Chitran covers his eyes and talks about the *manjchaL* (turmeric), or when he places his right fingers in his left palm and mentions *civapparici* (red rice), we could say that the gestures are part of the Tamil cultural paradigm. Gestures combine with the verbal expression of Tamil religious and cultural concepts to progress meaning-making and comprehension. Furthermore, just as the boundaries of languages become blurred in translanguaging settings, so too can the use and meaning of gestures. There is the potential that gestures can carry more than one meaning according to the cultural context in which they are enacted and interpreted (this has parallels to the trans-contextual mobility of objects mentioned in Archer and Björkvall [this volume] and Kress' [2010] proposition about the multiple meaning potentials of semiotic resources [Banda *et al.*, this volume]).

The interface between theories of gesture and approaches to multi-modality and translanguaging in multilingual contexts has been explored in this chapter; however, there is much more to be investigated and developed in this realm. While conceptualisations of translanguaging certainly acknowledge the salience of multimodality as part of semi-otic repertoires, they are yet to note the potential primacy of modes or signs other than verbal language in a translanguaging situation. In other words, in translanguaging settings, when speakers have varying linguistic repertoires (or language competencies), do other signs, like gesture, take on a larger functional load? Analyses of the use of semiotic repertoires in translanguaging situations need to incorporate the layering and combin-ing of various modes of communication. Thus, the concept of translan-guaging is due to evolve further to encompass not only the multilevel synchronicity of signs and modes, but also the multilevel synchronicity of meaning and interpretation.

Transcription symbols

[ ]	overlapping talk
=	latching
(0.5)	pause, timed
:	prolonged sound
<u>word</u>	stress or emphasis
.	final intonation
?	rising intonation
,	continuing intonation
$ $	gestural phrase
< >	gestural stroke
^ ^	post-stroke gestural hold

Acknowledgements

I would like to thank the members of the Year 9 Saiva class for par-ticipating in this project. In the preparation of this chapter, I gratefully acknowledge Chintana Sananikhone for creating the images, Dr Louisa Willoughby for her academic guidance and Monash University for the provision of a Postgraduate Publications Award.

References

Adami, E. (2017) Multimodality and superdiversity: Evidence for a research agenda. *Tilburg Papers in Culture Studies* 177, 1–28.

Backus, A. (2005) Codeswitching and language change: One thing leads to another? *International Journal of Bilingualism* 9 (3–4), 307–340.

Blackledge, A. and Creese, A. (2017) Translanguaging and the body. *International Journal of Multilingualism* 14 (3), 250–268.

Canagarajah, A.S. (2013) Theorizing a competence for translingual practice at the contact zone. In S. May (ed.) *The Multilingual Turn: Implications for SLA, TESOL and Bilingual Education* (pp. 78–102). New York: Taylor & Francis.

Fishman, J.A. (2006) A decalogue of basic theoretical perspectives for a sociology of language and religion. In T. Omoniyi and J.A. Fishman (eds) *Explorations in the Sociology of Language and Religion* (pp. 13–25). Amsterdam/Philadelphia, PA: John Benjamins.

García, O. and Li Wei (2014) *Translanguaging: Language, Bilingualism and Education.* Basingstoke: Palgrave Macmillan.

Goldin-Meadow, S. and Alibali, M. (2013) Gesture's role in speaking, learning, and creating language. *Annual Review of Psychology* 64, 257–283.

Gullberg, M. (2011) Multilingual multimodality: Communicative difficulties and their solutions in second-language use. In J. Streeck, C. Goodwin and C.D. LeBaron (eds) *Embodied Interaction: Language and Body in the Material World* (pp. 137–151). New York: Cambridge University Press.

Hutchins, E. and Nomura, S. (2011) Collaborative construction of multimodal utterances. In J. Streeck, C. Goodwin and C.D. LeBaron (eds) *Embodied Interaction: Language and Body in the Material World* (pp. 29–43). New York: Cambridge University Press.

Kendon, A. (2004) *Gesture: Visible Action as Utterance.* New York: Cambridge University Press.

Kendon, A. (2014) Semiotic diversity in utterance production and the concept of 'language'. *Philosophical Transactions of the Royal Society of London. Series B* 369, 20130293.

Krauss, R.M. (1998) Why do we gesture when we speak? *Current Directions in Psychological Science* 7 (2), 54–60.

Kress, G.R. (2010) *Multimodality: A Social Semiotic Approach to Contemporary Communication.* London/New York: Routledge.

Kress, G.R. and Van Leeuwen, T. (2001) *Multimodal Discourse: The Modes and Media of Contemporary Communication.* London: Arnold; New York: Oxford University Press.

Kusters, A. (2017) Gesture-based customer interactions: Deaf and hearing Mumbaikars' multimodal and metrolingual practices. *International Journal of Multilingualism* 14 (3), 283–302.

Kusters, A., Spotti, M., Swanwick, R. and Tapio, E. (2017) Beyond languages, beyond modalities: Transforming the study of semiotic repertoires. *International Journal of Multilingualism* 14 (3), 219–232.

Li Wei (2016) New Chinglish and the post-multilingualism challenge: Translanguaging ELF in China. *Journal of English as a Lingua Franca* 5 (1), 1–25.

MacSwan, J. (2005). Code switching and grammatical theory. In T.K. Bhatia and W.C. Ritchie (eds) *The Handbook of Bilingualism* (pp. 283–311). Malden, MA/Oxford: Blackwell.

Mahesan, N. (2003). *Brief description of a Saiva funeral service*. Sydney: Aum Muruga Society.

McNeill, D. (2005) *Gesture and Thought*. Chicago, IL: University of Chicago Press.

McNeill, D. (2006) Gesture and communication. In K. Brown (ed.) *Encyclopedia of Language & Linguistics* (2nd edn; pp. 58–66). Oxford: Elsevier.

Omoniyi, T. and Fishman, J.A. (2006) *Explorations in the Sociology of Language and Religion*. Amsterdam/Philadelphia, PA: John Benjamins.

Otheguy, R., García, O. and Reid, W. (2015) Clarifying translanguaging and deconstructing named languages: A perspective from linguistics. *Applied Linguistics Review* 6 (3), 281–307.

Payrató, L. (2002) Non-verbal communication. In J. Verschueren, J.-O. Östman, J. Blommaert and C. Bulcaen (eds) *Handbook of Pragmatics* (Vol. 8; pp. 1–35). Amsterdam: John Benjamins.

Perera, N. (2016) Tamil in the temples: Language and religious maintenance beyond the first generation. *Multilingua: Journal of Cross-Cultural and Interlanguage Communication* 35 (5), 535–559.

Perera, N. (2017) Talking Tamil, talking Saivism: Language practices in a Tamil Hindu temple in Australia. PhD thesis, Monash University.

Schegloff, E.A. (1984) On some gestures' relation to talk. In J.M. Atkinson and J. Heritage (eds) *Structures of Social Action: Studies in Conversation Analysis* (pp. 266–296). Cambridge/New York: Cambridge University Press; Paris: Editions de la Maison des sciences de l'homme.

Suseendirarajah, S. (1980) Religion and language in Jaffna society. *Anthropological Linguistics* 22, 345–62.

Woods, A. (2004) *Medium or Message?: Language and Faith in Ethnic Churches*. Clevedon: Multilingual Matters.

8 Translanguaging Practices in the Casamance, Senegal: Similar but Different – Two Case Studies

Samantha Goodchild and Miriam Weidl

Introduction

In more recent (socio-)linguistics research, it is often stated that most of the people in the world live in multilingual, superdiverse contexts (Blommaert & Rampton, 2011; Vertovec, 2007; among others). West Africa, where the current study is situated, has one of the highest levels of linguistic diversity in the world, yet remains under-represented, particularly in the translanguaging literature. An exception is Juffermans (2015), who investigated the languaging practices of multilingual speakers in the Gambia (see Banda et al.; Sherris et al., this volume for recent linguistic landscape and educational contexts, respectively). However, work on superdiversity and translanguaging tends to focus on language use in urban and educational environments (Blackledge & Creese, 2010; García & Li Wei, 2014), as does work on African multilingualism, although researchers such as Di Carlo and Good (2014) look at multilingualism and linguistic diversity in rural areas in northwestern Cameroon from an areal and ethnographically informed perspective.

In an area as multilingual and multicultural as West Africa, superdiversity is an accurate definition; in the following, we will demonstrate why translanguaging is the approach best suited to interpret and analyse spoken, interactive communicative events in such a context (Canagarajah, 2013; Juffermans, 2015). This chapter focuses on highly multilingual excerpts of multimodal interactions in two villages in Senegal, which are analysed as examples of fluid translanguaging practice. The research presented was conducted with people in the Casamance region of southwestern Senegal, where people's daily-lived experience is inherently based on two or more languages. All of the speakers are highly multilingual, with many participants engaging in translanguaging practices beyond speaking; passive comprehension of certain languages, reading/writing, in addition to gestures and body movement, all play an important role in everyday communication (as in Bradley and Moore; Perera; Sherris *et al.*, this volume). Social interactions and behaviour patterns support people's choices and the mixture of language(s), while influencing and possibly extending their individual linguistic repertoires. Communication can therefore only be situated in context and in-depth sociolinguistic research and analysis must take account of this. When considering translanguaging practices, we do not aim towards establishing generalisations but instead demonstrate actual language use and apply translanguaging as a convenient analytical approach to describe it. In this chapter, we investigate diverse practices in the region to build up a better idea of how people communicate in such a highly diverse, rural setting. By starting with analysis of the observed communicative event itself, and including ethnographic data on the speakers' linguistic repertoires, we can build up a better description of translanguaging practices in an African superdiverse context considering people's mobility, flexibility and adaptability.

Below, we provide a brief introduction to the research setting. Although we use the conventions of 'named languages' (see e.g. Lüpke & Storch, 2013) to describe the diversity of classified and non-classified languages in the area, we want to clarify that the notion of language with strict borders is neither applicable to the speakers' perceptions of the languages in question, nor our own.[1] The labels are used to give an overview and will be further problematised and discussed in the analysis. We conclude that the inclusivity of the translanguaging approach makes it an apt concept for analysing fluid linguistic practices in the Casamance.

Multilingualism and the Area of Investigation

Rooted in a firmly sociolinguistic tradition, the snapshot of research presented below originates from Goodchild and Weidl's (2016) research in the Lower Casamance, southern Senegal: specifically the villages of Essyl where Goodchild's work is based, and Djibonker where Weidl's work is based. The two villages as well as the broader Crossroads[2] area are shown by the dotted line in Figure 8.1, the focus area of the project with which we are affiliated. Although previous sociolinguistic studies exist, see for example Ducos (1983), most of the research carried out in the Crossroads area has concentrated on the documentation and description of languages, e.g. Sagna (2008) on Joola Banjal, Cobbinah (2013) on

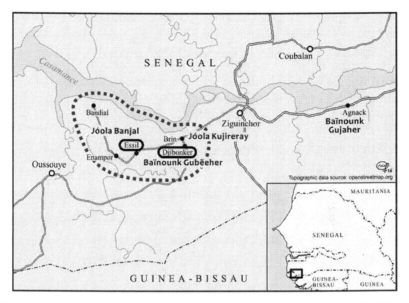

Figure 8.1 Crossroads area of investigation (www.soascrossroads.org; ed. Miriam Weidl)

Baïnounk Gubëeher and Watson (2015) on Joola Kujireray. The realities of language use in the area prompted a shift towards in-depth sociolinguistic studies on which we focus.

Area of investigation

Each village, or polity, on the map shown in Figure 8.1 is associated with a language of identification, which plays an influential role in the inhabitants' everyday lives. That is not to say that all of the residents speak the language actively, rather that it is bound to a unique cultural and linguistic representation: Joola Banjal to Essyl and the surrounding polity of Mof Avvi, Baïnounk Gubëeher to Djibonker and Joola Kujireray to Brin (Cobbinah, 2010; Sagna, 2008; Watson, 2015). Some of the languages are related: Joola Banjal and Joola Kujireray are closely related and share large amounts of lexical and grammatical features, whereas others are only distantly related to the Joola languages, such as Baïnounk Gubëeher spoken in Djibonker. However, multilingual repertoires of inhabitants vary depending on their lived experiences and often extend beyond languages of identification, which depending on their origin, often follow paternal inheritance patterns and may not be actively used.

Furthermore, all the people living in the area encounter, to differing extents, French, the official language of Senegal; Wolof, the most widely spoken language in the country, which is used as a national language of wider communication; and Joola Fogny (or another Joola language), one of the regional languages of wider communication. Depending on an individual's life history, it is common that even more languages have influential impacts according to different lived situations (Di Carlo, 2017; Dreyfus & Juillard, 2004; Lüpke, 2016). For people living and conversing in this highly multilingual and diverse area, it is not uncommon to actively use more than four (named) languages on a daily basis, and to passively be in contact with even more. All of these languages coexist as separate languages as an ideological perception, but within fluid and hybrid linguistic practices, meaning that people often mix them at a high rate in daily conversations (Cobbinah *et al.*, 2017; Lüpke, 2010). Conversely, they may be able to distinguish between them to a certain extent if they intend to do so or if it is necessary for certain communicative goals.

There are different reasons for the high number of languages in people's linguistic repertoires. For one, the long history of Senegal and West Africa, going far beyond the colonial periods, brought together people speaking a large number of different languages (Clark & Colvin Phillips, 1994; Nugent, 2007). Furthermore, the geographical location in relation to the colonial powers' border demarcations plays a significant role as the Casamance is located between Guinea-Bissau with Portuguese as the only language of instruction, and the Gambia with English as the formal language, and many trade routes pass through the area (Bamgbose, 2000). Looking more closely at individuals' expansion of their linguistic repertoires, these are mainly influenced by personal individual lived experiences and mobility. There can be voluntary motivations to expand repertoires as many people decide to acquire languages through more formal education or decide to do a 'linguistic residency' (Calvet & Dreyfus, 1990), meaning they move (or send their children) to a place to learn a certain language represented there. Mobility due to family responsibilities, moving into another household in a different linguistic environment, child fostering, as well as migration within extended families for support, is also common. Furthermore, (temporary) forced migration due to conflict, economic or professional reasons can initiate integration into a new linguistic environment, and can result in the acquisition of more languages. Traditionally in the Casamance region, upon marriage, the woman moves into her husband's family household, which is often in a different village and therefore likely to be a different linguistic environment. Even for an individual who remains in the same place during most of their lifespan, mobility plays a role in their repertoire as other people move and housemates, neighbours and traders exert influence on the linguistic setting (Dreyfus & Juillard, 2004; Lüpke & Storch, 2013; Singer & Harris, 2011).

All of the speakers presented in this chapter were affected by many of the aforementioned factors in different periods of their lives. As a result, even though the area is rural, most of the people living there have experience with urban settings. Some of these points will be exemplified in case studies in the following section, which illustrate the effects of mobility on people's linguistic repertoires.

Similar but Different: The Case Studies

The following examples are taken from data collected by Goodchild and Weidl from 2014 to 2017. In addition to observations of numerous sociolinguistic situations, people's detailed ethnographic information was collected, alongside linguistic biographies and interviews conducted on related topics, such as cultural practices and language attitudes. Both of the following examples, discussed in the sections titled 'Translanguaging Practice: Essyl' and 'Translanguaging Practice: Djibonker', are taken from video-recorded observed communicative events. Local transcribers with extensive multilingual repertoires and trained in multilingual transcription techniques carried out the transcriptions for the following examples. For transcription of non-standardised languages, the transcribers use an orthography that is based on the official Senegalese orthography for writing in national languages (Evers, 2011; République du Sénégal, 1971, 1977; Weidl, 2012). In the examples that follow, the transcribers also label the utterance according to which language they perceive is being spoken. When discussing repertoires, we use the terms that the participants themselves align with. We feel it is important to note that in using language names, we acknowledge that they have a lived reality for speakers (Canagarajah, 2013), although in using a concept such as translanguaging we aim to incorporate speakers' perceptions, others' opinions – such as transcribers' – and also sociolinguistic and linguistic analyses.

As a short example, we will look at RM1, who currently lives in Essyl, and her linguistic biography, before analysing an extract of a multilingual video-recorded conversation in which she features. RM1 is a key participant in Goodchild's research as she was initially introduced as a monolingual Joola Banjal speaker. Sagna (2016; in prep) describes Essyl as being characterised by societal monolingualism with Joola Banjal (he refers to Gújjolaay Eegimaa[3]) as the dominant language despite high levels of individual multilingualism. VB, her husband, initially referred to RM1 as being a monolingual Joola Banjal speaker; therefore, she was chosen as a key participant to account for individual monolingualism. However, over time, Goodchild found that the report of RM1's repertoire expanded considerably to include the named languages of French, Mandinka, Wolof and Kriolu, further to earlier reports of only speaking Joola Banjal. Therefore, she became an important case study for translanguaging, simultaneously demonstrating the importance of named languages for identity purposes in people's daily lives (Joola Banjal being the language RM1 identifies with) while engaging in fluid communicative practices using language that may not necessarily be ascribed to any particular ideological representation of named languages. In studying her linguistic biography, it becomes clear that many of the factors named in the previous section have played an important role in RM1's repertoire, but her mobility history, mentioned below, was particularly influential.

RM1 was born in 1955 in Enampor, a neighbouring village to Essyl in Mof Avvi, where Joola Banjal is also spoken. She did not attend formal schooling and reports that during her childhood she only spoke Joola Banjal. During her teenage years, she spent approximately five years in Dakar, the capital city of Senegal. There she stayed with relatives and learnt Wolof outside of the family home: in the family home she spoke 'Joola', a mix of Joola Banjal and Joola Fogny, although Joola Fogny is absent from her reported repertoire. As a young adult, RM1 migrated to work as a domestic worker in various places before returning to Mof Avvi, as is common for many young women from villages in this area (Lambert, 2002; Linares, 1992, 2003; Tomàs i Guilera, 2005). RM1 worked for two families in the Gambia: one was a Joola family in Brikama where they spoke Joola (which she did not further categorise) and Wolof. Then, she went to the capital city Banjul. The Aku family she worked for spoke English and Wolof. RM1 did not report acquiring any English, as she spoke Wolof in the house, but she did acquire Mandinka throughout her time in the Gambia. Later, she returned to the Casamance and worked in Ziguinchor for a French family. Working for this family, she informally learnt French while simultaneously acquiring Kriolu in the neighbourhood. RM1 then returned to her family in Enampor. When she married, she moved into her husband's house in Essyl where she has lived since. In each period of her life, when moving to a different location, RM1 has expanded her repertoire.

Translanguaging practice: Essyl

In the following example, an extract of conversation taken from a speech event in Essyl in which Goodchild participated (observations, fieldnotes and video recordings ESS150116SGa-c) will be analysed to demonstrate the multilingual, fluid nature of language use. The five women featured have the following self-reported linguistic repertoires. Due to limitations of space, it is not possible to describe each participant's linguistic biography as for RM1 above. Language names in Examples (1) and (4) are displayed in alphabetical order; however, this does not represent any comment on level of proficiency or language(s) of identity.

(1) **Self-reported repertoires of speakers in (ESS150116SGb)**

MM1	Joola Banjal, Joola Fogny, Wolof
DS4	French, Joola, Joola Banjal, Joola Fogny, Wolof
PB2	French, Joola Banjal, Wolof
RM1	French, Joola Banjal, Kriolu, Mandinka, Wolof
FT1	Joola, Mandinka, Wolof
AB2	French, Joola Banjal, Wolof

The following extract details a conversation between five women who are harvesting rice in RM1's field. In total, there are 14 women working together in a work group and RM1 is effectively in charge for the day and has to provide food for the women working for her (referred to in Line 08). The five featured participants have fallen behind the rest of the work group in their progress across the field. As they work, they also sing songs. In Examples (2) and (5), the speakers' participant codes are followed by a '→' sign, which shows the directly addressed interlocutor(s) to better understand the structure of this translanguaging conversation.

(2) **Extract from file (ESS1501116SGb 00:46–01:18)**[4]

01	DS4	→PB2	*Injé íjuenen mat'ujugom iilo iegul ma, uogal me gafóñ man ujaal ni go, ujaal go pe !*	Joola Banjal
			'if I knew how to sing I wouldn't be urging you to sing, if we decide to sing a song, let's sing it completely'	

02	PB2	→DS4	*Fétcé !*	Wolof (?)
			'leave me alone!'	
03	DS4	→large	*A-a, jiannen bugaa boube, gúuba gúbbañul*	Joola Banjal
		Group	'no, help these ones over here, two of you come back over here'	
04	PB2	→DS4	*Ee!*	Joola Banjal
			'Hey!'	
05	RM1	→small group	*Ñer elob yay etoge !*	Joola Banjal
			'You've done enough talking!'	
06	FT1	→RM1	*Al numbara... numbara...numbara !*	Mandinka
			'work hard...work hard...work hard!'	
07	FT1	→small group	*RM1 n'gandala aa!*	Wolof
			'RM1 is the boss!'	
08	AB2	→small group	*Tey mo ko yor !*	Wolof
			'today she's the one that has everything!'	

Although participants report Joola Banjal as being the dominant language spoken between women when working in the rice fields, the above example demonstrates that other languages are used as well. The naming of the above languages was carried out by a transcriber, and represents his interpretation of the utterances. It is important to note a couple of salient points: firstly, the identification of Line 02 as Wolof is questioned. Neither the transcriber nor PB2 the speaker were certain about which language this was and in fact the actual lexical content of the utterance was of limited importance to get her point across; in the recording, the accompanying tone and gesture mean her intention is clear (further demonstrating the importance of video recording in capturing the multimodality of language use – Adami; Bradley and Moore; Perera, this volume). Line 06 has been subject to various developing analyses resulting in the conclusion that the term 'translanguaging' is more representative of this example of language use rather than code-switching, as it is unclear if this example belongs to one code or not. At an early stage, the use of Mandinka in Line 06 by FT1 to RM1 was interpreted as being based on common knowledge of shared languages in their repertoires, and then in Line 07 FT1 turns back to the whole group and uses Wolof to include everyone (Goodchild, forthcoming), despite the shared multilingual repertoire among participants also including Joola varieties. However, the transcriber does not claim that Mandinka forms part of his repertoire; furthermore, after having previously analysed as detailed above, during March 2017 DS4 was observed saying the same phrase '*Al numbara, al numbara, al numbara*' to a group of masons, when she was passing by RM1's house where the masons were working. When Goodchild later queried what she had shouted to them, she replied that she wanted to encourage them to work hard in her language, Joola Fogny. However, if the above is analysed in terms of translanguaging, it does not mean that the text could not be interpreted using a code-based approach, but rather the above should demonstrate that how a code is defined is in itself multifaceted and the utterances may belong to different codes for different people and could even change according to when they were asked: i.e. Line 06 is Mandinka for the transcriber and is Joola Fogny for DS4 (at the time of asking). The inclusivity of the term is its strength, and in keeping this flexible approach further light can be shed on how people use language in such a highly multilingual setting. Therefore, from this example it should be evident that even a short excerpt can have multiple interpretations, all of which should be considered together, and using a term such as 'code-switching' would restrict these multiple interpretations. For example, restricting the use of 'Mandinka' to a defined *a priori* code does not allow for flexibility and multiple representations of languages with different meaning for different people, which are emblematic of the inherent complexity in translanguaging practices.

Translanguaging practice: Djibonker

This section provides an insight into a translanguaging practice recorded by Weidl in 2016 in Djibonker. Contrary to the example above, the conversation discussed below took place within the family household of LM and his wife KS2. All of the multilingual participants are very close and have well-established social rules and shared common knowledge. They originate from the Casamance and during the period of data collection spent most of their time together.

The following example shows a conversation of mainly three speakers (KS2, LM and IPS) and two more peripheral participants (PLC and TS1) who only appear briefly at the end of the extract, creating an

Figure 8.2   Recording setting (DJI170216MWa)

interesting multilingual constellation. The recording setting (see Figure 8.2) shows LM, TS1 and PLC producing traditional mud bricks to build a new house, KS2 is looking for a sack and later chasing a chicken and IPS is making Attaya, a green tea.

The self-reported languages of identification of the speakers vary. KS2 identifies with Joola Buluf, a Joola language spoken in Tobor further northeast, but she grew up and lived in Ziguinchor, the regional capital, before she came to Djibonker over 10 years ago to marry LM. She came into contact with more languages present in the village setting such as Baïnounk Gubëeher and Joola Kujireray. LM was born and grew up in Djibonker and identifies with Baïnounk Gubëeher; however, he has worked in different professions in the surrounding area, which has extended his linguistic repertoire. IPS's parents originate from Guinea-Bissau and he identifies with Arame. He has moved around Senegal and Guinea-Bissau and has acquired more languages through his experiences and interactions. He lives in the neighbouring village of Brin (see Figure 8.1), is a good friend of the family and is regularly present at the household. PLC is an inhabitant of Djibonker and has lived there all his life while identifying as Baïnounk Gubëeher. Even though he is well known by the family, in this scenario he is employed as a paid worker to accelerate the building process, a fact that changes his social status. TS1 identifies with Joola Kaasa and originates from Nyassia, a village linguistically very distinct from Djibonker. He is a professional builder and friend who came to live with the family during the construction works. All of the individuals in the conversation share more than one language in their multilingual repertoires (as can be seen below) and, due to their geographical location, are likely to be highly influenced by Joola languages, Wolof, French and possibly others. Yet, even though Baïnounk Gubëeher plays an important role in social interactions within Djibonker, it does not seem to have a big impact on the speakers coming from outside (IPS and TS1).

Their linguistic repertoires are self-reported as follows; the frequency of use of these languages is context dependent:

(4) Self-reported languages of speakers in (DJI170216MWa)

KS2   Baïnounk Gubëeher; Bayot; Joola Buluf; Joola Fogny; Joola Kujireray; Mandinka; Wolof

LM   Baïnounk Gubëeher; French; Joola Banjal; Joola Fogny; Joola Kaasa; Joola Kujireray; Kriolu; Wolof

IPS   Arame; Bayot; English; French; Joola Fogny; Joola Kaasa; Joola Kujireray; Kriolu; Wolof

PLC   Baïnounk Gubëeher; French; Joola Fogny; Joola Kujireray; Wolof

TS1   Bayot; French; Joola Fogny; Joola Kaasa; Kriolu

(05) Extract from (DJI170216MWa_cut01, 00:01–01:30)

01   KS2   →LM   *laurent ujukom juk imus ingar fubote*   Joola Buluf

'Laurent, did you see me taking a sack'

02   LM   →KS2   *eey fo nukane ñaa fubóm*   Joola Fogny

'Yes and the other one you have left is mine'

03   KS2   →LM   *eeee kob be yok írúp jaat nonom fubote fí ya nen de ŋar*   Joola Buluf

'Ee [laughs] wait when I take it, you are going to tell later that I took your bag'

04   IPS   →LM   *leegi lolu ngay kass*   Wolof

'So that is what you dig now [joking]'

05	LM	→IPS	*aw pop*	Joola Fogny
			'also you'	
06	KS2	→LM	*ujuk jaat iŋar fubote nonom fubote fubëm ulaŋen*	Joola Buluf
			'If you see me taking a sack you always tell me to return it'	
07	LM	→KS2	*ña ufu fujow yokk fuket de bala ungar fuke*	Joola Fogny
			'They have to increase first before you can take another one'	
08	IPS	→LM	*ŋga dann sac saku sonakos*	Wolof
			'Did you steal the 'Sonakos' sack'	
09	LM	→IPS	*boy man nironala kuy saac*	Wolof
			'Boy do I look like someone who steals to you'	
10	IPS	→LM	*ham ŋga muso fi bey gerte nga nan*	Wolof
			'You know, you haven't cultivated peanuts here and you ask [beg for a sack]'	
11	LM	→IPS	*gerte? yow man, man yow la*	Wolof
			'peanuts? You are, for you, I am like you'	
12	KS2	→all	*ginar bi la xam ni way dina def*	Wolof
			'I don't know about the chicken but I will do it'	
13	IPS	→KS2	*ban ginar?*	Wolof
			'which chicken?'	
14	KS2	→IPS	*fúfú la ko búgë dugël waye fokoi yeeg duma muna yeeg*	Wolof
			'I wanted to put it in there but where it climbed up, I won't be able to climb up there'	
15	LM	→KS2	*danga koy door mu dem*	Wolof
			'Hit it so it will go'	

16	LM	→PLC	*Umukuni*	Baïnounk Gubëeher
			'are you finished'	
17	PLC	→LM	*újegedi*	Baïnounk Gubëeher
			'stamping'	
18	TS1	→LM	*najuke asekol o ña muña o jibóóm*	Joola Kaasa
			'It [chicken] saw your wife and now it dances'	
19	LM	→TS1	*múnda ukat kasabote kujakut anine asaboterit mëmëk de*	Joola Fogny
			'Munda [nickname] stop the sabotage, men normally don't sabotage a lot'	

As the main speakers involved in this conversation have known each other for an extended period of time, it could be assumed that they would have either agreed upon a certain language or established a regular pattern of language use with each other. However, this is not the reality and far more factors play a role in the choice of language(s) and their mixtures. Interestingly, all of the speakers report their perception to stick to the Joola language with which they identify in this example. Only LM draws on Joola Fogny, the most widespread Joola language of wider communication in Senegal. However, these definitions are situated in this social, interactive context and might be interpreted differently in others, showing the fluidity of boundaries and named languages (see, e.g. Pozdniakov & Segerer, accepted).

In the first line, as could be anticipated from KS2, she addresses her husband in Joola Buluf, her language of identity, to point out a problem. However, since LM reported that it is important for him that his wife improves her Baïnounk Gubëeher, and the fact that they are in their household, where LM reports Baïnounk Gubëeher to be the central language, his response in Joola was somewhat marked. However, this is likely due to the presence of IPS and TS1, who are not proficient in Baïnounk Gubëeher and would therefore be excluded from the conversation.

In Line 4, IPS makes a joke addressed to LM in Wolof, which he responds to in Joola, since he is already in a Joola language mode. Only after IPS's iterated statement in Wolof, which builds on the conversation in Joola before, does LM adapt his answer to Wolof (Line 9). Then, KS2 makes a more general statement in Wolof about the chicken (Line 12), which is not addressed to anyone in particular. This translanguaging practice is used with the aim to prompt other interlocutors to interact; an intention that is clearly supported through a switch to one of the languages of wider communication in the area, as it is the most effective in order to reach the most individuals in the conversation. The conversation goes on in Wolof until LM addresses PLC to ask him if he is done with his work. He uses Baïnounk Gubëeher (Line 16), which is the shared language of identity of the two speakers while the other people are not included in their exchange. TS1 has followed the whole discussion about the chicken; interestingly he does not report speaking Wolof at all, but clearly understood what the conversation in Wolof was about. He makes fun of LM's wife (Line 18), which he expresses in Joola Kaasa, the Joola language he identifies with, and triggers LM again to answer in Joola. It could have been perceived as lacking respect if LM would have answered in Wolof, since TS1 is older and is the lead builder who does not want to be identified with Wolof. What can be seen in this data is that use of language(s) does not follow strict rules; it changes for reasons of context, interlocutor, intentions, ease, practicability, etc. Explanations of the decisions that speakers make in certain contexts can be found, to a certain extent, through in-depth sociolinguistic analysis, which must include detailed ethnolinguistic knowledge as presented above.

Additionally, Weidl analysed different lexemes from named languages throughout the conversation, which were intermixed into phrases as e.g. in Line 7 'yokk' originates from Wolof, meaning 'to add more' within a Joola utterance, which was not perceived as such by the speaker. 'Saku' (French 'sac' for sack) is used in the utterances based on Wolof instead of using a lexeme from Wolof 'mbuus' (Line 8), but for the same meaning, a lexeme from a Joola language 'fubote' is used in the Joola utterances. Further, LM uses the term 'boy', from English to address IPS (Line 9). He then uses the lexeme 'saboter' (French for sabotage) in a Joola utterance but fits it into the Joola grammatical system 'kasabote', with a noun class prefix for inanimate verbal nouns 'ka-' and then uses it as 'asabot-erit', with the 'a-' as a human subject prefix and '-erit' a negative habitual suffix (analysis in a private conversation with Rachel Watson, 2017).

However, these examples were only perceived as different languages by the researchers, not the speakers nor the transcribers. An analysis with a translanguaging approach (and not for example a code-switching approach) is appropriate here since the speakers' intentions are invisible and in retrospect they seem not to follow a certain clear distinctive intention, but are influenced by their social context and interactions and it is rather their conscious or unconscious choice to use the language(s) in that way. Therefore, in this interpretation the translingual fluidity is once again visible.

More than showing highly multilingual people who are translanguaging as a lived practice, this short excerpt further exemplifies that individuals are engaging in even wider multilingual practices than they are reporting.

Concluding Discussion of the Examples

The preceding sections present examples of translanguaging practices in two different settings. Although the participants in each of the examples have different constellations of linguistic repertoires and the contexts are sociolinguistically different, as described above, there are, however, similarities that can be discussed as both examples are pertinent to translanguaging.

First, both examples demonstrate that participants engage in wider multilingual practices than they report. This happens on the level of individual repertoire, as in the case of TS1 in 'Translanguaging practice: Djibonker' who did not report an active or passive knowledge of Wolof in his linguistic repertoire, but was clearly following the conversation of the other participants. This also happens on a situational level, as in 'Translanguaging practice: Essyl', where many of the participants report that Joola Banjal is the dominant language used by women in the rice fields. Although this may be the case, the observed linguistic practices of participants, observed over three separate occasions, each approximately 6 hours, with approximately 4 hours of recorded conversations, are not so strictly bound, in particular with regards to different varieties of Joola and Wolof, which are used fluently and frequently. Although underreporting is a common finding for participants across sociolinguistic settings, it is important to recognise that reporting may, of course, change over time. Therefore, reports of linguistic repertoires, as in the case of RM1 above may vary depending on interlocutor, setting, common knowledge and also trust. In this context, we are dealing with a fluid understanding of repertoire, where a participant is both 'monolingual' and 'multilingual'; furthermore, a participant is not restricted to the apparently available codes in their repertoire, but engages in wider translanguaging practices, creatively accessing their repertoires, whether they report it or not.

Secondly, through data obtained on reports of participants' repertoires, the reports of transcribers and also analyses by researchers, it is evident that in such a highly multilingual setting, where many of the languages are not standardised or codified, it is difficult to define or agree on what a code in fact is. Watson (Cobbinah *et al.*, 2017; Watson, in prep) has put forward a new way of conceiving languages as categories, which follows prototype theory. Therefore, through consensus, certain forms become prototypical of that language, be it a phonological or syntactic feature. It accounts for individual variation in language use, and furthermore, it also accounts for languages where there is significant overlap in structures, such as the closely related Joola languages. Perceptions by speakers and observers surrounding labelling of their translanguaging practices may be open, dynamic and changing depending on context, interlocutor, etc. As Canagarajah (2013) states '[...] labelled languages and language varieties have a reality for social groups. [...] They are constructs that are always open to reconstitution and relabelling'. A concept such as translanguaging is therefore more suited to our research context. A code-based approach is too rigid and whereas code-switching/-mixing assumes *a priori* codes, translanguaging includes the dynamicity of linguistic practices incorporating speakers' perceptions.

The Casamance, and the highly diverse multilingual situation represented there, presents a good setting for the elaboration and application of the translanguaging approach. This chapter has examined external influences that contribute to a high level of individual multilingualism, where participants have varied and diverse linguistic repertoires depending on their life trajectory. Using data taken from observed communicative events, we have demonstrated how the fluid, multilingual practices in this area are complex to analyse. An in-depth sociolinguistic investigation is particularly relevant as in such a superdiverse setting it is often not possible to pre-establish named languages or which code might be used.

It has been demonstrated that opinions on language use vary among participants, and an advantage to using a term such as 'translanguaging' is the inclusivity it presents to examine linguistic practices and to incorporate speakers' understanding of how they communicate. Particularly when dealing with such heterogeneous multilingual speakers, as in the contexts above, it is difficult to define what a social group is; nonetheless, labelled varieties do have realities and significance for people, but in varied ways. By using a concept such as translanguaging, there is no need to have established labels for practices that are fluid and changing and as Juffermans (2015) also states in using a term such as 'translanguaging' (which he refers to as languaging) the named languages are not the starting points of analysis.

In our analyses, we begin with the communicative event itself and take into consideration participants' perceptions of their repertoires, ethnographic data and other stakeholders' perceptions of languages used in order to arrive at a more holistic understanding of how people communicate with each other through translanguaging practices. We believe the way forward is to put the individual in the centre, but within their situated social interactions. Therefore, an approach such as translanguaging can draw in ethnographies, repertoires and local understandings of languages and languaging in order to build up a more nuanced description of the myriad possibilities of translanguaging practices in which people engage in such a highly fluid, multilingual setting.

Notes

(1) Formal linguists for example do not accept 'Joola' as a language, but rather a group of related languages. Yet, speakers often describe their linguistic practice as 'Joola', which reflects on their personal language use. However, if they want to refer to a specific Joola language they can, and their distinctions can even be more detailed than the one of formal linguists.

(2) For more information on the project 'Crossroads – Investigating the Unexplored Side of Multilingualism', see www.soascrossroads.org.

(3) For further discussion on language naming practices, see Goodchild (2016; forthcoming).

(4) Video clips are accessible at www.soascrossroads.org.

References

Bamgbose, A. (2000) Language planning in West Africa. *International Journal of the Sociology of Language* 141, 101–117. doi: 10.1515/ijsl.2000.141.101

Blackledge, A. and Creese, A. (2010) *Multilingualism: A Critical Perspective*. London/New York: Continuum.

Blommaert, J. and Rampton, B. (2011) Language and superdiversity. *Diversities* 13 (2), 1–21.

Calvet, L.-J. and Dreyfus, M. (1990) La famille dans l'espace urbain: Trois modèles de plurilinguisme. *Plurilinguismes* 3, 29–54.

Canagarajah, S. (2013) *Translingual Practice. Global Englishes and Cosmopolitan Relations*. New York: Routledge.

Clark, A.F. and Colvin Phillips, L. (1994) *Historical Dictionary of Senegal*. Metuchen, NJ: Scarecrow Press.

Cobbinah, A.Y. (2010) The Casamance as an area of intense language contact: The case of Baïnounk Gubaher. *Journal of Language Contact* 3 (1), 175–201.

Cobbinah, A.Y. (2013) Nominal classification and verbal nouns in Baïnounk Gubëeher. PhD thesis, School of Oriental and African Studies, University of London.

Cobbinah, A., Hantgan, A., Lüpke, F. and Watson, R. (2017) Carrefour Des Langues, Carrefour Des Paradigmes. In M. Auzanneau, M. Bento and M. Leclère (eds) *Espaces, Mobilités et Éducation Plurilingues: Éclairages d'Afrique ou d'ailleurs* (pp. 79–97). Paris: Éditions des archives contemporaines.

Di Carlo, P. (2017) Towards an understanding of African endogenous multilingualism ethnography, language ideologies, and the supernatural. *International Journal of the Sociology of Language* 1–20.

Di Carlo, P. and Good, J. (2014) What are we trying to preserve? Diversity, change, and ideology at the edge of the Cameroonian grassfields. In P.K. Austin and J. Sallabank (eds) *Endangered Languages: Beliefs and Ideologies in Language Documentation and Revitalisation* (pp. 229–262). Oxford: Oxford University Press.

Dreyfus, M. and Juillard, C. (2004) *Le plurilinguisme au Sénégal. Langues et identités en devenir*. Paris: Karthala.

Ducos, G. (1983) Plurilinguisme et descriptions de langues. *La Linguistique* 19 (2), 55–70.

Evers, C. (2011) Orthographic policy and planning in Sénégal/Senegaal: The détournement of orthographic stereotypes. *Working Papers in Educational Linguistics* 26 (1), 21–51.

García, O. and Li Wei (2014) *Translanguaging: Language, Bilingualism and Education*. Basingstoke: Palgrave Macmillan.

Goodchild, S. (2016) 'Which language(s) are you for?' 'I am for all the languages'. Reflections on breaking through the ancestral code: Trials of sociolinguistic documentation. *SOAS Working Papers in Linguistics* 18, 75–91.

Goodchild, S. (forthcoming) Multilingual people with monolingual perceptions: Patterns of multilingualism in Essyl, Basse Casamance, Senegal. In F. Lüpke (ed.) *The Oxford Guide to the Atlantic Languages of West Africa*. Oxford: Oxford University Press.

Goodchild, S. and Weidl, M. (2016) Documentation of Speakers' Linguistic Practices in Two Sociolinguistically Diverse Settings in the Casamance, Senegal. Conference Paper. Language Documentation and Description 5 SOAS University of London, 3–4 December.

Juffermans, K. (2015) *Local Languaging, Literacy and Multilingualism in a West African Society*. Bristol: Multilingual Matters.

Lambert, M.C. (2002) La marginalisation économiques des communautés joola à la fin du XXe siècle. In M-C. Diop (ed.) *Le Sénégal contemporain* (pp. 355–373). Paris: Karthala.

Linares, O.F. (1992) *Power, Prayer, and Production: The Jola of Casamance, Senegal*. Cambridge: Cambridge University Press.

Linares, O.F. (2003) Going to the city … and coming back? Turnaround migration among the Jola of Senegal. *Africa: Journal of the International African Institute* 73 (1), 113–132.

Lüpke, F. (2010) Multilingualism and language contact in West Africa: Towards a holistic perspective. *Journal of Language Contact* 3 (1), 1–12.

Lüpke, F. (2016) Pure fiction: The interplay of indexical and essentialist language ideologies and heterogeneous practices. A view from Agnack. *Language Documentation and Conservation Special Publication* 10, 8–39.

Lüpke, F. and Storch, A. (2013) *Repertoires and Choices in African Languages*. Boston, MA/Berlin: de Gruyter.

Nugent, P. (2007) Cyclical history in the Gambia/Casamance borderlands: Refuge, settlement, and Islam from c. 1880 to the present. *The Journal of African History* 48 (2), 221–243. doi: 10.1017/S0021853707002769

Pozdniakov, K. and Guillaume, S. (accepted) A genealogical classification of Atlantic languages. In F. Lüpke (ed.) *The Oxford Guide to the Atlantic Languages of West Africa*. Oxford: Oxford University Press.

République du Sénégal (1971) *Transcription des langues nationales*. Décret no. 71-566.

République du Sénégal (1977) *Application de la réglementation en matière de transcription des langues nationales*. Décret no. 77-55.

Sagna, S. (2008) Formal and semantic properties of the Gújjolaay Eegimaa: (A.k.a Banjal) nominal classification system. PhD thesis, School of Oriental and African Studies, University of London.

Sagna, S. (2016) 'Research impact' and how it can help endangered languages. *OGMIOS Newsletter 59*, 5–8.

Sagna, S. (in prep) A typological overview of Gújjolaay Eegimaa (Banjal). Unpublished manuscript.

Singer, R. and Harris, S. (2016) What practices and ideologies support small-scale multi-lingualism? A case study of Warruwi Community, northern Australia. *International Journal of the Sociology of Language* 241, 163–208.

Tomàs i Guilera, J. (2005) La identitat ètnica entre els joola d'Oussouye (Húluf, Bubajum áai). Doctoral thesis, Universitat Autònoma de Barcelona.

Vertovec, S. (2007) Super-diversity and its implications. *Ethnic and Racial Studies* 30 (6), 1024–1054.

Watson, R. (2015) Verbal nouns in Joola Kujireray. PhD thesis, School of Oriental and African Studies, University of London.

Watson, R. (In prep) Language as category: Using prototype theory to create reference points for the study of multilingual data. Unpublished manuscript.

Weidl, M. (2012) Das Medium Sprache in Senegal: Spracheinstellungen der Wolof mit dem Fokus auf den Bildungssektor; Probleme, Schwierigkeiten und Ansätze zu Lösungsver-suchen. Diplomarbeit, Institut für Afrikawissenschaften, Universität Wien.

9 The Paradox of Translanguaging in Safaliba: A Rural Indigenous Ghanaian Language

Ari Sherris, Paul Schaefer and Samua Mango Aworo

The experiences of one Safaliba language community in Ghana are offered as an example of a translanguaging approach to education by an indigenous society that affirms both the intrinsic value and practical utility of the minority language. The community also utilizes a more traditional view of language for identity-politic purposes and for insight into literacy problems and strategic solutions. We document and analyze transcripts of translanguaging from Safaliba adults and children (6–10 years of age). The results validate Safaliba activists' intuitions that translanguaging has a legitimate and valuable place in their children's education, despite the outsider status of the Safaliba language and translanguaging in official Ghanaian education policy.

Introduction

Ghana has a population of 27.6 million people and 73 indigenous living languages; no single language's first language speakers make up a majority (Lewis *et al.*, 2016). Safaliba is spoken as a first language by 7000–9000 people, most inhabiting seven towns and villages in a 120-square kilometer area west of Tamale and south of Wa. This rural area is one of the more linguistically diverse rural parts of Ghana, with at least 11 other indigenous languages spoken within a radius of 50 kilometers (e.g. Gonja, Choruba, Vagla, Deg, Birifor, Dagaare, Waali, Lobiri, Jula, Siti and Kamara), whose speakers engage with the Safaliba communities regularly in marketing, farming and other social contexts.

The main medium and goal of formal education in Ghana since before independence has been the English language; in popular understanding, the goal of education and literacy has been equated with an ability to read and write English (Opoku-Amankwa & Brew-Hammond, 2011). In Ghana, as in some other African countries, any use of what some still call the vernacular is often framed as undesirable in educational settings (Mwesigire, 2014; Onuh, 2015).

However, in actual classroom practice, at least some Ghanaian schoolteachers do make use of local languages to better communicate with students and to explain the concepts being taught; after all, if the goal of schooling is to 'teach for understanding of the subject matter, then all resources, including the various languages which are familiar to learners, should be used alongside the official unfamiliar language' (Opoku-Amankwa & Brew-Hammond, 2011: 102). Opoku-Amankwa and Brew-Hammond frame this multilingual communication as 'code-switching', but suggest that the term 'translanguaging' is potentially more rewarding for the educational context. We agree, affirming that in a 'translanguaging space' (Li Wei, 2011: 1234), languages creatively interact together, in addition to and alongside one another, and the free use of all the linguistic repertoires of both students and teachers improves educational experiences and participation.

As is the case with most indigenous languages in Ghana, Safaliba has few books and no government status for use in government forums, documents or schools, in part due to a *de facto* language education policy that officially supports educational materials and instruction in only nine of Ghana's languages.[1] Nevertheless, Safaliba is experiencing an awakening among the Safaliba teachers in Mandari, Ghana, the largest Safaliba-dominant town (Sherris, 2017), and in the academic literature (Bodua-Mango, 2012, 2015; Schaefer, 2009, 2015; Schaefer & Schaefer, 2003, 2004).

As has been documented for other indigenous peoples elsewhere (Coulthard, 2008; Patrick, 2012), indigenous activism, self-determination, pride in the links between the indigenous language and identity, and issues related to land and governance are evidenced among the Safaliba (Sherris, 2015). Local Safaliba subsistence-farmer-teacher-activists and their allies are resisting dominant school discourses to teach Safaliba children to read and write their language in formal and informal settings (Sherris, 2017). This chapter draws on data from traditional Safaliba storytelling, hip-hop, community interaction and early childhood Safaliba literacy materials and teaching practice to explore the Safaliba revitalization that is manifested in the movement to bring Safaliba into formal schooling via literacy instruction.

We deploy a theory of translanguaging to explain the data (Baker, 2011; Blackledge & Creese, 2010; Canagarajah, 2006; García, 2009;

García & Li Wei, 2014; Hornberger & Link, 2012; Li Wei, 2011; Otheguy *et al.*, 2015). We contend that translanguaging is an unmarked practice in Safaliba, a communicative approach that expands the meaning-making capabilities of Safaliba in traditional storytelling and contemporary hip-hop. Because translanguaging as a construct is free of any deficit characterization, it potentially represents a pathway for the widest cross section of emergent Safaliba readers to embrace a socially and culturally relevant, communicatively rich and creative Safaliba literacy that organically arises from Safaliba orality.

At the same time, we are also cognizant of the need for the category *language* for identity-politic purposes particularly with respect to language rights (Skutnabb-Kangas & Phillipson, 2017), the policies of nation states and the communicative intuitions and educational development goals of the Safaliba-speaking community. The Safaliba data suggest that linguistic phenomena such as phonology, morphology and syntax significantly determine the specific ways that Safaliba speakers translanguage; and recognition of differences in linguistic structure between Safaliba and other languages is vital for understanding some of the specific factors (such as pronunciation and semantic categorization) that have proved challenging to Safaliba children's success at school in the past.

The identity-politic stance of Safaliba activists is that Safaliba is a separate and distinct language and deserves, like English or Gonja (a hegemonic regional indigenous Ghanaian language[2]), to be recognized as such and become a separate part of the school curriculum. At the same time, they have utilized a translanguaging approach in the materials they have developed for Safaliba literacy, in the hope that this will increase the success of schooling for their children, lower the dropout rate and lead to greater learning.

There is some tension in these efforts between the ease of adopting new vocabulary items from English versus the concern of elders to reintroduce to a younger generation the semantically equivalent Safaliba words from a rich oral tradition. The Safaliba Chief of Mandari, for instance, urges that eliminating borrowed words is the best path for Safaliba when he said to a group of high school students, 'We want to instill our culture back! The Safaliba language is one way. We have to think of ways to expand it'. Nevertheless, he himself translanguaged using English loanwords in his talk with Primary 1 students, and when this was brought to his attention during a check of the transcriptions, he laughed and said, 'You caught me'.

Some presentations of translanguaging argue very strongly for the priority of 'idiolects' and 'repertoires' over and against 'languages'.

However, to do so in this case would marginalize the identity-politic efforts of the Safaliba activists as well as the evidence of real-world effects in children's educational experience of what is traditionally understood as 'linguistic structure'. An uncompromising stance on the primacy of 'translanguaging' in this context hinders comprehension of the social and educational issues at hand in the Safaliba context as well as the status issues vis-à-vis indigenous languages recognized by Ghana Ministry of Education practices. Paradoxically, it is recognition of these factors that allows us to use the basic concepts of translanguaging to argue for a broader and more inclusive approach to education in linguistic minority communities, as well as to develop specific remedies at the instructional level.

This chapter, consequently, recognizes the continued work of descriptive linguists to chart a traditional, albeit normed or mostly static view of Safaliba as a status-raising endeavor in the eyes of the nation state and its academia, while also contributing to the documentation of a fluid, dynamic view of the language and supporting such among community members in their language practices. Although it is traditional to view language as static, language also exhibits itself as 'waves of behavioral movement merging one into another in intricate, overlapping, complex systems' (Pike, 1972 [1959]: 129)[3]; see Larsen-Freeman, Bricolage). In essence, we argue to live the paradox that both conceptualizations of human linguistic phenomena have valid contexts of usage and need not be framed as essentially oppositional.

Translanguaging

The term 'translanguaging' was coined in the early 1980s by Cen Williams (1994, 1996, cited in Baker, 2011: 288) to conceptualize the use of alternate languages during receptive (reading/listening) and productive (talking/writing) lessons in Welsh bilingual education. Teachers utilizing a critical translanguaging pedagogy, at times maintaining boundaries between languages in order to offset and even resist hegemonic control by dominant languages and at other times providing affordances for negotiating meaning and communication, was described by Blackledge and Creese (2010).

The conceptions of translanguaging as 'the act of deploying all of the speaker's lexical and structural resources *freely*' (Otheguy *et al.*, 2015: 297) and as '*multiple discursive practices* in which bilinguals engage in order to *make sense of their bilingual worlds*' (García, 2009: 45) are particularly useful for our context. Furthermore, the pedagogical practices of alternating languages across reading, writing, listening and speaking can all be beneficially categorized as *translanguaging*; the term also covers code-switching, code-mixing, creolization and vocabulary borrowings, a creative use of language (Li Wei, 2011).

Translanguaging situates language and literacy in real-time interactive production. It also detaches the conception of communication from an artificially fixed linguistic framework and fosters movement across idiolect, dialect, variety and register. Hence, translanguaging valorizes the indigenous creativity in each extract of communication we discuss in this chapter: storytelling with its roots in pre-colonial traditions and hip-hop as decolonized interactional expressiveness, children's verbal interaction with adult Safaliba community members and the talk-to-text moves of a pedagogy of reading instruction that strikes an ecolinguistic balance that nurtures grassroots literacy.

'To translanguage or not' is not an either/or reality among the Safaliba activists, even when it runs into corrections from older speakers of the language. The identity politics of resistance is sometimes strengthened when Safaliba stands apart from other languages to establish its status and individual nature. Indeed, the subject positioning by activists passionate about their cause is creating the conditions for children to learn to read Safaliba, bringing it into the school to teach its written form. It is, in a real sense, a political act, a form of decolonization of schooling through resistance to the government curricula for reading instruction. The translanguaging within the Safaliba school curriculum is a nod to *real* language, *real* take-over of school, real-time decolonization of a different sort, an opening to the creative incorporation of languages into Safaliba as a member of a multilingual communicative space (see Perera, this volume).

Methodology

This is an ethnography with data from Safaliba speakers in Mandari, Ghana, comprising reflective and descriptive fieldnotes, photos and 20 hours of video recordings of adults talking to children, children talking to their teacher, community storytelling and a hip-hop workshop.

Transcriptions and translations as well as reflections and fieldnotes were verified through iterative readings by Safaliba teacher-activists, a form of member checking. Discussion of Safaliba linguistic categories and generalizations are from the descriptive analysis based on 25 recorded and transcribed Safaliba oral narratives and 13 written texts from Safaliba speakers from Mandari in Schaefer (2009). These oral narratives include both traditional wisdom stories and individual narratives, and were recorded for the research in contexts designed to match the situations where such narratives typically occur, with only Safaliba speakers present. Each narrative was told by a Safaliba adult to a group of other Safaliba speakers, all of whom had been vetted by members of the larger Safaliba-speaking community as exhibiting broadly typical Safaliba speech patterns. The performance of the traditional stories included the opening, audience response, group singing and closing, which typically comprise such performances, while the individual narratives were given in a conversational setting that included less-formalized interaction between narrator and audience.

The Safaliba language population is fairly homogeneous and comparatively few in number, with the majority of the speakers remaining in or near the traditional area where the Safaliba have apparently lived for at least the last 500 years[4] (Schaefer, 2015). This homogeneity suggests that observations from Mandari data can be reasonably assumed to have valid application to the rest of the Safaliba-speaking population.

Translanguaging in non-school social contexts

Adult social interaction commonly exhibits translanguaging: the linguistic repertoire of adult speakers regularly includes elements from multiple languages that are brought into play for various communicative purposes. The following examples are from a humorous narrative told to entertain and the lyrics of a local musician giving a presentation on hip-hop to interested Safaliba youth.

The narrative, finding humor in both the colonial-era 'white man' as well as local stereotypes of the neighboring Vagla ethnic group, was composed in the early 1980s (Mbatumwine, 2007). The story incorporates some actual Vagla conversation as well as an imaginative rendition of the English attributed to the 'white man' (Excerpt 1). Non-Safaliba elements are italicized.

Excerpt 1:   Vagla and English repertoire elements in Safaliba storytelling

1   Ba ye ká, 'Ɖ yaọ! M mɛɛ Sumaani dabba la!'
         <They said, 'Uh-oh! My father Sumaani is coming!' >

2   Ká ọna ŋ kenne nee.
         < Meaning that they said it was he who was coming.>

Although some members of the Safaliba audience would understand the Vagla excerpts, the text includes interpretation of some of the more complex Vagla phrases. Since most Safaliba speakers have limited English comprehension, the speaker creates an imaginative 'English' for Safaliba ears, which diverges from normative English speech (Excerpt 2).

Excerpt 2:   Vagla and English repertoire elements in Safaliba storytelling

1   O máŋ ye ká, '*Dɛ bɔɛ de kat dɛ tot! Maŋkɛsɛ!*'
         <He would say, '*The boy the cat the tot! Matches!*'>

Except for the word 'matches', the rest of the 'English' has no objective meaning; it is explained by the narrator as a humorous impression of the white man's speech. The repetition of 'dɛ/de' possibly represents the high-frequency word 'the', which some of the audience may recognize as 'English' (Excerpt 3).

Excerpt 3:   Vagla and English repertoire elements in Safaliba storytelling

1   Yini Boronisi ọŋ máŋ bọlɛ nẹẹ: '*Dɛ bɔɛ de kat dɛ tot! Maŋkɛsɛ!*'
         <It's as if he was speaking English: '*The boy the cat the tot!
         Matches!*'>

These excerpts demonstrate typical Safaliba use of non-Safaliba repertoire elements. We label such usage as translanguaging because these elements are used without any outside coercion and represent the speaker's own freedom and choice in communicative strategies. We do not categorize it as code-switching or other terminology that can imply boundaries and judgments that intrude into indigenous ways of knowing and habits of mind. As a decolonizing move in theory and research with indigenous communities (Paris & Winn, 2014; Tuhiwai Smith, 2012), we acknowledge variation in language while denying relevance to terms that potentially represent outside impositions.

The next example (Excerpt 4) is from T.I.P. MoreLife, a hiplife artist who raps in Dagaare, Gonja, English, Safaliba and Wali initially at a hip-hop workshop. Hiplife is a phenomenon that combines highlife and hip-hop, two genres of Ghanaian music (Omoniyi, 2009).

The hip-hop workshop transpired in an open yard outside of the Chief of Mandari's palace on 28 March 2016. A canvas shade covering was set up on stakes and teachers and youth brought plastic yard chairs for the workshop. There were 22 participants including the Chief of

Mandari, teachers and youth. Speakers, a microphone and a laptop with hip-hop background beats was set up and connected to electricity from the chief's palace. After the chief was introduced and spoke about the value of extending the oral Safaliba traditions to contemporary music, T.I.P. MoreLive, the hip-hop artist, spoke about how he constructs his work and its value. Mandari youth also spoke about the value of Safaliba and the desire to explore and celebrate their language and cultural practices through this medium. Then T.I.P. shared the iteration of the hip-hop rap discussed below. This rap excerpt blends Safaliba and English (to our knowledge, this is the only example of Safaliba hip-hop).

Excerpt 4:   Safaliba hip-hop

1   *Yeah. Beah. Beah. Click. Click. Yaŋ kwa huuh!*
            <Let's go!>
2   *Welcome to Mandari*, Ɲmandarɛ ŋ posiriye!
            <Mandari Greetings!>
3   Bɔnɔ kpaŋ maŋ dɛ wa kɔttɛya!
            <I have brought you something!>
4   *So* nɛra zaa yoo ɔ tobee!
            <'*so*' everyone should open their ears!>
5   Tɛ gbagba yala maŋ dɛɛ waa!
            <this message belongs to us!>
6   *So* ŋ sɔsɛra, yá wa wonne!
            <So come and listen!>
7   *God bless* nɛra zaa haŋ zɛnɛ chɛ wonne wonne!
            <'*God bless*' everybody who listens! Listens!>
8   *This is Safaliba language*
9   *Yeah Safaliba language*
10   *This is Safaliba language—it's about—yeah!*
11   Ɲmandarɛ nɔma ba niŋɲe mɔɔya ka ana ŋ wa tɔma zee
            <Mandari people are always serious when it comes to work>
12   Ba so nɔɔrɛ kanyiti a lɛ woore taasɛ zee, ba ba zɛnna kotɛ sɔba yala a di te too bɔnya
            <They are united, patient, they love each other>
13   Ba lɛ woore saamba yala
            <They love strangers>
14   A dɛ jirima kɔ' nɛŋkottu *Yeah*
            <and they show respect to elders, '*yeah*'>
15   *This is Safaliba language Yeah*

This excerpt evidences word-, phrase- and clause-level translanguaging, primarily of English elements. The extent of English usage might reflect an assumption that even in rural areas Ghanaian hip-hop audiences include such English items in their repertoires. Lines 3–7 are mostly in Safaliba, function as the rap's chorus and reach out to the audience, requesting they listen to the message of the song. The English word 'so' in Lines 4 and 6 is commonly used by Ghanaians to express a causal relation and is taken from English. The expressions 'God bless' and 'yeah' are also examples of translanguaging, using English that is likely to be part of the repertoire of the listeners.

The direct messaging about Safaliba as a language (Lines 8–10) is, ironically, in English-only and switches up the messaging language. Its function is to draw attention to a language, Safaliba, which is little known by Ghanaians outside the Bole District. This English usage may be an example of what Omoniyi (2009: 124) calls 'linguistic convergence in performing in the dominant official language'. As such, it also shifts the audience, increasing it to Ghanaians, many of whom would not understand Safaliba unless they are Safaliba. T.I.P. extends the discourses from local to global. He later even records a longer version of this excerpt, which of course links to the mobility of hip-hopianized Safaliba, a very new genre phenomenon for this language (see Archer & Björkvall, this volume, on discourses; Banda et al., this volume, on translocality). Lines 11–15 reach out in Safaliba to the Safaliba people to praise them in ways that valorize traditional values. This establishes a friendship footing for T.I.P. and possibly reasons for his advocacy of Safaliba as a language, knowing as he does that Safaliba and the Safaliba people are unrecognized in schools.

Translanguaging in oral educational contexts

Our data from educational contexts are from a classroom ethnography where the first author videotaped, wrote fieldnotes and collected artifacts and documents during the 2015–2016 academic year. The third author of this chapter, Samua Mango Aworo (called Samua Aworo in daily interactions and in our discussion), was the lead activist for Safaliba-in-the-schools (Sherris, 2017).

Among many other Safaliba-rich literacy practices, teacher-activist Samua Mango Aworo takes his Primary 1 students on weekly field trips by foot to visit different community members, who then demonstrate and talk about the various roles they play, such as bicycle repairing, blacksmithing, cattle herding, drumming, yam cultivating, shea nut processing, etc. The children discuss these excursions later in the classroom.

Excerpt 5 from the children's field trip to a bicycle mechanic shows the interplay between an educational translanguaging context and the children's growing linguistic repertoires.

Excerpt 5: Bike repair visit
BM: Bike mechanic; S1-2: students; T: teacher

1 BM: Ɛɛh tɔ, *sipuusi* mẹŋ, ka *sipuusi* ẹŋ na ye ka ẹ́ na ti, ẹŋ isi *hopu* nẹẹ wa sa, ẹ so naaŋ *sipuusi* nẹẹ ẹ haŋ na daŋnẹ faarẹ.
<Okay, as for a *spoke*, if it is a *spoke* you plan to fix, when you finish removing the *hub*, you have the *spoke* that you start with.>

3 BM: Kà ẹna ŋ iŋŋi kpaŋ nẹẹ wa sa, ẹ naa ŋmaa *hopu* nẹẹ bɔkọ kpaŋ a la basẹ chɛ lɛ iŋŋi kpaŋ.
<After you have finished fixing the first one, you will jump one of the holes of the *hub* and then fix the next.>

4 S1: Kà ẹ iŋŋire *sipuusisi*, ẹ máŋ gáta naaŋ a bɔgọrọ.
<If you are adjusting the *spokes*, you skip every other hole.>

5 BM: Kà ẹna ŋ wa isi *kɔtɔpinsi* nẹẹ sa, a nyẹaa pọọ so *sẹpaana* ẹŋ na *lugisi*.
<After you have finished removing the *cotter pins*, the 'heart' (spindle) has a *spanner* you use to *loosen* it.>

6 BM: Kà ẹna ŋ wa *lugisi* nyẹaa pọọ nẹẹ sa, ọ mẹŋ gba nẹẹ, *girisi* nɔɔ ẹŋ na *girisuu* sarẹ chɛ ka ẹ́ iŋŋi *booronsi*.
<After you have finished *loosening* the spindle, it too needs *grease*, you have to *grease* it before you put in *ball bearings*.>

7 S2: Kà ẹ ye maalẹ ọ nyẹa poo, ẹ máŋ *luusi* naaŋ ọ nyẹa poo *pin* nẹẹ naaŋ, chɛ isuu a iŋŋuu kaaŋ nẹ *boorosisi*, chɛ lɛ pagẹ a nyẹa liŋsi ka *pin* nẹẹ nya iŋŋi.
<When servicing its 'heart' (spindle), you have to *loosen* the spindle's *pin*, remove it and add oil and *ball bearings*, then close the spindle's covers and put back the *pin*.>

Many of the technical terms referring to tools or to different parts of the bicycle are from the bicycle mechanic's English repertoire (e.g. hub, loosen, pin, spanner). However, the Safaliba word for heart or chest is used to refer to the spindle/crank (Lines 5–7). The English word for 'grease' was used by the mechanic (Line 6) instead of the comparable Safaliba term *kaaŋ* 'oil'; however, the children used the more familiar Safaliba word (Line 7) in their own discussion of the visit.

Translanguaging involves the freedom of the speaker to use whatever resources are in their repertoire. Thus, while the bike mechanic uses the borrowed term *sɛpaana* 'spanner', the blacksmith (Excerpt 6) refers to his pliers as *nyɔka* and his chisel as *kerige* (both words of Safaliba origin), but calls his hammer *hama* (from English), his punch *kutupiŋ* (from Safaliba *kutu* 'iron' plus English *piŋ* 'pin').

Excerpt 6:   Blacksmithing visit

1   Nyɔka o̱ máŋ dege̱ a nyɔge̱ a kutuze̱aŋ,
           'It is the pliers which he uses to hold the red iron',

2   chɛ de̱ *hama* ŋmɛɛra a kerige ka a kutu ŋmaa.
           'then takes the *hammer* and hits the chisel for the iron to be cut'. ...

7   Kutupiŋ o̱ máŋ dege̱ a vutte a bɔgo̱rọ.
           'It is the punch which he uses to create a hole'.

Words from English are often used for items outside the traditional material culture or practice; what is 'borrowed' from English is the core semantic content and the basic phonological form of the word. Borrowings, translations and cognates are considered to be translanguaging pedagogies (García & Li Wei, 2014; García *et al.*, 2017). This type of translanguaging in adult-speaker speech provides validation for its use in Safaliba literacy instruction with children.

Words and phrases of English origin are typically adapted to the phonology, morphology and syntax of Safaliba. As evident in the previous examples, English consonants and vowels are mapped onto similar Safaliba counterparts. Since Safaliba syllables are largely limited to CV, CVV or CVN, English words with multi-consonant onsets or codas are re-syllabified: 'spokes' (CCVCC) becomes *sipuusisi* (CVCVCVCV), Line 4 in Excerpt 5.

English morphology and syntax are not frequently employed in Safaliba translanguaging (Excerpt 7). Safaliba morphological constraints shape adaptation so that the word for motorcycle (*moto*, from English motor) is pluralized by adding *–si* (a common plural-marking suffix for nouns) and *loore* (from British English lorry) is pluralized as *looresi*. Except for rare cases where an entire phrase or clause is adopted, English syntax elements are not common in Safaliba translanguaging; after all, English 'not all lorries' is expressed in Safaliba as *loore zaa naane̱* 'lorry each it-isn't'.

Excerpt 7:   Fuel-seller visit

1   Ká *motosi* nɛ *motokiŋsi* ŋ nyuure *patrol*.
    (He said that *motorcycles* and *motor-kings* use *petrol*.)

2   Ká *loore* zaa naanɛ ŋ nyuure *patorol*.
    (He said that it is not all *lorries* that use *petrol*.)

3   Ká *looresi* anime nyuure naaŋ *dɛɛzelɛ*, ka anime mɛŋ nyuure
    patorol.
    (Some *lorries* use *Diesel*, and some use *petrol*.)

Viewing phonological, morphological or syntactic adaptations as part of translanguaging and therefore legitimate communicative expressions allows the children an expanded range of 'acceptable' lexical and phrasal options to 'do school'. Learning can take place using the children's working repertoires without insisting on 'proper' English pronunciation or word formation, which is often at variance with the children's phonological development as young emergent multilinguals.

When schoolteachers recognize that Safaliba phonology has its own patterns and constraints that affect children's pronunciation in predictable ways, this may help to counteract the impression that they are speaking 'bad' or 'broken' English. Furthermore, when older students become aware of their own linguistic patterns,[5] they are more able to strategize and transition to pronunciations and speech patterns that more closely match societal and academic expectations.

Translanguaging in child-authored school materials

Until recently, Safaliba children's experience of primary school largely consisted of the repetition and memorization of English words and sentences, frequently with little knowledge of their basic meaning or normal usage. Use of non-English repertoires in school was discouraged. Now, the awareness that translanguaging is a normal part of social communication permits a wider acceptance of the practice in formal schooling.

During the 2015–2016 school year, Safaliba activists created 35 eight-page Safaliba–English bilingual books. Most of these were taken from Primary 1 students' re-telling of their community field trips. Approximately 15–20 minutes after each visit, the children sat in groups of four to six participants, discussed with one another what they learned, then dictated their thoughts to teacher-activist Samua. A week or two later, they would each receive a copy of a little book created from their classroom discussion and illustrated with photos taken during the field trip; they would practice reading with each book for a week.

In these printed materials, the freedom inherent in a translanguaging approach is evident. The printed word is often attributed a high degree of normative power (a common Ghanaian saying is 'Book no lie!'), so the presence of linguistic variation in these materials goes a long way to affirming the value of the children's linguistic capacity and efforts. Initial reactions in the community did include concerns that Safaliba terminology might become permanently replaced by English-origin words; however, over time the overall positive effects were recognized.

Excerpt 8 shows how the children's repertoires were represented in referring to a fuel hose, whether the item was described with a Safaliba descriptive phrase or whether the borrowed English word was used.

Excerpt 8:   Fuel-seller visit

1   Ká ẹ máŋ dẹgẹ naaŋ bọnnẹẹ haŋ so bɔkkọ nẹẹ a tọŋ a patorol poo.
           (He said that you use the thing that has a hole in it [the hose] and put it in the petrol.)

2   Ẹ máŋ dẹgẹ naaŋ *hoosi* nẹẹ a iŋŋi galaŋ poo chɛ ŋmɛɛla.
           (You use the *hose* and put it in the gallon measure, and start turning [the pump].)

Interestingly, the little books also provided opportunities for the students as well as adults to explore meanings and semantic connections of which they were unaware. This was the case with the word for 'yeast', which came up in field trips to a brewer of traditional guinea-corn beer and a maker of local donuts. It was not formerly realized that the yeast used for brewing (called *bọra*) is essentially the same 'thing' as the commercial yeast (called *yiisi*) used for baking bread (foods made of wheat flour were introduced to the culture during the colonial period). After the semantic connection was made, some adults advocated using *bọra* to also refer to the modern commercial yeast used for bread. However, regardless of discussions among the adults about terminology, the schoolchildren were free to use whatever term was most salient to them (Excerpts 9 and 10).

Excerpt 9:   Brewer visit

1   **Bọra** bá máŋ iŋŋi ka á isigi, sarẹ ka á ɛ nyuubu.
           (They add **yeast** for it [the guinea-corn mixture] to ferment, before it is ready for drinking.)

Excerpt 10:   Donut-maker visit

1   Ká *yiisi* nẹ yaaŋsọŋ zaa ba máŋ iŋŋaa.
            (She said that they add *yeast* and salt to it [donuts].)

Though the field trips and little books can lead to expanding or
reinforcing English-based vocabulary, the main goal is to let the children
feel fully at liberty to create, read and write material using whatever
repertoire they control. The concepts and presentation of some of the
field trips proved to be so unfamiliar that English vocabulary couldn't
be absorbed. In these cases, the children used their existing Safaliba
repertoire to describe what they had heard and observed. We frame this
too as a form of translanguaging since the children are free to use their
full repertoire without requiring particular vocabulary from a particular
language. After the visit to the nurse (Excerpt 11), the children described
the medical instruments by their function.

Excerpt   11: Nurse visit

1   Bọnọ kpaŋ eŋŋa bá máŋ vɛnẹ ka ẹ́ dọ a asẹ ka bá kaa a sọba
            tẹgẹsẹgọ.
            (They let you stand on a certain thing for them to check the
            person's weight [=the scales].)

2   Ba máŋ dẹgẹ naaŋ bọnọ a iŋŋi ẹ bakkọ poo ka bá kaa, kà a sọba
            eŋŋa togili beẹ kà ọ maaya.
            (They use a certain thing and put it in your armpit and
            look at it, to see whether a person body is hot or cool [=the
            thermometer].)

Similarly, no effort was made to ensure consistency in children's
terminology from one field trip to another. The titles for the following
books illustrate this (Excerpts 12 and 13), where 'turner' is the literal
equivalent of one common Safaliba term for the driver of a vehicle:

Excerpt 12:   Lorry driver visit (book # 25)

1   Tẹ haŋ tẹ' Loore Dmɛɛla Zee
            (We Went to the Lorry Turner's [=driver's] Place)

Excerpt 13:   Taxi driver visit (book #28)

1   'Tẹ haŋ tẹ' Tazẹ *Dẹrava* Zee
            (We Went to the Taxi *Driver's* Place)

Discussion

The Safaliba translanguaging data, as well as Safaliba sociocultural and educational contexts, have implications for our definition and use of the term 'translanguaging.' Each excerpt in this chapter demonstrates 'the deployment of a speaker's full linguistic repertoire without regard for watchful adherence to the socially and politically defined boundaries of named ... languages' (Otheguy *et al.*, 2015: 283; Perera, this volume). Each is particular to a context – traditional storytelling, contemporary hip-hop, classroom interaction and community talk. In the examples of schooling, both the transcripts of classroom talk and those for reading use translanguaging for pedagogical reasons.

At the same time, the Safaliba do want to raise the status of their ethnic group, as Mandari's Safaliba Chief indicated. Not unlike most of West Africa, the Safaliba environment in rural Ghana has been multilingual for centuries (Banda et al.; Goodchild & Weidl, this volume), yet in the postcolonial political realities, identity politics plays an important role in gaining recognition as a legitimate language for government schools and school materials development. Traditional storytelling, hip-hop, pedagogical practice and adult talk present Safaliba as a living language, strong in its intergenerational transmission. Through the work of teacher-activists like Samua Aworo, Safaliba is slowly gaining a footing in local government schools. Decolonizing schooling, in part, is occurring because of Safaliba's growing presence in materials development (Sherris, 2017).

In the educational linguistic space, we do not perceive any irreconcilable disagreement between the two perspectives on language, between 'translanguaging' in critical sociolinguistic theory (Blommaert and García, Bricolage) and descriptive linguistic analysis, particularly if each retreats from a hard and fast ideological stance that bans the other. In fact, it is only by affirming important aspects of both viewpoints that we can support effective community strategies to change the educational system in ways that bring results with practical benefit to the community as well as to the individual students.

For us, the valorization of the community members and their efforts to use their language and transform the educational system requires that we defer questions of linguistic ideology to the linguistic and cultural perspectives of the Safaliba people themselves, who do maintain (again, in agreement with basic descriptive linguistics) that the many positive (and they would add, necessary and non-negotiable) aspects to conceptualizing their language have a reality beyond the sum of individual community members' linguistic repertoires. To a certain extent, this highlights a tension between the individualistic perspective of Otheguy *et al.*'s (2015) definition of translanguaging, and the more community-oriented 'indigenous' values held by the Safaliba people. We might also frame our work in a Complex Dynamic Systems Theory (Larsen-Freeman, Bricolage) as, perhaps, Pike (1972) hinted at as early as 1959.

All research is ideologically driven, none is neutral; we believe the ideologies of language and translanguaging both describe the same phenomena (Kress, Bricolage), albeit differently, and both are often useful at different times and for different purposes. Indeed, there may even be a creative tension along a continuum from the imagined boundedness, singularity and stasis of a language to its imagined translanguaging, unbounded, multiple and shifting forms.

The promise translanguaging holds for education is no less significant a phenomenon for which to discuss and develop pedagogy. The classroom excerpts of talk and text in this chapter are representative of the fact that most 'meaning' communicated is done through the local language. Here, 'translanguaging' is used both to help the children acquire concepts that are lexicalized in English but not Safaliba as well as to learn concepts in both languages. We might extrapolate that as children advance into higher grades, translanguaging might help them acquire English lexical items that have Safaliba equivalents, thus allowing them to acquire English vocabulary, and eventually syntax. Instead of rote memorization, banning local language and restricting educational success to few who might cope in an oppressive environment, these students will have succeeded in education through a natural and meaningful translanguaging process, making the best use of all resources available in their rich social context and heritage.

Notes

(1) These nine were not necessarily selected due to population or extant literature, but apparently as a result of various historical factors; one of the nine, Akan, is represented in formal education by instructional materials in three different dialects.
(2) Gonja is one of the nine indigenous Ghanaian languages with government sponsorship for lower-primary reading instruction; it has, in descriptive terms, little morphosyntactic similarity to Safaliba and is not widely used or understood by Safaliba children or adults.
(3) In fact, Pike (1972 [1959]: 129) lamented that '[i]t is extraordinary that in the twentieth century we should still be viewing language almost entirely from a static, particle-like view rather than in a dynamic fashion' – and this was almost six decades ago!
(4) That is, prior to the arrival of the Gonja, dated to the 1500s by Wilks (2000: 99). This situates the Safaliba as a linguistic community perhaps not quite so unlike the

so-called 'primordial villages' referenced in Pratt (1991): indeed, most Safaliba people do know most of the fellow members of their linguistic community, and in fact most consider one another to be 'family' in one form or another.

(5) For instance, Safaliba phonology does not include the palatal fricative written in English as 'sh'; thus, Safaliba speakers often pronounce English 'fish' as 'fis'.

References

Baker, C. (2001/2011) *Foundations of Bilingual Education and Bilingualism*. Bristol: Multilingual Matters.

Blackledge, A. and Creese, A. (2010) *Multilingualism: A Critical Perspective*. London: Bloomsbury Publishing.

Bodua-Mango, K. (2012) Coordinators in Safaliba. Thesis, University of Science and Technology, Trondheim.

Bodua-Mango, R.K. (2015) The phonology of a Safaliba three year old child. Thesis, University of Ghana, Legon.

Canagarajah, S. (2006) The place of Englishes in composition: Pluralization continued. *College Composition and Communication* 57 (4), 586–619.

Coulthard, G. (2008) Beyond recognition: Indigenous self-determination as prefigurative practice. In L. Simpson (ed.) *Lighting the Eighth Fire: The Liberation, Resurgence, and Protection of Indigenous Nations* (pp. 187–224).Winnipeg, CA: Arbeiter Ring Publishing.

García, O. (2009). Bilingual education in the 21st century: A global perspective. West Sussex, UK: Wiley-Blackwell.

García, O. and Li Wei (2014) *Translanguaging: Language, Bilingualism, and Education*. London: Palgrave Macmillan.

García, O., Johnson, S.I. and Seltzer, K. (2017) *The Translanguaging Classroom: Leveraging Student Bilingualism for Learning*. Philadelphia, PA: Caslon Publications.

Hornberger, N., & Link, H. (2012). Translanguaging and transnational literacies in multilingual classrooms: A biliteracy lens. *International Journal of Bilingual Education and Bilingualism*, 15 (3), 261–278.

Lewis, P., Simons, G. and Fennig, C. (eds) (2016) *Ethnologue: Languages of the World* (18th edn). Dallas, TX: SIL International. See http://www.ethnologue.com.

Li Wei (2011). Moment analysis and translanguaging space: Discursive construction of identities by multilingual Chinese youth in Britain. *Journal of Pragmatics*, 43(5), 1222–1235.

Mbatumwine, A. (2007) Why Sigimaa fears the white man. Unpublished manuscript.

Mwesigire, B. (2014) Why we must be vigilant in the defense of local languages in African schools. See http://spynewsagency.com/why-we-must-be-vigilant-in-the-defence-of-local-languages-in-african-schools/ (accessed 10 June 10).

Omoniyi, T. (2009) 'So I choose to do am naija style': Hip hop, language, and postcolonial identities. In H.S. Alim, A. Ibrahim and A. Pennycook (eds) *Global Linguistic Flows: Hip Hop Cultures, Youth Identities, and the Politics of Language* (pp. 113–139). New York: Routledge.

Onuh, A. (2015) African Schools Punish Children For Speaking Vernacular. See http://answersafrica.com/african-schools-punish-children-for-speaking-vernacular.html (accessed 10 June 2016).

Opoku-Amankwa, K. and Brew-Hammond, A. (2011) 'Literacy is the ability to read and write English': Defining and developing literacy in basic schools in Ghana. *International Journal of Bilingual Education and Bilingualism* 14 (1), 89–106.

Otheguy, R., García, O. and Reid, W. (2015) Clarifying translanguaging and deconstructing named languages: A perspective from linguistics. *Applied Linguistics Review* 6 (3), 281–307. doi: 10.1515/applirev-2015-0014

Paris, D. and Winn, M. (eds) (2014) *Humanizing Research: Decolonizing Qualitative Inquiry with Youth and Communities*. Los Angeles, CA: Sage.

Patrick, D. (2012) Indigenous contexts. In M. Martin-Jones, A. Blackledge and A. Creese (eds) *The Routledge Handbook of Multilingualism* (pp. 29–48). London: Routledge.

Pike, K.L. (1972 [1959]) Language as particle, wave, and field. In R.M. Brend (ed.) *Kenneth L. Pike: Selected Writings* (pp. 129–143). The Hague: Mouton.

Pratt, M.L. (1991) Arts of the contact zone. *Profession* 91, 33–40.

Schaefer, P. (2009) Narrative storyline marking in Safaliba: Determining the meaning and discourse function of a typologically suspect pronoun set. Dissertation, University of Texas at Arlington. See http://dspace.uta.edu/bitstream/handle/10106/1669/Schaefer_uta_2502D_10219.pdf?sequence=1, accessed date January 1, 2018.

Schaefer, P. (2015) Hot eyes, white stomachs: Emotions and character qualities in Safaliba metaphor. In E. Piirainen and A. Sherris (eds) *Language Endangerment: Disappearing Metaphors and Shifting Conceptualizations* (pp. 91–110). Amsterdam: John Benjamins.

Schaefer, P. and Schaefer, J. (2003) *Collected Field Reports on the Phonology of Safaliba* (Collected Language Notes, 25). Legon: Ghana University of Ghana.

Schaefer, P. and Schaefer, J. (2004) Verbal and nominal structures in Safaliba. In M. Dakubu and E. Osam (eds) *Studies in the Languages of the Volta Basin II* (pp. 183–201). Legon: Department of Linguistics, University of Ghana.

Sherris, A. (2015, October) Resisting Oppression: The Case for Safaliba. First Conference on Multilingualism in Africa: Resources or Challenge? University of Ghana, Legon.

Sherris, A. (2017) Talk to text Safaliba literacy activism: Grassroots Ghanaian educational language policy. *Writing & Pedagogy* 9, 163–195.

Skutnabb-Kangas, T. and Phillipson, R. (eds) (2017) *Language Rights* (vols 1–4). London: Routledge.

Tuhiwai Smith, L. (2012) *Decolonizing Methodologies: Research and Indigenous Peoples*. London: Zen Books.

Wilks, I. (2000) The Juula and the expansion of Islam into the forest. In N. Levtzion and R.L. Pouwels (eds) *The History of Islam in Africa* (pp. 93–115). Athens, OH: Ohio University Press.

Williams, C. (1994). *Arfarniad o Ddulliau Dysgu ac Addysgu yng Nghyd-destun Addysg Uwchradd Ddwyieithog,* [An evaluation of teaching and learning methods in the context of bilingual secondary education]. Unpublished Doctoral Thesis (University of Wales, Bangor).

Williams, C. (1996). Secondary education: Teaching in the bilingual situation. In C. Williams, G. Lewis, and C. Baker (Eds.), *The language policy: Taking stock,* (pp. 39–78). Llangefni, UK: CAI.

10 Heterarchic Commentaries

Ari Sherris and Elisabetta Adami

For each of the empirical studies presented in Chapters 3–9 of this volume, we now offer a possible reading and expansion for future work along two perspectives, i.e. that of Complexity Theory and that of Social Semiotics (as sketched in the Bricolage, Chapter 2 of this volume, in Diane Larsen-Freeman's and Gunther Kress' answers, respectively). These commentaries are a discursive move that sketches next steps in sign-making and translanguaging from heterarchic rather than homoarchic discourses. An inflexible ranking of complexity (CT) or social semiotics (SocSem) theories – a homoarchic discourse – would not be sufficiently in tune with the different ecologies of knowledge and meaning-making that each of the ethnographies in this book attempts to articulate. Liminality, fluidity, porousness, variation, mobility and change resonate through the actual observation of the making of signs and translanguaging in urban, rural and educational spaces.

We use the adjective *heterarchic* in the title of this chapter to emphasize differing *synergies* that might suggest themselves to the reader within and – we hope – between our social semiotic and complexity *takes* in these commentaries. Unlike the adjective *synergistic*, heterarchic immediately brings to our minds *hierarchic* as an antonym, which is useful, since neither theory unilaterally explains or is framed by the other, metaphorically or meta-theoretically. Were we to call this chapter 'Synergistic Commentaries', our concerns about a hierarchy might have been less transparent. At the same time, we are cognizant that ranking (i.e. a hierarchy) might arise from a dataset in a particular place and with respect to particular data, but a ranked or linear imposition of either theory would suffer from a fallacy of imitative form. Just because domain or discourse-specific significations of visual data, for instance, might be supported by translanguaging or vice versa does not mean that

SocSem or CT takes control of the other or is ranked as a metatheory while the other is ranked as a context-germane operational theory. Decisions to prioritize one theory or take over the other are not how theory is best handled in any sort of ethnographic journey. Like research questions, theory in ethnography is best left to liminal spaces that shift, transform and remain fluid.

We admit that the 'archy' stem (from the ancient Greek 'archeia', meaning 'government' or 'leadership') is still problematic, since it assumes power or control; we conceive of the notion of 'heterarchy' as akin to Deleuze and Guattari's (1980, 1987) 'rhizome', which allows for multiplicity and transconnections in knowledge that avoid any pre-determined hierarchy. For the moment, however, given that these two metatheories have not yet been used intertwined in any actual work, we believe it is more sensible to stay on the threshold, by labeling these commentaries 'heterarchic', and in this way, we hope to open a door that will enable future interconnections. Readers will see in the commentaries that there is abundant room for starting to cross that threshold.

A Complexity Theory (CT) Take. Adami (Chapter 3) analyzed multimodal sign-making in a butcher shop in the Leeds Kirkgate Market (UK), a super-diverse context. She collected data in and outside the butcher shop through photographs, fieldnotes and interviews. A CT analysis would reshape the examination of the butcher shop from a static, non-temporal study to a dynamic one, with time playing a role, one that adds even more complex relationalities, conveying, possibly, a representation of changing, flexible, meanings for the rich disembodied resources in the study, particularly if a fine-grained analysis of ensembles of gaze, talk and hand gesture inside and outside the shop is included. What do other cultures make of the cat in the window, for instance? This would extend the analysis across micro- and mesa-genetic timescales of face-to-face customer encounters from varied linguacultures (Agar, cited

in Larsen-Freeman, Bricolage) with a cohort interacting with each other and with the material resources mentioned, as well as with other material resources not mentioned, such as through transactions with credit cards, cash bills and coins, possibly. Moreover, the physical spatial dimensions of the stall, the size and shape of the counter, lighting, sounds and the role of cutting, weighing and wrapping meat selected by customers would enter into the trans-sign-making. These would be documented in real time and analyzed. Stimulated recall analysis could also be used to determine subject positioning and meaning-making throughout super-diverse transactions.

A Social Semiotic (SocSem) Take. As mentioned in the conclusions of the chapter, also in a social semiotic approach, the study could be further integrated (always through ethnographic investigation) to include actual face-to-face interactions between the butcher and customers, and expanded to include other semiotic resources, particularly with observation through time, to see not only changes in the butcher's rearrangement of signs in his shop but also the development of shared semiotic/communicative repertoires with customers through multiple interactions.

As to approaching different sociocultural demographics of customers to see what kinds of meanings they make of the lucky cat, a social semiotic stance on 'culture' takes a different approach though. It assumes that national cultures are an ideological construct; particularly in today's diversity, individual's values, repertoires and meaning-making practices are rather influenced by fragmented and multifaceted variables in lifestyle (which include not only personal trajectories and encounters, but also different social positioning toward hegemonic values and tastes). A quantitative survey on how people from different nationalities (whatever that may mean) make meaning of the lucky cat would give only a rough indication of correlation, obscuring, rather than revealing, the specificities of motivations and the many variables that affect an individual's meaning-making. Further investigation could instead compare other settings (such as public offices, for example) and see if these are adequately shaped to facilitate communication in contexts where linguistic resources are little shared.

A Complexity Theory (CT) Take. Archer and Björkvall (Chapter 4) analyzed discourses *in* and *around* 'upcycled' artifacts. A possible future CT agenda might be to explore smooth and abrupt transformational relationalities in state and phase spaces *in* and *around* discourses of artifact 'upcycling' entailing a multisite ethnographic design. This would occasion a study of dynamic adaptations, enactments and distributed process(es) in, say, discourse, gesture and movement that play out *in* and *about*, for example, a doorway curtain as it is being imagined and then made from trash on a beach as well as its journey to local and distant markets. As such, CT would re-center the spatial separations of *in* and *around* as state and phase relations. This might capture a complex ensemble of modes in the soft-assembly of discourse and artifact in real-time process(es). This is not just a question of a metaphoric turn, nor is it simply a question of the hermeneutics of '*in* and *around*', but a reconceptualization of materiality as state and phase space, thereby extending ways Archer and Björkvall discursively constructed authenticity. This is not to deny materiality; it is to admit that even shape, color and size are not just *in* an object – but constructed through discourses and mode ensembles and subject to smooth and abrupt shifts. It would also be a dynamic conception that unifies the material relationalities across discourses that are themselves relationalities in state space. Knowledge of shape, color and size are all relational, historical, co-constructed and soft-assembled. They are narratives as well as materials as are the narratives of upliftment, poverty, the environment and women's struggles. A CT take would extend the current work and potentially contribute to a complexity turn in SocSem theory.

A Social Semiotic (SocSem) Take. Social semiotics treats all phenomena in terms of their meaning-making potential – with meaning intended in all its possible aspects, not only informational, but also aesthetic, emotional, interpersonal, intertextual and orientational. It is concerned with the specific relation between resources that are used to make meaning, the people who make these meanings and the wider social dynamics that influence how we make meaning of these resources/how we use these resources to make meaning. Archer and Björkvall show how materiality, shapes and colors (among others) of objects make meaning not 'as such', or for their intrinsic characteristics, but through discourses that are entexted[1]/embedded in their social production, uses and circulation. The whole world (and its contradictions) is condensed in the specific discursive shaping of these artifacts-as-signs. Further social semiotic research on upcycling as a global/local sign-making practice could go deeper in analyzing data that link a particular artifact, its circulation and commercialization, with broader aesthetic and commercial dynamics (in terms of taste and lifestyle construction), and – through possible integration with ethnographic methods – with the specific values and meanings (and possible new creative uses and re-uses) that both producers and consumers of these artifacts-as-signs make of them. This could reveal the diversified sociocultural positioning of different meaning-makers in respect to corporate appropriation and re-production of discourses such as environmentalism, exoticism and sustainability (to cite a few), as well as contextualize further the social value and meaning of upcycling today.

A Complexity Theory (CT) Take. Banda, Jimaima and Mokwena (Chapter 5) explore how Zambians (and one Chinese owner) engage with affordances of material Chinese signage, signifiers all, in rural Zambian landscapes. The chapter uses observations, photos and interview data to examine what is signified when Zambians have no knowledge of Chinese and repurpose Chinese signage. Findings indicate the Chinese signage is resemiotized as reference points when giving directions to get somewhere or talking about a place, as well as a name for a place (e.g. 'PamaChinese' or 'Chinese Inn'). A CT study might expand the enquiry to explore the prevalence of the emergence of resemiotization from the (inter)actions with and around the Chinese signage among a broader cross section of Zambians and an expanding sector of international Chinese living in rural Zambia. Of particular interest perhaps might be how second-generation Chinese-Zambians from rural multilingual homes where Chinese, English and an indigenous Bantu language (perhaps Tonga or Nayanja) are spoken might refashion meaning from signage. A CT multinational multi-site ethnography might explore Chinese signage and their resemiotization throughout rural sub-Saharan Africa. Perhaps similar patterns might be shown across sub-Saharan rural contexts and different indigenous languages and Chinese signage. Of keen interest in a CT study might also be the geo-centric and ego-centric positionality of different marked and unmarked ways of giving directions to get to different places and possible shifts that might result in repurposing (inter)actions of different interlocutors from a variety of indigenous sub-Saharan languages in a multinational study.

A Social Semiotic (SocSem) Take. A social semiotic approach to Banda *et al.*'s data would refocus them from language to other resources, including font, layout, image, color size and their positioning. It would also expand from the signage to further intertextual relations with objects, space and the built environment, to investigate the influence of Chinese corporations and re-semiotization of their intervention in Zambian society, as traceable in the materiality of the human landscape, and in the meaning-making and sign-making of people inhabiting it.

A line of investigation of the social dynamics of the entering of these Chinese agents could examine the possible changes in the aesthetics of the landscape (again in the use of all resources, rather than only language, in terms of images, colors, materialities, fonts, architecture, etc.), to trace socio-economic tensions and conflicts, as in the dynamics of possible gentrification and renovation, but also in possible mixing of styles/aesthetics, both from above (from Chinese corporations and from the local government/institutions) and from below (in terms of appropriation by villagers in their sign-making), which could reveal the many facets of change (also in terms of taste) in the multiple social stratifications that transnational dynamics of capital may have on the area.

A comparative analysis with urban areas in the same country and with other rural areas in other countries could ascertain similarities and differences in the relations between semiotic changes in the landscape and socio-economic changes as an effect of 'foreign' capital investments (and migration). Finally, interviewing the designers of signs and observing their practices could provide insights into the motivations behind their design choices.

A Complexity Theory (CT) Take. Bradley and Moore (Chapter 6) explored resemiotization in two projects: a puppetry performance in Ljubljana, Slovenia and performance poetry in Leeds, UK. The authors, quoting Iedema (2001: 41), define resemiotization as shifts in meaning-making 'from context to context, from practice to practice, or from one stage of practice to the next'. A CT study might explore the same data to identify and follow the trajectories of three possible types of attractor[2] in these two creative productions and their semiotic transformations: fixed point (FP) attractors, cyclical or closed loop (CCL) attractors and chaotic or strange (CS) attractors. Larsen-Freeman and Cameron (2008: 56–57) define FP attractors as 'the simplest type, representing a system moving into a stable, preferred state and remaining there'. They define CS attractors as periodic movement 'between several different attractor states' and they define CCL attractors as 'a region of state space in which the system's behavior becomes quite wild and unstable, as even the smallest perturbation causes it to move from one state to another'. The self-organizing and emergence of discourses within and across embodied semiotic repertoires, materials and ensembles of modes in each project has been partially described through a nexus analysis (Scollon & Scollon, 2004), but state space, i.e. the 'dynamic behavior of elements or agents at a particular point in time' (Larsen-Freeman & Cameron 2008: 44), has not been examined and might add a finer-grained analysis of attractors to resemiotization.

A Social Semiotic (SocSem) Take. In a social semiotic perspective, Bradley and Moore's work operates two epistemological innovations, i.e. one on 'resemiotization' and the other on 'translanguaging', which deeper social semiotic investigation could bring further forward. While Iedema's (2001) 'resemiotization' involves semiotic change from the 'temporal' to the 'durable', Bradley and Moore analyze changes from the 'durable' (a goat-as-sign, and a written poem) to the 'temporal' (a performance in both cases). The latter, in its turn, leaves further traces, and is re-semiotized in the video-recording, in the props used by the actors and in the very chapter hosted in this volume. This shows that products and processes are intertwined in ceaseless semiosis, and could be investigated further in all domains.

The authors consider these semiotic transformations as translanguaging; social semiotics would consider them as re-semiotization pure and simple, possibly with 'translanguaging' as one of them, involving only the resources of either speech or writing. Further work could go deeper into the dynamics of these transformations, to see the agency of different sign-makers and their roles, as well as possible conflicts, and how semiotic changes are affected by their assessment of the needs of their audience, as well as their perception of the social values/uses (provenance) of the resources used (along with their materiality, which the authors consider), and the possible innovations brought about in the specific signs being made.

A Complexity Theory (CT) Take. Perera (Chapter 7) examined gaze, gesture and translanguaging among second language (L2) heritage learners of Tamil as they interacted in an urban Australian Tamil Hindu Temple classroom where they learn both the Tamil language and Tamil Saivism, a branch of the Hindu religion. Perera presented evidence of different ways that gaze and gesture support language learning. A CT study might re-examine the 10 hours of videotapes that comprise the three terms of study for any transformations in the role of gaze, gesture and translanguaging from the beginning of the academic school year to its conclusion. The transformations of gesture and gaze might be shown to have self-organized as language knowledge developed and the roles of translanguaging might also be shown to have transformed. Exploring the soft-assembly and co-construction across classroom (inter)actions might be useful for teachers. The open-systems nature of a CT study may also show individual learner paths of transformation and change in gaze, gesture and translanguaging particularly, but not exclusively around language as they develop among learners. With respect to the soft-assembly and co-construction of lexical and syntactic resonances of translanguaging, this study might utilize conversation analysis (CA). If CA is systematically studied across the 10 hours of videotapes, it is quite likely that traces of individual learner trajectories of liturgical phonological, morphosyntactic, lexical and semantic/pragmatic repertoire dynamism will be evidenced. A CT study could explore interaction over a 1–2 year future period, and might afford knowledge of dynamic learner language flows, transforming repertoires and the twin roles of gaze and gesture in L2 language and content learning for heritage learners at micro/mesa timescale levels.

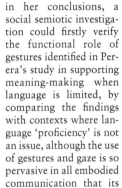

A Social Semiotic (SocSem) Take. As Perera notes in her chapter, gestures and other modes in face-to-face interaction have been subject to investigation in several traditions of multimodal research, including multimodal interaction analysis (Norris, 2004) and multimodal conversation analysis (e.g. Mondada, 2014), to cite only a few. These perspectives focus mainly on the interactants' situated co-construction of meaning and coordination of actions, with less focus on the wider social context. The relation between sign-makers' situated interaction and meaning-making and the wider social context is instead the specific focus of social semiotics. Following from Perera's indications for further research in her conclusions, a social semiotic investigation could firstly verify the functional role of gestures identified in Perera's study in supporting meaning-making when language is limited, by comparing the findings with contexts where language 'proficiency' is not an issue, although the use of gestures and gaze is so pervasive in all embodied communication that its 'mere' supporting function is questionable (see also Gullberg [2011], who did not find significant difference in gesture use between native and non-native speakers). A social semiotic study could shed light on the sign-maker's embodied knowledge and positioning specifically toward religion, as 'entexted' in gestures, by considering the relation between a specific gesture as a signifier/shape and the criterial aspect of the religious phenomenon that is signified. This could reveal the sign-maker's specific interest and take on the specific phenomenon, following Kress (1993, 2010). A social semiotic investigation of interpersonal meanings of gesture and gaze could also reveal power roles in the interaction and in relation to the subject issue.

A Complexity Theory (CT) Take. Goodchild and Weidl (Chapter 8) analyzed translanguaging in extracts of conversations from speech events that took place in Essyl and Djibonker, towns in southern Senegal. A CT study might explore the videotapes of the participants and continue to make more of them, particularly, but not exclusively, of the family as they interact in different domains to identify different degrees of stabilizing and varying patterns in translanguaging discourse as well as affordances for gesture and gaze. In such a CT study, an ethnographic design might video document translanguaging as one phenomenon in the semiotic repertoires of each of these speech communities. Over several years, the data might prove particularly productive for understanding the open, dynamic flow of translanguaging, its soft-assembled and co-constructed complex patterns. As Ellis and Larsen-Freeman write (2009: 92) 'Language is intrinsically symbolic. As speakers communicate, they coadapt their language use on a particular occasion'. Because many of the languages in this study are not codified, a usage-based theory (Ellis & Larsen-Freeman, 2009) of language could be a starting point, particularly one that built in research from conversation analysis in order to identify mutually elaborating resources (e.g. gesture and gaze) woven into the fractal patterning of the phenomena of usage-based communication and semiotic meaning-making. Indeed, this could be a seminal study of the development of a usage-based social semiotics. And in an under-documented language at that.

01	DS4	→PB2	*Injé ijuenen mat'ujugom iilo iegul ma, uogal me*	Joola
			gafóñ man ujaal ni go, ujaal go pe !	Banjal
			'if I knew how to sing I wouldn't be urging you	
			to sing, if we decide to sing a song, let's sing it	
			completely'	
02	PB2	→DS4	*Fétcé !*	Wolof (?)
			'leave me alone!'	
03	DS4	→large	*A-a, jiannen bugaa boube, gúuba gùbbañul*	Joola
		group		Banjal
			'no, help those ones over here, two of you come	
			back over here'	
04	PB2	→DS4	*Ee!*	Joola
				Banjal
			'Hey!'	
05	RM1	→small group	*Ñer elob yay etoge !*	Joola
				Banjal
			'You've done enough talking!'	
06	FT1	→RM1	*Al numbara... numbara...numbara !*	Mandinka
			'work hard...work hard...work hard!'	
07	FT1	→small group	*RM1 n'gandala aa!*	Wolof
			'RM1 is the boss!'	
08	AB2	→small group	*Tey mo ko yor !*	Wolof
			'today she's the one that has everything!'	

A Social Semiotic (SocSem) Take. While Goodchild and Weidl focus on language use, a social semiotic take on the context would consider how interactants use all resources to communicate, to shape their roles and the relationships among them. The uncertainty of attribution to a given language code highlighted by Goodchild and Weidl, which is a very significant finding for linguistic research, would be an assumed tenet of a social semiotic investigation of these interactions. Social semiotics assumes that signs are not 'used' but are newly made every time a resource is employed. Hence, differently from what has been suggested as a CT take, the alternative to a semiotics and linguistics of codes would not be a semiotics of use. Rather, in a social semiotic perspective, it would be a matter of understanding how interactants, because of their interest (understood as the focusing of their social histories onto the situation at hand, cf. Kress, 2010), draw on the resources materially and socioculturally available to them to signify (always anew) in the situation at hand. Given the video data available, a social semiotic study would simply ask different questions, e.g. how do interactants manage power, or how is this reflected in the way they interact semiotically? How do they establish relations among them? How do they express, manage and resolve conflicts? How do they manage misunderstanding and communication breakdown, and how do they construct sharedness in semiotic repertoires as well as in knowledge? Which resources (with which provenance) do they draw upon, for which functions? What does this tell us about the broader social context in which they live?

A Complexity Theory (CT) Take. Sherris, Schaefer and Aworo (Chapter 9) analyzed Safaliba translanguaging in extracts from traditional storytelling, contemporary hip-hop, classroom interaction and community talk from Mandari, a rural town in northern Ghana. A CT study might continue to collect data from the town of Mandari using a multi-site ethnographic design. If translanguaging is the study of emergent patterns of language use by real people, a CT ethnography would serve this purpose well. Expanding on Agar's (2004: 21) position that 'ethnographic research rests on a fractal-generating process',[3] Larsen-Freeman and Cameron (2008: 243) comment that ethnography is the search for 'processes that apply iteratively and recursively at different levels to create patterns, variations which emerge from adaptations to contingencies and environment'. Larsen-Freeman and Cameron (2008: 110) also discuss 'language use as a fractal, not linguists' descriptions of language' and cite 'Zipf's findings for English, Latin and Chinese' (cited in Larsen-Freeman and Cameron (2008: 109)). Might Safaliba translanguaging and other aspects of its usage be fractal-like (Larsen-Freeman, 2017a)? The jury is still out, of course. Finally, the multigenerational aspect of the current ethnographic work might continue to build on Schaefer's (2009) corpus and extend language usage patterns to younger ages 6–30 year olds, enriching our knowledge of Safaliba as an open, dynamic and complex system.

Excerpt 4: Safaliba Hip-hop

1 *Yeah. Beah. Beah. Click. Click. Yaŋ kwa huuh!*
   <Let's go!>

2 *Welcome to Mandari, Dmandarε ŋ posiriye!*
   <Mandari Greetings!>

3 *Bɔnɔ kpaŋ maŋ dε wa kɔttεya!*
   <I have brought you something!>

4 *So nεra zaa yoo ɔ tobee!*
   <"so" everyone should open their ears!>

5 *Tε gbagba yala maŋ dεε waa!*
   <this message belongs to us!>

6 *So ŋ sɔsεra, yá wa wonne!*
   <So come and listen!>

7 *God bless nεra zaa haŋ zεnε chε wonne wonne!*
   <"God bless" everybody who listens! Listens!>

8 *This is Safaliba language*
9 *Yeah Safaliba language*
10 *This is Safaliba language—it's about—yeah!*

A Social Semiotic (SocSem) Take. A social semiotic investigation of Sherris, Schaefer and Aworo's context would ask different questions and would consider 'data' differently; the storytelling, the hip-hop song, the classroom and the community interactions would be considered in their overall semiotic realizations instead of considering only the language used. With these multimodally composed data available, the analyst could ask how knowledge is communicated, how 'culture' is entexted and how all social components of the specific context surface though the texts, representations and interactions that are produced. In this, also issues of dominant/hegemonic and minority cultures (in their broader socio-economic and political variables) could be investigated semiotically, in the gestures, the visuals, the clothing, the objects, the music, the built environment, as well as in the language and how sign-makers position themselves in relation to them. This would enable a more holistic investigation of identity and negotiation of identities, which considers power and agency as semiotically realized. Multi-site socio-semiotic ethnographic investigation would allow for cross-cultural comparison, while a longer-term type of investigation could also trace trajectories of influence across contexts.

Conclusion

The SocSem and CT takes overlap around temporal and spatial entanglements that were originally culled from the seven empirical chapters at the core of this book. However, the commentaries wove in and beyond the phenomenal world originally articulated by each chapter, with suggested differences of emphasis. Not even close to the last word on research in the spaces discussed across the empirical chapters in this book, the Heterarchic Commentaries are different openings, imaginaries that emerge from reflections and dialogues about next steps in research. Neither Elisabetta nor Ari are searching for a simple equation, logarithm or formula for research. As Diane Larsen-Freeman (2017b: 38) maintains, 'Complexity theory encourages the search for ways to access the relational nature of dynamic phenomena, a search that is not the same as the pursuit of an exhaustive taxonomy of factors that might account for behavior of any given phenomena'.

Conceived of as 'a theory of all sign systems as socially constituted, and treated as social practices' (Hodge & Kress, 1988: vii–viii), with 'texts and contexts, agents and objects of meaning, social structures and forces and their complex interrelationships together constitute[ing] the minimal and irreducible object of semiotic analysis', social semiotics has been developed to 'provide this possibility of analytic practice, for the many people in different disciplines who deal with different problems of social meaning and need ways of describing and explaining the processes and structures through which meaning is constituted' (Hodge & Kress, 1988: 2). Yet, in parallel with Larsen-Freeman's approach on CT quoted earlier, 'Social semiotics is not "pure" theory, not a self-contained field. [...] interdisciplinarity is an absolutely essential feature of social semiotics. Social semiotics is a form of enquiry. It does not offer ready-made answers. It offers ideas for formulating questions and ways of searching for answers' (van Leeuwen, 2005: 1).

Bringing this volume together has been a journey that has led Elisabetta to start embracing dynamic ethnography and Ari to start engaging with the semiotics of communication. In the Heterarchic Commentaries, each of us offers our individual perspective on a further possible CT and SocSem investigation of the data of each of the other chapters; readers will notice that each theoretical stance shows traces of mutual influence embracing dynamic ethnographic and semiotic resources beyond language. As a hoped-for next passage in the journey, we both envisage working toward a possible integration of the two approaches as an overarching meta-theoretical rhizomatic approach that weaves multiple methodological tools together for understanding the intricate dynamics of communication and meaning-making today. We hope that readers, provoked by the works of the volume, will want to join us in a dialogue for starting such an enterprise.

Notes

(1) Larsen-Freeman and Cameron (2008: 45–47) write, 'In a vivid spatial metaphor, a complex dynamic system is visualized as wandering across a landscape, up hills and down through valleys.... A state space is a collection of all possible states of a system.... A phase space is a state space with at least one dimension relating to change over time'.

(2) Larsen-Freeman and Cameron (2008: 50) define an attractor as 'a region of a system's state space into which the system tends to move'.

(3) Kramsch and Whiteside (2008: 660) define fractals as 'patterns of activities and events which are self-similar at different levels of scales'. Michal Agar (2004: 21) writes, 'In its pure mathematical form, a fractal is a simple algorithm applied over and over again at different levels of scale'.

References

Agar, M. (2004) We have met the other and we're all nonlinear: Ethnography as a nonlinear dynamic system. *Complexity* 10 (2), 16–24.

Deleuze, G. and Guattari, F. (1980) *Milles plateaux*. Paris: Éditions de Minuit.

Deleuze, G. and Guattari, F. (1987) *A Thousand Plateaus: Capitalism and Schizophrenia*. Minneapolis, MA: University of Minnesota Press.

Ellis, N. and Larsen-Freeman, D. (2009) Constructing a second language: Analyses and computational simulations of the emergence of linguistic constructions from usage. *Language Learning* 51 (1), 90–125.

Gullberg, M. (2011) Multilingual multimodality: Communicative difficulties and their solutions in second-language use. In J. Streeck, C. Goodwin and C.D. LeBaron (eds) *Embodied Interaction: Language and Body in the Material World* (pp. 137–151). Cambridge: Cambridge University Press.

Hodge, R. and Kress, G. (1988) *Social Semiotics*. Cambridge: Polity Press.

Kramsch, C. and Whiteside, A. (2008) Language ecology in multilingual settings: Towards a theory of symbolic competence. *Applied Linguistics* 29 (4), 645–671.

Kress, G. (1993) Against arbitrariness: The social production of the sign as a foundational issue in critical discourse analysis. *Discourse and Society* 4 (2), 169–191.

Kress, G. (2010) *Multimodality. A Social Semiotic Approach to Contemporary Communication*. London: Routledge.

Iedema, R. (2001) Resemiotisation. *Semiotica* 37 (1/4), 23–40.

Larsen-Freeman, D. (2017a) The Fractal Shape of Language. A presentation at the 18th World Congress of Applied Linguistics, 27 July.

Larsen-Freeman, D. (2017b) Complexity theory: The lessons continue. In L. Ortega and ZhaoHang Han (eds) *Complexity Theory and Language Development: In Celebration of Diane Larsen-Freeman* (pp. 11–50). Amsterdam: John Benjamins.

Larsen-Freeman, D. and Cameron, L. (2008) *Complex Systems and Applied Linguistics*. Oxford: Oxford University Press.

Mondada, L. (2014) The local constitution of multimodal resources for social interaction. *Journal of Pragmatics* 65, 137–156.

Norris, S. (2004) *Analyzing Multimodal Interaction: A Methodological Framework*. London: Routledge.

Schaefer, P. (2009) Narrative storyline marking in Safaliba: Determining the meaning and discourse function of a typologically-suspect pronoun set. (Dissertation, University of Texas at Arlington). Retrieved from http://dspace.uta.edu/bitstream/handle/10106/1669/Schaefer_uta_2502D_10219.pdf?sequence=1 Date retrieved: January 1, 2018Scollon, R., & Scollon, S. W. (2004). *Nexus analysis: Discourse and the emerging Internet*. New York: Routledge.

Van Leeuwen, T. (2005) *Introducing Social Semiotics*. London: Routledge.

Index

Note: Page numbers followed by n indicate footnotes. Page numbers in *italics* refer to figures.